INVITATION TO RESEARCH IN PRACTICAL THEOLOGY

Practical theology as a subject area has grown and become more sophisticated in its methods and self-understanding over the last few decades. In doing so, it has become increasingly methodologically sophisticated and theoretically self-aware. This book provides a complete and original research primer in the major theories, approaches and methods at the cutting-edge of research in contemporary practical theology. It represents a reflection on the very practice of the discipline itself, its foundational questions and epistemological claims. Each chapter examines different aspects of the research process: starting with experience and practice, aspects of research design and epistemology, communities of learning, the influence of theological norms and tradition on the practice of research, and ethical considerations about what constitutes 'the good' in advanced research.

The uniqueness of this book rests in its authoritative overview of current practical theological research across a range of traditions and approaches, combined with a comprehensive introduction to research methodology. It offers worked examples from the authors, their colleagues and research students that serve to illustrate key ideas and approaches in practical theological research.

The four authors are all internationally-leading scholars and rank amongst the most influential figures in practical theology of their generation. The book promises to be of interest to students, teachers and researchers in practical theology, especially those looking to conduct original practice-based enquiry in the field.

Zoë Bennett is Director of Postgraduate Studies in Pastoral Theology for Anglia Ruskin University and the Cambridge Theological Federation.

Elaine Graham is Grosvenor Research Professor of Practical Theology at the University of Chester and Programme Leader of the Doctor of Professional Studies in Practical Theology.

Stephen Pattison is Professor of Religion, Ethics and Practice and H.G. Wood Professor of Theology at the University of Birmingham. He is director of the Doctor of Practical Theology programme at the University.

Heather Walton is Professor of Theology and Creative Practice in the School of Critical Studies, University of Glasgow and Director of its Professional Doctorate in Practical Theology.

INVITATION TO RESEARCH IN PRACTICAL THEOLOGY

Zoë Bennett, Elaine Graham, Stephen Pattison and Heather Walton

 Routledge
Taylor & Francis Group

LONDON AND NEW YORK

First published 2018
by Routledge
2 Park Square, Milton Park, Abingdon, Oxon OX14 4RN

and by Routledge
711 Third Avenue, New York, NY 10017

Routledge is an imprint of the Taylor & Francis Group, an informa business

© 2018 Zoë Bennett, Elaine Graham, Stephen Pattison and Heather Waltont

British Library Cataloguing-in-Publication Data
A catalogue record for this book is available from the British Library

Library of Congress Cataloging-in-Publication Data
A catalog record for this book has been requested

ISBN: 978-1-138-47854-1 (hbk)
ISBN: 978-1-138-47856-5 (pbk)
ISBN: 978-1-351-06824-6 (ebk)

Typeset in Bembo
by Apex CoVantage, LLC

CONTENTS

PREFACE

This book represents the tip of an iceberg in terms of collaborative working. While the conventions of publishing make it appear that there are 'only' four authors who have worked together and who take responsibility for this text, it is actually the product of work in many communities of practice and research within practical theology. More people than can possibly be mentioned here by name have contributed to it, directly and indirectly. The authors would like to thank them all, especially those who may feel that we have forgotten them by failing to list their names here.

So, first, we would like to thank all the students and colleagues who have worked with us since 2003 on constructing and participating in the UK professional doctorate in practical theology: some 120 people or more to date. The former include all those who at various national summer schools and other events have engaged with us about this book and helped us to shape and steer it.

We have had many helpful colleagues who have engaged in and around the doctorate to bring it into being and to help it prosper. Amongst the most influential of these have been Chris Baker, Mark Cartledge, Doug Gay, Ken Jeffrey, Steve Knowles, Dawn Llewellyn, David Lyall, Wayne Morris, Harriet Mowat, Leah Robinson and Vernon Trafford.

A group of doctoral students and graduates generously came together to give us the benefit of their experience and perceptions in response to some of our draft material at a workshop in Birmingham in February 2016. This was kindly sponsored by the British and Irish Association for Practical Theology. We want to thank those who attended and who also provided subsequent feedback: Susy Brouard, Susan Van Scoyoc, Mark Pryce, Nick Ladd, Steve Dixon, Linda Robinson and Anna Sorensen.

Nearing the end of the process of writing this book, we decided to involve more former students, graduates and colleagues, both from the professional doctorate and beyond. We would particularly like to thank those who have taken the trouble to write pieces about their own experience of undertaking research in practical theology. We have included many of these pieces in whole, or in part, through the book and we will introduce and acknowledge the authors when they appear in the text. Thank you so much, all of you, for immeasurably improving this text and helping it to breathe with the fascinating lived experiences that you have shared with us.

If this book has a physical epicentre or home, it should probably be located in the John Robinson Room at Gladstone's Library, Hawarden, North Wales. This is a congenial and friendly place in which to meet, talk and write. We recommend it to other would-be authors, and thank the Warden, Peter Francis, and staff for their quiet, effective hospitality. We also met in each others' homes, on Skype, and in railway carriages and cafés around the UK. This is the pleasant, but demanding, reality of collaborative work; we owe one another a real debt of hospitality and care.

We would also like to thank Jack Boothroyd and his colleagues at Routledge who have been very helpful in transforming our rather tardy manuscript into a publishable volume.

It is a hackneyed truism to say that all academic work is in the way of being midgets standing on the shoulders of giants. But it is nonetheless true that practical theological research as we have come to inhabit and understand it, and we ourselves, have been considerably shaped and influenced by personal and academic relationships with teachers and colleagues, many of them in the context of meetings and membership of the British and Irish Association for Practical Theology. They have been important members of our community of practice through their writings and friendship even if some are no longer directly participating in it.

Working together to write a book collaboratively over five years deepens and tests relationships. For us, this volume is the culmination and celebration of over twenty years' work together in practical theology in the UK. We are happy (and relieved!) to report that we are firmer friends now than when we started. We hope our readers will have as much stimulation and pleasure from reading it as we have had in writing it.

Zoë Bennett
Elaine Graham
Stephen Pattison
Heather Walton
September 2017

NOTES ON THE AUTHORS

Zoë Bennett is Director of Postgraduate Studies in Pastoral Theology for Anglia Ruskin University and the Cambridge Theological Federation. Zoë read Classics and Theology at Cambridge, and has held various posts in adult theological education, including Director of Pastoral Studies at Westcott House, Cambridge.

Her publications include *Introducing Feminist Perspectives on Pastoral Theology* (2002), *Using the Bible in practical theology: historical and contemporary perspectives* (2013), *Your MA in Theology: a study skills handbook* (2014) and, with Christopher Rowland, *In a glass darkly: the Bible, reflection, and everyday life* (2016).

In 2016 she received the prestigious Lanfranc Award for Education and Scholarship, awarded annually by the Archbishop of Canterbury for outstanding achievement in the field of adult theological education.

Elaine Graham is Grosvenor Research Professor of Practical Theology at the University of Chester and Programme Leader of the Doctor of Professional Studies in Practical Theology. Her first degree was in Sociology and Economic & Social History from the University of Bristol; she also has a Master's degree and PhD in Social and Pastoral Theology from the University of Manchester, where she taught for over 20 years.

Her publications include *Making the Difference: Gender, personhood and theology* (1995), *Transforming Practice: pastoral theology in an age of uncertainty* (1996, reprinted 2002), *Representations of the Post/Human* (2002), *Words made flesh: writings in practical and pastoral theology* (2009), *Between a Rock and a Hard Place: public theology in a post-secular age* (2013), *Apologetics without Apology: speaking of God in a world troubled by religion* (2017) and, with Heather Walton and Frances Ward, *Theological Reflection: Methods* (2005).

Elaine is a former President of the International Academy of Practical Theology and honorary Canon Theologian at Chester Cathedral.

Stephen Pattison is Professor of Religion, Ethics and Practice and H.G. Wood Professor of Theology at the University of Birmingham. He is director of the Doctor of Practical Theology programme at the University. Stephen read Theology at the University of Cambridge before going to Edinburgh to undertake a PhD. After a period working as a hospital chaplain he taught Pastoral Studies at the University of Birmingham, then moved into National Health Service management, before returning to HE, first as senior lecturer in health and social welfare at the Open University, then as head of Religious & Theological Studies at Cardiff University and finally back to the University of Birmingham.

His publications include *A Critique of Pastoral Care* (1988, 3rd Edition 2000), *Alive and Kicking: Towards a practical theology of illness and healing* (1989), *Pastoral Care and Liberation Theology* (1994), *Faith of the Managers: when management becomes religion* (1997), *Seeing Things: Deepening relations with visual artefacts* (2007) and *Saving Face: Enfacement, shame, theology* (2013).

Having served for nine years on the Ethics Committee of the Royal College of General Practitioners, Stephen was made an Honorary Fellow of the College in 2013.

Heather Walton is Professor of Theology and Creative Practice in the School of Critical Studies, University of Glasgow and Director of its Professional Doctorate in Practical Theology.

She studied Literature and Theology at Lancaster University before travelling to South Africa on a World Council of Churches scholarship, and undertaking research on racial justice for the Methodist Church in Britain. She was tutor at the Northern Baptist College in Manchester where she also taught one of the first undergraduate courses in feminist theology in the UK with Elaine. She has an MA in Creative Writing from Goldsmiths University of London and a PhD in Theology, literature and critical theory from the University of Glasgow.

Her publications include *A Tree God Planted: Black People in British Methodism* (1985), *Literature, Theology and Feminism.*(2007), *Imagining Theology: Women, Writing and God* (2007), *Writing Methods in Theological Reflection* (2014), *Not Eden: Spiritual Life Writing for this World* (2015) and, with Elaine Graham and Frances Ward, *Theological Reflection: Methods* (2005).

Heather is Executive Editor of the journal *Literature and Theology* and served as President of the International Academy of Practical Theology from 2015–17.

INTRODUCTION

This book does two things. First, it reflects deeply on the practice of research in practical theology from the perspective of practising researchers. Secondly, it witnesses to the highly creative and transformative potential of practical theological research. It will not tell you exactly how to do a particular research project, or provide you with a comprehensive list of methods or approaches (though you will hear plenty about those as the book goes on). But it should help you to see why your research is important and enable you to locate yourself critically within this fascinating, important activity. This is not a text book about how to do research. It is a critical, reflective companion to the world of practical theological research that provides stimulus, rationale and questions for interrogating and undertaking that work. It also provides worked examples from the authors, their colleagues and students that firmly root the book in a large and growing 'community of practice' in practical theological research.

Practical theology as a subject area has grown and become more sophisticated in its methods and self-understanding over the last few decades. In doing so, it has become increasingly self-conscious and theoretically self-aware. *The Wiley-Blackwell Companion to Practical Theology* (Miller-McLemore, 2012) brought together fifty-seven leading scholars from ten countries and represented an important, milestone attempt to scope and summarise the discipline internationally. Since its publication, a number of significant overview books have appeared. These begin to reflect more critically and self-consciously on the fundamental nature of practical theology and the engagement of scholars within it (including Cahalan and Mikoski, 2014; Bass et al., 2016; Dillen and Wolfteich, 2016; Mercer and Miller-McLemore, 2016). They witness to a strong commitment to the creative potential of practical theology. They particularly reveal a growing emphasis on the importance of their authors' own reflexivity and personal engagement in practical theological work. The term reflexivity denotes 'the role the self plays in the generation of all forms of knowledge about the world' (Walton, 2014, p. xvi). One of the things this present work seeks to do, then, is to pick up on and extend this notion of reflexivity, *specifically in relation to research*, as opposed to within practical theology generally.

This book emerges from the particular context of the United Kingdom; from a distinctive religious and academic environment, from rich and diverse research projects, and from communities of active practitioner-researchers, many trained on professional doctoral research programmes. It offers a research-based perspective on the cutting edge of the evolution of practical theology. In particular, it teases out the ways in which research emerges from and returns to practice, often developing elements of reflexivity to generate both practical wisdom (*phronēsis*) and creative imaginative possibilities (*poiesis*).

It also offers a vision of the diverse, innovative nature of research in practical theology. In the *Proslogion*, the eleventh-century Italian-Franco-British theologian, Anselm of Canterbury, famously defined theology as 'faith seeking understanding'. The present work represents an attempt to articulate the nature and potential of practical theological research so that research in this field might find greater understanding. If you like, we try to describe and evaluate the 'inhabited action-guiding world-views' (Pattison, 2007, p. 7) and practices underpinning research so that practical theological researchers can better comprehend their own activities and the significance of these. Locating this activity within the wider fields of life, practice and theology should enable a fuller understanding of the value of research, its possibilities and limitations.

Fifty years ago, it would not have been possible even to think of writing a book of this kind in this area. Practical theology was basically a subject taught to Protestant students for ministry as an 'applied' arm of systematic theology and biblical studies, rather than an area of postgraduate research and active enquiry. Starting doctoral work in 1979, Stephen asked Duncan Forrester, Professor of Practical Theology and Christian Ethics in Edinburgh, 'What methodologies do we use in practical theology?', to receive the reply, 'There are none!' Things have changed a lot since then. With the growth of higher education, professionalism and the need for further training and education, the field has expanded exponentially in terms of research. There is now no shortage of methods and approaches that can be adopted, and the engagement of practical theology with other disciplines, particularly the social sciences, has been notable. Indeed, it has been a central element in its growth and consolidation as a recognised, legitimate field of research within the academy.

The present authors have been active participants in the growth of practical theological research as students, researchers and, latterly, as supervisors of the ever-increasing number of doctoral students in this burgeoning area (there are currently more than one hundred students undertaking research projects in the professional doctoral programmes that we jointly run in the United Kingdom, and many others undertaking PhD studies and other opportunities).

We find, slightly to our dismay, that we have about a century of practical theological research engagement between us! Given this level of experience and involvement, we felt that the time was right for us to try and summarise our learning about the nature and practice of research in practical theology, and to attempt to articulate our philosophy and theology of what this activity has taught us. But we did not just want to share such understanding and wisdom as we might have. We also wanted to bear witness, constructively, to the ways in which we have seen practical theological research activity transform our doctoral students and colleagues – hence the inclusion of their words and experiences that breathe life into this book. For us, the best kind of practical theological research emerges primarily out of practice and communities of practice.

This book itself is a product of our own collaborative community of practice as we have sought to understand and challenge each other on what we have been trying to do for the last few decades severally and together. We have been working particularly closely together around the UK-based professional doctorate in practical theology since 2003, and even more so since we decided to write this book together in 2012. Both of these projects have served as catalysts for our common practices of mutual reflection and reflexivity. This book is the direct outcome and product of that shared journey. As far as possible, we have tried to shape it to mirror the processes of our own research, as well as that of others. This means that we must foreground our own context overtly, starting, as we believe all practical theological research must, from lived experience and context in the here and the now.

As we have already indicated, we write from a very particular perspective and context. Practical theological research is an international activity with very different settings, concerns and preoccupations both within and outwith the Western world. While we are engaged with and appreciative of the perspectives of non-British practical theological researchers, and indeed have been privileged to work with many students from, for example, Hong Kong and parts of Africa, the primary *Sitz im Leben* for this work is the United Kingdom. We are all holders of full-time academic posts in non-collegiate public universities. While all of us have close links to churches and other faith communities – and for Zoë her location in the ecumenical and inter-faith context of the Cambridge Theological Federation is important – our perspective is inevitably shaped by the pressures on public universities, mechanisms of research funding and the need to work credibly in a non-confessional environment. For that matter we are all white, middle class, non-metropolitan in our origins and places of residence and work, and would self-identify on a continuum between liberal and radical in terms of our commitment to Christianity. What we bring to and have learned from research may be very different from the experiences of colleagues in other contexts. We hope they can learn from our experience, as we hope to learn from theirs. We aim here to make overt our commitments, passions and concerns, seeing this as a necessary part of locating and undertaking practical theological research that takes contemporary experience and practice seriously as sources of theological and other kinds of knowledge.

You will find out more about us and our own research work as the book progresses. You will also hear about the experiences and insights of other researchers in practical theology, for this is a diverse activity and different voices and perspectives are integral to it. Where we allude directly and at length to our own research and experience, or to that of our colleagues, material is distinguished in freestanding text boxes. So one way of reading this book might be simply to work through those boxes, seeing them as primary objects in an exhibition, while the rest of the text could then be seen as a commentary upon them. We have all written each of the chapters, and they are different from each other in style, structure and approach as determined by their subject matter.

But what about you, the reader? We envisage that you might be a professional practical theologian, but perhaps more likely a postgraduate student. You have come into the discipline of practical theology and are trying to understand the space that you have entered, and what your options in terms of research might be. Perhaps you are fascinated by practical theology, perhaps confused – or even disillusioned. But you want to be able to locate and articulate the value and place that you are in, to know what the room is that you have entered, why it is as it is, and how it is furnished.

Some people feel on entering practical theology that they have found some kind of home, a place that they value and instinctively feel welcome in, but they don't understand what this home is. Others may feel that it is not so much a home as a temporary resting place, even a crack in a rock where they have a moment to look at life differently. Whatever your metaphor for indwelling or engaging with practical theology, we want here to give you material to think with, and to react against, as you try to find your way through the ever-changing world of research. We hope this book will help you to understand and locate yourself in this world so that you can act more effectively, intentionally and responsively within it.

One of the problems with research in general, and practical theological research in particular, is that it is often confusing, with different elements and aspects moving around all the time, like being on a boat at sea. We want to validate this sense of confusion and to affirm that questions that arise from practice, if honestly faced, really can produce more coherent and plausible theories and theologies than issues that are just explored in an abstract or disinterested way. We have seen this happen and will demonstrate the fruitfulness of staying with difficulties in research as the book evolves. Alongside this, we want to show that practical theological research can be transformative as well as analytically rigorous; can also be an engine for the development of practical wisdom and insight together with creative innovation in thought and practice; and, in its deep engagement with practice, can generate theological exploration and insight in the contemporary world. Furthermore, we want to suggest that practices of research might themselves be world-revealing and become spaces of divine epiphany where 'God take[s] place' (Bergmann, 2008, p. 82). This kind of profound disclosure involves costly, self-involving, deep reflection and reflexivity.

We are not content to see practical theological research as bits and pieces of incoherent endeavour that somehow haphazardly touch upon practice, theology and theory. At the heart of this book is a clear conviction that such research has its own coherence and integrity. We hope to demonstrate this, and to advance the theory and understanding of the fundamental nature and directions of practical theological research, drawing on the cutting-edge experience of our own research and that of some of our colleagues.

The shape of this book and how to use it

This book can be seen as a reflection on the practice and practices of practical theological research. Like the people who pursue such research, and the living human contexts in which it takes place, the reality of research is complex and recursive. Matters of method, philosophy, practice, theory and theology swirl around one another, mixing and mingling at all points. While the academic results of particular research projects may look neat and systematic in the way they are represented, the course of research is seldom simple, being replete with uncertainty and difficult decisions throughout. The chapters and structure of this book, while presented in the linear form pre-supposed by writing, are not so much about discrete topics, but more different 'takes' and perspectives on the research endeavour as a whole. So, for example, at every point in practical theological research issues of the aims and ends sought ('ethics'), the ways and means of exploring reality ('framing the view') and the place of traditions ('tradition') can come into play and be in active dialogue. Thus there is no sense in which one dimension of the conduct of advanced research can be completely isolated from any other. Yet clearly, some issues and perspectives may be more salient at different moments on the research journey, although this may be a matter of emphasis rather than a complete turning away from other considerations.

That being the case, we have found it challenging to order the chapters in a particular way. Arguably, the present configuration broadly reflects the chronological order in which people might conceive, design and complete a research project in practical theology, starting with practice and ending with ethics. On the other hand, it would be just as plausible, and, indeed, as valid, to start at the other end.

We suggest that readers begin by reading Chapter 1, which is where we, as authors, locate ourselves and our concerns. Thereafter, any chapter that meets an obvious need or strikes the imagination will be as good an entry point as any. There is, intentionally, a certain amount of repetition and doubling back on topics in the different chapters. This reflects the circling, iterative nature of the research journey.

In Chapter 1, we begin – as we believe all practical theological researchers should – by trying to be clear about our own context and commitments. Theologies and research projects don't emerge from thin air. So it behoves us to make clear the ground from which we start our journey. Beyond that, the chapter sets out more of our vision of the kind of practical theological research we pursue in terms of a set of key theses which characterise our approach.

Chapter 2 progresses to looking at one of the most important attributes of contemporary practical theological research: reflexivity. Researchers are integrally implicated in their research at all points in the process. Their awareness of themselves and their own subjectivity as an integral part of coming to know is a key to arriving at research questions that are practically and theologically important and to the research process and the outcomes and uses to which research may be put. To be properly reflexive is to move beyond reflection, traditionally a very important part of practical theology, into a space that is potentially transformative. This is one of the most exciting, demanding and daunting aspects of contemporary practical theological research.

Reflexivity is occasioned by and feeds into practice, which is the starting and ending point for this kind of research. So Chapter 3 explores concepts of practice and the significance of using this as a place for working theologically. We assert here that attention to practice must be considered to be a primary source for the conduct of research at all points, and is essential for developing theoretical and theological insight and understanding. Attending to experience and practice, in fact, produces better and more urgent theological questions.

Whilst the norm in the arts and humanities has generally been that of the individual scholar working alone, reflexivity, practice and research in general are not necessarily solitary activities. Research often grows out of communally-generated needs and perceptions. Equally, it is usually pursued with others in what have come to be known as 'communities of practice'. In Chapter 4 we consider the importance of such communities in and for research, examining how these might work to help develop greater insight, understanding and support for researchers. Much of this chapter reflects directly on the experience we have had together, and with students, of doing theological research in community. Getting beyond the solitary, library-bound researcher is an important catalyst in contemporary practical theology as we have experienced it.

Those who seek the reflexive road from practice to theology in the company of others in communities of practice will have come from inhabited worlds of belief and practice, whether overtly religious or not. These native worlds of practice and understanding may be a resource and a challenge in practical theological research, as assumptions may be interrogated and actions questioned on the research journey. Chapter 5, then, critically evaluates the importance, opportunities and obstacles posed by recognising the traditions from which researchers come.

Action-guiding world-views and traditions are by no means confined to the overt realm of faith communities. Research approaches and methods themselves are value-laden and make huge assumptions about the nature of reality and the ways in which it can be explored and known. So Chapter 6 looks at the frames of reference that inform various approaches and methodologies in research to help make researchers more aware of the assumptions upon which they work.

The unearthing of assumptions behind research activity, a theme which runs throughout the book, what might be called 'creative suspicion' or perhaps 'critical naïvety', is taken up in Chapter 7 on ethos. This chapter raises fundamental questions about the 'good' that is being pursued in doing research and the possible goods or harms that might emerge as research proceeds. If research is worth undertaking, it is important to understand what its costs and benefits might be. For, demanding and absorbing as it is, there are real disadvantages in its pursuit as well as positive aspects for all participants, including individual researchers themselves.

John Ruskin, the nineteenth-century social and aesthetic philosopher, wrote, 'Mostly, matters of any consequence are three-sided, or four-sided, or polygonal; and the trotting round a polygon is severe work for people in any way stiff in their opinions' (cited in Bennett, 2013, p. 86). We believe practical theological research to be a matter of considerable consequence. The multi-perspectival picture we present here shows that practical theological research is at least polygonal, if not four-dimensional, and the 'trot' demanded around it to do it justice is extremely demanding. We are all in some ways stiff, holding on to what we know and seeking to justify our rigidities. But the fact that we cannot quite fix, or get a grip on, the totality of this activity shows that it is a living, human activity, a practice that reflects and illuminates its subject matter. Long may we all continue to be perplexed, challenged and made to grow in our sympathies and commitments socially, communally and individually. It is right that there should be no end to our exploring and striving to understand more, and better. Belonging to a community of practical theological researchers means that it is not possible just to stand still. There is more to be learned around the next angle of the polygon about ourselves, about the world, and about the divine.

Some guiding themes in practical theological research

We conclude this introduction with a kind of appendix outlining some guiding themes in practical theological research. It has been a very interesting, creative process for us to try and capture something of the distinctiveness and diversity of research in practical theology, together and in conversation with other researchers. To that end, we spent a lot of time together formulating a set of four themes that could help to crystallise important aspects of this activity and so might run through the whole book. Ultimately, we decided against using these themes overtly to structure this text. However, we include them here as one way of capturing the experience of research as it has appeared to us. You may find them useful to reflect with and against as you read on.

The four themes that underlie and characterise the kind of practical theological research commended and analysed in this book are:

- Rooted
- Changed
- Lost
- Claimed

As practical theological researchers, we have found ourselves, to a greater or lesser extent, rooted, changed, lost and claimed – sometimes simultaneously.

Rooted

Everyone approaching research in practical theology comes from somewhere, has an identity, a context, a background, a home, a community of reference For some, this rootedness may be very clear, articulate and much valued. They may come from a particular religious or theological tradition and community with its own distinctive context, identity and way of understanding and doing things. For others, rootedness and attachment may be less clear or more multivariate; they may have little articulate understanding of presuppositions and pre-commitments until, perhaps, they engage in the process of research and then this becomes more apparent.

The whole idea of doing critical research is rooted in a particular academic tradition, heavily influenced by Enlightenment rationality and the notion that humans individually and collectively have the means and the right to explore the universe with their rational powers. And theology, particularly Christian theology, is rooted in two thousand years of the experience of communities that have tried to understand and articulate the meaning and importance of faith and commitment to the divine. Practical theology itself emerges from particular academic traditions and ideas that value practice and the exploration of the significance of the divine, the non-negotiable 'really real' in the present.

In practical theological research, people's concerns impelling them to research are rooted in practices and understandings, many of which are inherited – we start in the middle. This place of departure can be a cherished or a difficult place, but it is where we begin. It needs to be recognised and understood, perhaps to be returned to with new eyes and/or renewed commitment as the research process takes its course. There is no view from nowhere. If we think we are nowhere or nobody, it is impossible to undertake research – for whom would it have any value and to whom would we communicate it or regard ourselves as responsible to? So understanding, critiquing, valuing and returning to our multiple rootednesses is important. Dialoguing and moving between our various contexts, and those of others, is part of the process and richness of practical theological research. We must not finally forget where we have come from or where we are trying to go, even if the process of research often obscures and confuses these points *en route*.

Changed

Practical theological research is not just about being rooted in a place, time or tradition; it is also about a journey of change and transformation. It often begins with a real desire for new or deeper knowledge and understanding, perhaps because someone has been engaged with some kind of practice for a long time. A frequent starting point for research can be a conscious desire to develop, to see and understand things differently, or perhaps a suspicion that things cannot continue as they are. There may be a yearning for change and development in practice or thought. So change and development are often sought.

However, the kinds of changes and transformations in theory and practice that might occur in the practical theological research journey may be partly or wholly unexpected. The familiar becomes problematic or looks different as research is undertaken and perspectives and engagements change. Sometimes, people find themselves alienated or distanced from their starting point, wondering why they were ever inhabitants of that world in the first place and trying to find better ways of understanding that may not be instantly to hand. At other times, finding a bigger, more adequate insight or approach may be a joy, occasioning moments of recognition and conscious growth. Continuing to move forwards with purpose and intent to better understand and engage is demanding, requiring a real commitment to a process which involves the whole of the embodied self and sometimes, indeed, organisations and whole communities of people.

Like all good educational activities and particularly within the horizon of praxis, practical theological research brings about change at many different levels, professional, personal, communal and academic, theoretical and practical. At its most fruitful, this kind of research can eventuate in questions of 'So what . . . (is to be done, made or understood differently)?' 'How might . . . (our work be undertaken better, more creatively and imaginatively)?' 'What if . . . (this were to be understood or created differently)?'

Lost

The process and outcomes of research in practical theology can be characterised by change, even transformation, as the world is seen and acted within differently. As researchers we hope that this proves to be worthwhile, but it does not happen without effort or cost. One of the most important virtues that practical theological researchers need to acquire is what Keats described as 'negative capability': a capacity to live with uncertainty and lack of clarity without grasping prematurely for certainty. The acquisition of new insights and knowledge destabilises the familiar, taken-for-granted and homely, so that researchers can find themselves estranged from their native knowledge bases and understandings in a state of exile that may prove temporary or permanent.

Sometimes this kind of living with uncertainty can be very uncomfortable, placing researchers in a place of vulnerability, uncertainty, even profound ignorance. What used to mean a lot is now no longer helpful; familiar intellectual landmarks and habits are left behind in a kind of fog. Lack of confidence in this kind of context is appropriate – we can only learn when we are open to the new, but the new by definition may be difficult and indeterminate. There are moments in research where you might not even know or understand what you don't know! This can be disabling, producing feelings of inadequacy, incompetence, even imposterdom – I don't know what to think or do, and I have no right to call myself a practical theologian!

Curiosity can be hugely enjoyable and valuable as it produces 'aha' moments of real grasp and understanding. These moments of joy and satisfaction do emerge; but they do so out of intentional effort, often in the face of great uncertainty, not just by good fortune. The research journey can be very demanding as different approaches and methods unfold and may or may not yield the kinds of insights sought. There is many a dead end street in research and it tends to proceed by fits and starts which are experienced very differently by researchers than is reflected in the apparently straightforward linear accounts of research that emerge in completed theses, books and articles.

Being able to tolerate being lost in ways that are creative and constructive within complex possibilities of knowledge and approach is as vital as it is demanding in practical theological research. Many researchers will have had cause to think of the people of Israel in the desert or Jacob wrestling with the angel as they have lived with their own sense of not knowing quite where things are going, what kind of resources will become available, and what awaits at the end of the project. Being lost, we would contend, is integral to any kind of learning and research process.

Claimed

The people of Israel did not venture into the desert to explore it for its own sake. They were seeking, in solidarity with each other, a better place where they would be free of oppression, and following the promptings of the divine that claimed their attention and existence so that striving and moving forward in hope were sacred obligations.

In practical theological research, there is a similar commitment to the claims of that which lies within and beyond the mundane and ordinary. New experiences, voices, perspectives and insights emerge that demand new ways of seeing, thinking and acting. A kind of call, or invocation, is heard. The world does not look the same; agendas and priorities have to be re-ordered, it is impossible not to perceive and engage differently as a kind of imperative.

The call of the 'other', that which has been ignored or unseen, can emerge and prompt innovation and commitment. Paying close attention to that which is there, and truly valuing it, can itself produce a sense of awe and wonder as the all-too-familiar becomes unfamiliar and then wondrous. This can happen with people, traditions, ideas, places, actions. It may be that the plight of others, previously unrecognised, lays upon us an ethical and humanitarian claim. Or there can then be a sense of finding or renewing a sense of identity, or being re-located, perhaps even of coming home. A number of people when they discover the field of research in practical theology feel that somehow they have found and named the place that they can call home intellectually and practically, a place where they can be themselves as researchers where their concerns and taken seriously. And this can lead them to offer accommodation and help to other seekers in the way of practical understanding and creativity. New knowledge, insights and understanding can be gained, articulated shared providing a profound sense of community and excitement in learning and practice as people recognise things about their fellow human beings, and about themselves and their traditions, that were previously opaque and obscure.

There is a sense, then, in which practical theological research can help to sanctify or give profound value to the commonplace in embodied human existence. This provides a kind of spirituality to both the ends and the means used in research as depth is disclosed and seekers become finders and sharers of understanding. This kind of depth of engagement is a sort of calling or vocation, a summons to go further and understand more for the sake of valuing life itself. Thus, far from being an abstract, disembodied search for academic accolades or conformity, research in practical theology enables researchers to be claimed by, and committed to, new understandings of the 'really real' with all the moral and aesthetic demands that this implies.

The four themes identified above emerge from, and inform, our epistemology in practical theology as well as owing much to, but not being limited by, theological traditions. This is an epistemology based as much in the thickness of practice, commitments, bodies, attachments and emotions as it is in cognitions and reasons. It is based on the phenomenology, or lived experience, of undertaking practical theological research. Words may help in gaining a sense of what is being pointed to here, but they will not really reveal the fullness of what is pointed towards. This is, of course, a common problem in theology!

The themes themselves are more like entangled, interconnected threads of different ideas and meanings, poly-and multi-valent. They represent focal viewpoints in fields that have no clear fences or boundaries. In many ways, they overlap and breathe together. Pulling them out separately to anatomise them is actually a profound distortion of the way that they appear within the organic complexity of the research process in practical theology. The artist Damien Hirst (of dead, pickled shark fame), says that to really see a living thing, you have to kill it. It feels like fixing in formaldehyde to allow scrutiny is what we are doing here. But as in anatomical science, it can be useful to try and freeze-frame a living process to get a sense of its main features.

References

Bass, D.C., Cahalan, K.A., Miller-McLemore, B.J., Niemann, J.R. and Scharen, C.B., 2016. *Christian practical wisdom: What it is and why it matters.* Grand Rapids: Eerdmans.

Bennett, Z., 2013. *Using the Bible in practical theology.* Farnham: Ashgate.

Bergmann, S., 2008. Making oneself at home in environments of urban amnesia: Religion and theology in city space. *International Journal of Public Theology*, 2(1), pp. 70–97.

Cahalan, K.A. and Mikoski, G.A., eds., 2014. *Opening the field of practical theology: An introduction.* Lanham: Rowman and Littlefield.

Dillen, A. and Wolfteich, C., eds., 2016. *Catholic approaches in practical theology: International and interdisciplinary perspectives.* Leuven: Peeters.

Mercer, J.A. and Miller-McLemore, B.J., 2016. *Conundrums in practical theology.* Leiden: Brill.

Miller-McLemore, B.J., ed., 2012. *The Wiley-Blackwell companion to practical theology.* Chichester: Wiley-Blackwell.

Pattison, S., 2007. *The challenge of practical theology: Selected essays.* London: Jessica Kingsley.

Walton, H., 2014. *Writing methods in theological reflection.* London: SCM Press.

1

LOCATING OURSELVES

Starting where we are

Practical theological research is rooted and grounded in the contemporary material and embodied world. This type of research attends to the text of the present as well as to theological traditions. It takes the present moment and the complexity of contemporary bio-social reality as an important *locus theologicus*, a place where theology is constructed and understood in the light of divine reality. Religious and theological practices, insights and truths are mediated through contemporary social and material realities; they are generated for and by people seeking better to understand faith and action.

That being so, the people who undertake practical theological research work are themselves integrally and reflexively bound up with the kinds of insights and theologies they produce in practice and in theory (Cahalan and Mikoski, 2014, pp. 6–7). There is no view from nowhere, no theology or research finding that does not have a human, with a context and perspective, behind or within it. So, as authors of this book, we need to be as clear as we can about our starting points and assumptions so readers can locate us and see exactly where we are coming from in our approaches to research.

In this chapter, then, we take you into our shared and separate practical theological research worlds to provide a series of insights into the nature of practical theological research as we understand and try to practise it. We do this using two different, but complementary, means. First, we each individually locate ourselves and some of our concerns and contributions in practical theological research *via* personal narratives of engagement. Who are we? How did we get involved in practical theology, and in practical theological research? What are our passions and concerns? Why do we believe that practical theological research is worth undertaking? What have we gained from, and offered to, the research endeavour? These are some of the questions that will allow readers to evaluate the nature and worth of our approach to practical theology, and to see the kinds of research that we ourselves engage in. It will also enable you to infer the continuities, similarities and differences between us in terms of commitments, interests and methods. Practical theological research is pluralistic and variegated. We don't all do the same things to the same extent.

Having introduced and located ourselves in practical theological research in selective, discursive narratives, we then try to express the key preoccupations and synergies that characterise the kind of research that we are commending here in a more abstract way. To do this, we set out a series of seven brief key theses about the character of practical theological research. This terse expression of the assumptions that we both hold in common and commend as key to our approach to practical theological research will reveal the sorts of approaches to research we value. They may, or may not, embody useful insight and wisdom, but at least by the end of the chapter you should have a clear understanding of the nature and types of practical theological research expounded and adumbrated in the remaining chapters of this book. And you will also have seen, *via* the use of both narrative and propositional approaches, something of the breadth and depth of trying to characterise the different features, types and levels of practical theological research.

Practical theological research through the living human document: introducing the authors

Research in practical theology is undertaken by particular humans in specific historical and social contexts. In this section of the chapter we each introduce aspects of ourselves and our concerns in the form of personal narratives that give a sense of where we have come from and what we do in relation to practical theological research. Narrative can, of course, be over-valued and misrepresented as an uncomplicated, truthful and authentic form of communication (Eakin, 2004). But it is one way of representing key aspects of ourselves and our concerns to readers so they can evaluate the nature and integrity of our overall approach to research. It also allows you to see something of the variety and different motivations and methods that can impinge on practical theological research.

Each of us has been shaped by communities, traditions and ideas, theological and other. We have not sprung from nowhere; we owe who we are and how we see the world to many others, academics, theologians, communities, families, friends, the living, the departed. Some of these we allude to directly, but the thickness of human life and experience expressed in narrative form resists the labelling of ideas and experiences with relevant academic references. Within every thesis or book in practical theology, there is a real person with commitments, passions, concerns, biases and values trying to get out. Here we try to give a sense of this integration of person and research, mindful, too, that our narratives demonstrate all-too-human inconsistencies and that together they provide not so much a synthetic view of the 'wholeness' of practical theological research and its practitioners, but more a vision of its pluralism, partiality and incoherence. We are on a journey together as friends, colleagues and practitioners. We have much in common, but part of the stimulus to research is what differentiates us and what we have yet to discover, individually and collectively. Welcome, then, to our joint and several worlds.

Zoë Bennett

My commitment to writing this book arises from a calling, a vocation, to be a teacher, and in two ways. The first is historical, and partly serendipitous. In 1995 the Cambridge Theological Federation, the institution I work for, validated an MA in pastoral theology with Anglia Ruskin University (then Anglia Polytechnic University). As the only person on the staff who understood the educational language of aims and objectives, of module definition sheets and the paraphernalia of contemporary pedagogy in higher education, I became programme director. Ironically, I have a deeply humanistic and experiential philosophy of education, preferring process to objectives, and human development to grading. From this engagement with practical theology came my involvement in the UK's professional doctorate in practical theology. For me, the first aim of this project is to clarify for myself, and to bring to speech, all that I have learned from collaborative working on the professional doctorate – both that which I already know I have learned, and that which I have learned but which hasn't yet become conscious.

The second connecting element between the practice of pedagogy, my vocation as a teacher, and the commitment to this book goes deeper into my life-experience and identity. I became a pastoral and practical theologian initially by accident, but this move reflected my lifetime commitment to, and ongoing study of, learning and teaching processes.

Having studied Plato's Socratic Dialogues in school, with an eccentric and brilliant teacher whose pedagogical approach suited my temperament perfectly, I have retained the excitement or the vision of those lessons. We were expected to react directly to the text (no secondary literature); we were asked the big questions which were there in the text as if the most important thing was our own growth in wisdom and understanding ('do *you* think that there are aesthetic absolutes as well as moral absolutes? And *are* there moral absolutes?'); we spent whole lessons in discussion and collaborative thinking (translating the text was a technicality done at home). This gave me a deeply rooted humanism, which included the importance of human experience, of my own judgement, and of historical perspectives and the value the seemingly strange and other. Experiential education for me is not primarily about techniques of getting people to learn things by participation and by doing; it is crucially about 'drawing out' (Latin *e-ducere*) what is there inside human beings but untapped, unexplored, untheorised.

Accounts of Socrates' dialectical approach emphasise the posing of contraries to elicit progression. Equally important for me is the 'Rogerian' attention to human experience as the ground of worthwhile human knowing (Rogers, 1969). The teacher midwifes the birth of what is within, but yet unknown and unspoken. Such philosophical and practical commitments found a natural partner in practical theology, with its dialectic or 'critical conversation' between experience, tradition and self, between what is happening, what is given, and personal voice.

The key values and beliefs I hold in my practice of pedagogy I hold in my theology: self-reflexivity, epistemological reserve, practice/experience as a location of radiant immanence in which we may find 'God'. I have found in my co-authors enough common ground here to speak of a shared world. I want to make our account of that available to others within our communities of practice who embrace the same understandings, priorities and loves, especially those who either have not been able to articulate them yet, or who or feel partly ashamed of them and would value solidarity. And I want to commend this way of understanding and practice to others for whom it is alien.

The next life-stage for me after the Socratic school experiences (during which I had no explicit religious commitment) was a long immersion in an 'open evangelical' Christian culture. Here I was engaged in deep, regular reading and discussion of the Bible, public and private. From this inheritance came my ineradicable love of the Bible. In reaction to it came my later wrestling with the Bible in suspicion and anger (for example, in relation to the treatment of women in Christian traditions). But I have never let go.

Navigating between the values, commitments and world-views of these two formative influences has been a personal journey happening alongside my development as a practical theologian.

> *Studying some years later for an MPhil in Cambridge I had a burning question in my mind and heart: 'what kind of animal is this "Bible"?' Inerrant or infallible (the argument in my evangelical world), or neither? In any way connected with theology, or not? (I was naïvely shocked when I found no one else brought a Bible to the Faculty Christology Seminar). I chose the route through the MPhil entitled Christian Theology in the Modern World, despite the attractions of the New Testament route to an evangelical classicist soaked in Scripture and the Greek language, because I wanted to grasp a wider context for biblical interpretation – to understand the Bible's use and its relationship to theology, faith, and practice.*
>
> (Bennett, 2016, p. 24)

I came to doing my own doctorate in practical theology much later, when I had already published a good deal. I therefore chose the route of PhD by Published Work. For this I submitted work published over the preceding ten years, and wrote a critical commentary on how this work made a significant and coherent contribution to knowledge in my field. 'Coherent' was the problem. How could I suggest that work on feminist theology, ecumenical pedagogy in practical theology, the dialectic between the Bible/Christian tradition and experience/practice, not to mention research on John Ruskin, made a coherent whole? A friend said to me, 'When you can see what the connection is between feminist theology and John Ruskin you will have got it'! 'Impossible', I said.

The key, I discovered, was in self-reflexivity. *I* was the key. My commitment to these various projects all stemmed from something inside me: a dissatisfaction with how things are, a curiosity, a questioning of the *status quo*, a sense of being on the margins and the search for an alternative perspective. Above all, they were all connected to a need to get some critical space, to sit in a different place, to ask questions of what was taken for granted because what was taken for granted was so often damaging to me or to others. I called my thesis *Finding a critical space: Practical theology, history and experience*; it closes thus:

> *The substantial question which gives coherence to this submitted body of work is the search for a critical space within experience and tradition from which to do the work of practical theology, and the contribution which an historical perspective, as exemplified in my work on John Ruskin, may offer to this. It is about having 'a place to stand', or to change the metaphor, spectacles through which to look. Archimedes' place from which to lever the globe, however, or 'heaven' as the spectacles from which to view the earth, may superficially suggest that critical space as being above and beyond this world. On the contrary, my work locates the critical space on offer to us in the messy history and experience of human beings – and to be found in the examination of a particular historical figure (John Ruskin) and in the self-critical exploration of our own . . . context . . . and practices . . . .*
>
> (http://arro.anglia.ac.uk/313911/)

As I confessed earlier, my engagement with practical theology happened in an unplanned and unexpected way. I similarly tumbled into research on John Ruskin when my university took his name as part of its own. Did this great Victorian polymath, art critic and social critic have anything to offer practical theology? I found gold. Ruskin's commitment to, and exploration of, good 'seeing' offered practical theologians for whom seeing, along with judging and acting, is a central practice, rich material. His use of the Bible in his engagement with the social realities he saw offered a challenge, and crucially, a perspective from somewhere which wasn't my own, a critical space. Most of all, he offered companionship along the road. Here was a human being who in a different time and place had wrestled like me with the tensions, destructive and creative, between the Bible in which he was soaked and the contemporary public and private realities of his life, and who was afraid of neither the public nor private dimensions of this wrestling. My using Ruskin as a paradigm for an engagement with historical thinkers and practitioners could enrich the discipline of practical theology immeasurably.

> *Without better seeing there is no better acting. I have argued that John Ruskin can contribute to our endeavour through his discussions of how important it is to see well and how it is we might do so, but, even more than this, his example of seeing well across a range of disciplines and objects of sight. What is more he demonstrates the telling of what we see 'in a plain way', and how that clarity of 'plainness' is achieved through integrity, passion, and disciplined attention to how we represent what we have seen in the public world in a way which does the work we want it to do with our audience.*
>
> *Furthermore, Ruskin's lifelong engagement with the biblical text, in virtually daily reading of it, constant personal note taking and much use of it in published work, and all this in the context of a deep existential and intellectual awareness of the Victorian 'crisis of faith' through which he lived, make him for the practical theologian a precious source of material for reflection and a companion who constantly stimulates the imagination and challenges the faculties. He can enrich both the content and the method of practical theology.*
>
> (Bennett, 2011, p. 202)

My most substantial published work on Ruskin is also primarily a work on the Bible (Bennett, 2013). It is to the Bible I have returned, working with a biblical scholar, Christopher Rowland (Bennett and Rowland, 2016). I have come to engage with the Bible in ways which are very different from those of my earlier life. I value the stimulus to the imagination which it invites and the critique of, and challenge to, contemporary realities which it offers, most powerfully through the horizon of hope which emerges constantly, prophetically and apocalyptically from its words, stories and images. As a crucial element in the practice of living a reflective, self-reflexive and critical life the Bible has become part, for me, of this commitment which predated its advent in my life: for a human being 'the unexamined life is not worth living' (Plato, *Apology 38a5–6*).

Elaine Graham

I had a conventional Anglican upbringing and remember taking my confirmation and its preparation very seriously. But as a teenager I couldn't find a place to express that: at school, religious matters were monopolised by a group of (what I would now identify as) conservative Evangelical girls associated with a local charismatic Baptist congregation. They were a very distinct sub-culture in the school, especially in the Sixth form, and projected an image of Christianity in terms of all the things you *weren't* allowed to do – and for girls, what you shouldn't aspire to (male headship was supreme). I wasn't able to articulate it this way at the time, but

I instinctively perceived this as a form of religion that represented human diminishment, rather than fulfilment.

And yet I was always very interested in the ethical and social dimensions of life. I took the world and its woes very seriously. I wasn't old enough to vote in the referendum in 1975 when the British electorate voted to *join* the EU (or Common Market), but in my diary (yes, of course, I kept one) I remember noting that the British people should trust in the future and join with the larger vision of European unity. It was also a time when issues of climate change and the environment were emerging – I read Rachel Carson's *Silent Spring* (1962) as a teenager and was very troubled by it. But I didn't have a framework to put any of that into, although even at the time I know I was searching for something: some kind of larger cause or community that would help me make sense of the world and into which I could channel my convictions.

University provided the opportunity to explore that side of things more deeply: I signed up for a few Christian groups. I felt most at home in the Anglican Chaplaincy, but as a social science student – I was hardly aware of theology or religious studies as academic subjects – out of politeness I attended some Christian Union meetings including a lunchtime prayer session organised by the 'Social Science Christian Fellowship'. This involved turning my back on the main foyer of the Economics building, which was crammed with everyone waiting to go to lunch with their friends, and walking down a long, narrow corridor to a small room in which the faithful remnant were gathered. The leaders would invite us to pray that those studying Marxist sociology and economics would not lose their faith. Yet I felt unable to identify with a version of faith that saw the world as a threat: even the self-imposed isolation of a group which was cloistered in prayer whilst the hubbub of the lunchtime crowd echoed down the long corridor, seemed significant. I did not feel at home in a group that could not engage with the new and challenging ideas that I was beginning to encounter in my degree. Could I be a 'real' Christian as well as a serious social scientist?

Thankfully, the University Anglican Chaplaincy offered a more affirming synthesis of faith and academic study; and through this, I was directed towards the Student Christian Movement (SCM). I attended a weekend conference which was like a conversion experience. It turned my world upside down, and disturbed many of my conventional, middle-class assumptions. But at the same time I knew this was what I'd been looking for all along. It was like drinking rocket fuel. I most valued the lack of intellectual inhibition. SCM assumed that students should be applying the same level of seriousness to their political and moral beliefs as they would to their academic studies; and that one's future career, garlanded with the fruits of a degree earned with tax-payers' money, would also be the subject of serious consideration, as something for which one was accountable to a wider community. Since I didn't know what I wanted to do after University, I went to work for SCM.

The SCM of the late 1970s and early 1980s was working hard to recover from a Trust dispute of the mid-1970s, when a group of senior friends challenged the student leadership for adopting radical political causes that seemed to depart from the movement's historic role as a key player in the development of world mission and ecumenical movements. Working with grass-roots student groups, I came to see that it was not the political stances of that time *per se* which were at fault, but the failure to make connections between campaigns beyond the university and the theological well-springs of ecumenical Christianity. I realised the importance of a process that led students to see that link for themselves, as I had done – and eventually came to identify as a hermeneutic of action and reflection.

When I undertook a Master's programme in social and pastoral theology in the mid-1980s I began to translate the commitments that guided my work with students into the field of academic theology. At that time, I was catching the wave of two important moments in the development of practical theology as a discipline: the transition from 'pastoral studies' to 'practical theology', and a rejection of models of 'applied' theology in favour of practical theology as beginning and ending in practice. I was influenced by an article written by Tony Dyson in the early 1980s which captured the beginnings of that new wave and was influential in constructing an agenda. Dyson believed that the option for psychotherapy which predominated at that time was 'symptomatic of the search for a trouble-free zone of inwardness' (Dyson, 1983, p. 20); difficult issues concerning the relative authority of Scripture, tradition and church practice upon contemporary ministry tended to be bracketed out. The urgent and vital challenges to the churches of secularisation and cultural pluralism, economic and social injustice, even questions about personal identity and the self, were submerged by cosy sentiments of 'warm personalism' (Dyson, 1983, p. 3). Presciently, he warned that the male-dominated nature of the Church and the theological tradition required a thorough-going reconstruction of its core beliefs and assumptions regarding the human person, the nature of power, spirituality and care in favour of more inclusive, rigorous and progressive understandings.

I took up some of those leads. My master's dissertation examined the lack of attention to the pastoral needs of women in the literature, concluding that its dominance by a clerical, androcentric paradigm silenced the voices and lives of women (Graham, 1989, 1990). In my doctorate, I followed my instinct that theological understandings of the human person as gendered remained almost completely unexamined. So my PhD set out to interrogate what different disciplines were saying about gender identity, gender roles and gender relations, and what the implications might be for the way theology talked about what it means to be human (Graham, 1995).

My research helped to propel that move from 'pastoral studies' to 'practical theology': a transition beyond the therapeutic and clerical paradigms, to embrace deeper investigation of the conditions under which the 'action-guiding world-views' of Christian communities are actually engendered. It also meant moving the practical theological agenda away from training for ordained ministry towards an understanding of the whole church as a community of practice – as the context in which 'ministry' of many kinds took place, from Christian formation and nurture, to worship, to pastoral care, to community engagement and outreach, to public statements on social issues.

> *The earliest developments of Christian writing and talking about God, the beginnings of coherent and public communications about the meaning of faith and the nature of Christian truth-claims arose in response to very specific practical circumstances . . .*
>
> *First, theology informs the processes that enable the formation of character . . . Second, theology assists in building and maintaining the community of faith (including determining where the normative boundary of faithful practice might lie, and thus the distinctiveness of the collective identity of Christians). Third, theology enables the relating of the faith-community's own communal identity to the surrounding culture, and the communication of faith to the wider world . . . These three core tasks – of adult formation and nurture, of corporate identity, and of gospel and culture – are fundamental to the conduct of theological reflection that seeks to engender 'talk about God' in ways that are capable of informing the practice of faith in all these dimensions.*
>
> (Graham, Walton, and Ward, 2005, p. 10)

Looking back I can see how, in my early experiences were sown the seeds of my subsequent attraction to practical theology: a concern for the practical and ethical dimensions of religion; a conviction that there are no 'no go' areas for Christianity, intellectually or materially; that even if the beliefs of a divided Church may compromise its credibility, its authentic mission is to be found in its practices of service and justice; and a sense that there are no easy answers and the journey of enquiry has to be rigorous and self-critical.

But taking this one step further (as I had begun to do in a book springing directly from my doctoral research) I had come to the conviction that theology was practical insofar as we can see faith practices as constituting a kind of 'performativity' in respect of theological truth-claims (Graham, 1996). 'Theology' was primarily an enacted discipline, and only secondarily written down. Again, the influence of postmodern and liberationist thinking is evident upon me here: theology is practised as orthopraxis first, and systematised as orthodoxy second.

> *A vision of God embedded in human encounter and renewal animates genuinely disclosive practical wisdom: words made flesh in a community which fosters a generosity to others . . .*
>
> *Just as identity in the postmodern condition is contingent, performative and provisional, so theological truth-claims are to be seen as forms of phronēsis, or practical knowledge: faith and truth cannot be separated from practical action, which is the very vehicle and embodiment of the Word made flesh . . .*

> *Can we regard authentic pastoral practice, therefore, as that which draws us into encounter with the 'Other', towards a deeper understanding of our own identity-in-relation? Pastoral theology is an interpretative discipline enabling faith-communities to give a public and critical account of their performative truth-claims. It attempts to capture glimpses of Divine activity amidst human practice. Pastoral theology aims to put to the test the conviction that the imperatives of hope and obligation are enshrined in transformative practice that seeks to realise a larger vision yet to come.*
>
> (Graham, 2000, p. 113)

Stephen Pattison

I have been employed as a University academic in practical theological research and teaching for over thirty years. This was an accident! I never intended to spend most of my adult life like this. While training for ministry in the Anglican Church, I enrolled for a pastoral studies course involving placements and reflection at Edinburgh University. Having been a rather reluctant theology undergraduate, I found myself involved in an area which was practically stimulating and intellectually challenging. Like many people, I had found a home in practical theology that I did not even know existed, or that I was seeking (Stoddart, 2014). This was the beginning of a lifetime of enquiry into theology and practice (Pattison, 2007, pp. 11–23).

Let's start with my reluctance. I was brought up on a diet of biblical studies (including biblical languages) and historical theology. The course I did ended abruptly at 451 CE. But I was committed to living, twentieth-century Christianity. I wanted to be able to help people live fuller and more hopeful lives illuminated by commitment to a living God. My degree programme provided no bridges between the world of doctrines, ideas and history and contemporary people's lived experiences.

It was a revelation, then, to discover in the world of practical and pastoral theology that there were ways of bringing contemporary experience and theological understandings and commitments together to mutually interrogate and illuminate each other. In confronting terminal illness on a placement, it was not necessary to mouth words of scripture or doctrinal truisms, it was possible to remain silent or to become curious about why the traditions of Christianity were often apparently so at odds with lived experiences. If God loves us so much that we are created in God's image, why do people live short lives or die excruciatingly painful deaths? While there might not be answers to difficult questions, it was possible to live with and contain them; a respectful silence might yield more compassionate and realistic responses that honestly and reverently engaged with experiential realities. Honestly enquiring into contradictions, paradoxes and difficulties arising in experience was the only sensible way to engage, rather than trying to maintain a fairy-tale world in which, as one patient said to me as a student chaplain, 'You're the person who goes around and says everything is alright when it isn't alright at all.'

I learned that the theological world was not an enclave to be protected in its hermetic separateness, but a spacious room, full of questions and different perspectives to be vigorously explored. The God I was committed to was bigger than I had thought, and could accommodate big questions and contradictions. I could use my intellect and experience to try and engage openly with the 'really real', however difficult that might be in theory and in practice. My world had become larger and fuller, if not simpler. Subsequently, whenever I have found areas of difficulty arising either in theological theory or in experience (my own and others) I see them as areas for curiosity and enquiry. This feels like keeping faith with, and in, reality.

So to research. Research in French is *rechercher*, only a hair's breadth away from *recherché*. The *recherché* is obscure, hidden, irrelevant, confined and exclusive. Research can be understood as the kind of thing that scientists do when they discover hitherto unknown and fundamental truths and facts about the universe. This kind of research seems grand and overtly useful in a very public sense.

And that is not what I am indicating as my passion and practice here. A philosopher put it well when he said that his so-called research was really thinking hard about ideas and perceptions so that he could better understand the worlds humans inhabit. This is often the nature of humanities research, and it is the kind of research that I engage in within the framework of practical theology. Much of my attempt to understand the world consists in trying to understand how others think about the world in disciplines like sociology, neuroscience, art theory and so on, and then trying to correlate this with my own pre-commitments, understandings and experiences, including theological insights, perceptions and methods. I characterise this as practical theological conversation – you try to get relevant insights, methods and perceptions talking to each other, and out of this you develop different understandings of practice, experience and the world (Pattison, 2000b). Such conversations are directed towards helping people to fully indwell their worlds and experiences rather than living uncritically in them as inevitable and unchangeable.

Sometimes people tell me I have helped to explain their world to them so that they can see how it works and how they fit into it in terms of their assumptions, practices and behaviours. They feel more self-aware and in charge of their experience. Here are a couple of examples of what I mean.

Some years ago, I was making a presentation based on research/enquiry I had undertaken for a book, *The Faith of the Managers* to a group of senior executives from a global computer company (Pattison, 1997). At the end, one of the participants thanked me and said, 'You have just explained to me why I no longer want to work for X' (the company in question). What had my published enquiry done to help this person? In the book, I had asked the question, 'What might the application of theological insights, practices and methods reveal about the assumptions, practices and theories of management in secular organisations?' I was working on the hunch that the sphere of management was an inhabited faith world, a world of commitments, beliefs, attachments and practices that were unexamined and unarticulated as such. The inhabitants of this world were believers with limited critical awareness of the limits and implications of their beliefs. In my book, I invited readers as a thought experiment to become critical inhabitants of their faith world, to assay and test it, not with a view to abandoning it, but with a view to taking responsibility for it: I had myself been an inhabitant of the world of management, working in the National Health Service. Thus, from a theological perspective I questioned the way in which management theories seemed to require employees' total commitment, like religious adherents, that they often seemed to focus on the teachings of guru-like consultants and theorists whose charismatic authority was unchallenged, that they seemed to divide the world up between good (within organisations) and bad (outside organisations) and that they had an over-optimistic view of controlling the future without having a sense of what theologians call sin and what risk managers might call unintended harmful effects.

This particular conversation allowed me and others to have a more critical perspective on one particular inhabited action-influencing world-view. The book has continued to provoke response, particularly outside the theological world in management and organisational theory. This is particularly rewarding as I believe that if theological work is worth doing at all, it should be intelligible and helpful to people beyond theology and the church, as well as to those within. God is not confined to the church. Theology should be a public undertaking in pursuit of the common good.

> *The theory and practice of management, seen as analogous to the enacted theologies of religious faith communities, could learn much from the experience of such communities and their theologians, both in terms of the methods they employ to consider issues and of the questions and answers they pose. Becoming articulate and critical about one's faith and belief assumptions does not necessarily entail becoming uncommitted to action or belief. It does, however, allow the possibility of escaping from the kind of unrealistic, over-optimistic, one-sided naïve belief that characterises much management thinking and practice . . . . (B)elievers who are self aware and critical of their faith may be more judicious about their practice, less belligerent in their claims and attitudes and, just possibly, less destructive in their effects on the world.*
>
> (Pattison, 1997, p. 155)

Another enquiry that has attracted interest and correspondence from people in a variety of conditions and spheres has been work that I have done on shame (Pattison, 2000a). Shame is a universal human condition, but one that little theological work had been done on until the late 1990s. I had a research fellowship that allowed me to conduct a complex interdisciplinary conversation with disciplines and perspectives such as psychology, sociology, biology, and cultural history to gain an all-round perspective on this complex subject. I was interested in it because years before I had had to write an essay on chronic guilt; I had identified in doing that

that the condition which blighted my life was a sense of shame. However, I did not understand what shame was, how it was acquired, and what its outworkings and solvents were. Work that had been done across disciplines in the 1980s and 1990s enabled me to evolve a theory of chronic shame as toxic unwantedness. This allowed me to reprise Christian teaching and practice in relation to shadowy and unnameable conditions of personal and social misery, exposing some of the limits of a theology of atonement that focuses on guilt (associated with committing offences and then making reparation) rather than on the nature of being a person and having an accepted place in the human community, which has to precede guilt and responsibility.

The book not only enabled a positive, creative critique and response to the shortcomings of Christian thought and practice, its insights have been taken up into disciplines like literature and drama. Most gratifying is that a number of individuals have contacted me to say that they recognise themselves and their experience in its pages; this enabled them better to understand themselves and their situations so that they could seek support or change. The book has also inspired others to research the topic.

> Shame . . . presents enormous challenges to Christian thought and practice. It problematises the 'goodness' of this theological tradition, the truthfulness of its narratives about a caring God, and effectiveness of its practical responses. If these challenges are veiled or ignored this might indicate that practical theologians are more interested in defending and exemplifying the 'truth' of certain a priori assumptions and positions than they are in understanding human experience and promoting human flourishing. If this is the case, theology risks being wilfully deceived and deceitful at the expense of human well-being. It can be seen as glossing over the uncomfortable and unspeakable rather than honestly facing it.
>
> (Pattison, 2000a, pp. 13–14)

I hope it is now clear why it might be worthwhile practising research and enquiry in practical theology. First, complex interdisciplinary enquiry is stimulating and enjoyable, increasing a sense of the wonder and incomprehensibility of the world. Secondly, recognising and exploring this complexity is an honest response to the ways in which divinity and human experience are understood and interpreted. Thirdly, this kind of enquiry can make a difference to those involved in it and those who use its insights, methods and findings. It can make the world more complex and more inhabitable, more strange, but also better known. This is empowering, increasing a sense of responsibility and agency. To engage in practical theological research and enquiry is to understand theory and practice differently. Thus experience seeks understanding and finds a place where it is recognised, complexified, and, hopefully, transformed. There's no escape from the limits and possibilities of life and creation, so we'd better explore them to the full.

Heather Walton

In my early 20s, I was appointed by the British Methodist Church to a position whose brief was to promote racial justice in the institutional and congregational life of the Connexion. That a young, white woman was given this role was indicative of the ambivalence with which such antiracist work was viewed. I was bright, enthusiastic and prepared to work hard for the meagre salary offered. I was also politically aware, with experience of political activism in South Africa and the UK. However, my experience of ethnically diverse churches was limited; most importantly, I was white. I did not have the forms of authority (in terms of status, experience or identity) that would aid me in my work or carry credibility amongst Black Methodists. Indeed many seasoned campaigners believed that my appointment signalled that the church was not seriously committed to combatting racism in its own context. They were probably right!

Although young and naïve I was not unaware of these problems and decided upon, what appeared to me then, the most sensible solution. No-one actually knew how many Black Methodists there were in the UK, what positions of leadership they exercised in churches, what their experience had been, or what constituted a healthy, diverse congregation. The most useful contribution I thought I could make would be to devote my energies to research in these areas. A researcher's job was to present accurate empirical data that was a true reflection of reality and could be used to facilitate considered responses to issues of ethical and theological concern. Surely, I told myself, any skilled, perceptive, objective person could generate this important data; its validity should not be compromised by their social location.

I was guided in this research project by committed academics from the Research Unit on Ethnic Relations at Aston University. I was initiated into the processes of questionnaire design, data analysis, ethnographic study and interviewing techniques. It was a fascinating world and I loved it. I was seduced by statistics and captivated by case studies. However, I was troubled by some of the demands my (fairly mainstream) sociological mentors were making. It is not enough, I was told, to construct a well-designed questionnaire. You must gain a better understanding of the living context of your questions. You must immerse yourself in the life of multi-racial congregations, hang out with young black people, including the justifiably angry ones; talk to the fearsome but compassionate elders; ask advice and learn some wisdom. This process was life changing – but very painful.

Ethnography is the multi-layered study of cultural forms as they exist in everyday contexts . . . A key part of this approach to research has always been the self-conscious use of the self as research instrument – indeed the

> *acute, observing self is the guarantor of the authenticity of data. Autoeth-*
> *nography takes this process a good deal further. Instead of the researcher*
> *being a disciplined observer of social processes 'out there' the project is*
> *brought much closer to home. The focus in autoethnography is upon the*
> *analysis and communication of those experiences that have shaped the*
> *researcher themselves. Personal experience becomes a data source . . . This*
> *recognition of the significance of particular, located and embodied experi-*
> *ence has been made possible by the postmodern reflexive turn in epistemol-*
> *ogy. It is critically linked to liberative movements such as feminism, postco-*
> *lonialism, and queer theory which all have emphasised the importance of*
> *the standpoint from which we view the world.*
>
> (Walton, 2014, p. 3)

Alongside my research work, I was developing as a worship leader at church and was working with a small gospel choir of teenage girls. I helped them construct, through role playing and improvisation, dramatic representations of their experience of being young black women in the church. These short performance pieces were powerful; they were soon performing them beyond local churches at synods and national meetings. However, they were not as profoundly resonant as the music that accompanied them – composed by the choir members themselves and combining their current experience with a deep, creative tradition linked to their denominational roots, but drawing on spiritual resources far beyond those of contemporary Methodism – or indeed Christianity.

After three years my research report was produced (Walton, 1985). Despite its limitations it has since served some useful purposes in the process of communal reflection. However, I was left with an awareness that what I had produced, my mirror on the church, was a very one-dimensional image, perhaps not the vital resource it might have been. A sense that I had only just begun to understand the rich potential for other ways of generating knowledge propelled me to undertake postgraduate study in applied social research. My studies confirmed that while research might include counting, observing and elucidating it has the potential to be much more than this. Furthermore, my personal tensions concerning the role of a researcher (I had long abandoned the notion of objective observation) were mirrored in academic debate. Fierce arguments were taking place between scholars representing a bewildering variety of methodological positions. The choice of research methods, it appeared, was not simply a matter of choosing the best tools for the job. Innocent-looking techniques of data collection carried with them fundamental understandings about the nature of reality itself. I quickly understood that beliefs about existence (ontology) predicate which ways of knowing are judged valid (epistemology) and these shape the research approach and design (methodology) that eventually constructs our picture of the world.

Many years on my reflections on these matters, deepened through participation in many different projects and contexts, have distilled into the conviction that the research journey is itself a spiritual quest. The researcher must take the risk of journeying out of their own safe space and entering new worlds in which they will be changed and formed. They must abandon the illusion that they can present a true mirror of an existing situation whose veracity is confirmed either by their theological framework or their methodological rigour. A dialogical process is what makes good research – a truly attentive listening to the other. This requires a certain self-emptying, a letting go, and a willingness to let the process change the person whose own self is the vulnerable research instrument employed. The products of this research are seldom tidy data sets; the more dialogical and transformative the process has been the less control the researcher has over the outcomes.

Although I admit to find the noisy debates about methodologies and methods very interesting, I do think that most forms of social research have the potential to be undertaken in a manner which acknowledges the dialogical and transformative nature of a research process and the researcher's own place within it. My early sociological mentors were committed to large-scale, survey-based research believing it has the potential to be socially transformative. But they painfully educated me to acknowledge that I had to leave my own comfort zone and engage deeply with the context I was researching if I was to learn how to ask important questions. The seriousness with which they took the 'spiritual discipline' of research preparation has stayed with me and is one of the main reasons that I am unwilling to join with those who regard so-called 'empirical research' as an oppressive way of knowing that inevitably produces reductive representations of cultural life.

Whilst I have no desire to denounce other approaches, my own journey has been more and more towards reflexive research methods that entail a deep focus upon particular instances. Practical theology, I believe, has tended to identify social research with the process of understanding classes of persons or social processes at work within religious communities. However, there is much to be gained by engaging again with that tradition of social research which has emerged through anthropology and cultural studies and which gazes with wondering attention upon particular instances in everyday life and celebrates the amazing creative resources of persons in mundane and everyday contexts. Like parables, attention to epiphanic moments generates wisdom that begins with, but extends beyond, the concrete and particular. One of my most beloved academic writers is the French cultural theorist Michel de Certeau. He brings his early training as a Jesuit to his social research. The discipline of spiritual formation within this tradition emphasises the revelatory potential of every human circumstance and every specific human encounter. Once again careful attentiveness and the willingness to be transformed in meeting the other are the guiding principles of this research practice. Furthermore it acknowledges human beings as being what de Certeau calls 'unrecognised producers, poets of their own acts, silent discoverers of their own paths in the jungle of functional rationality'. In other words, we are makers of our social worlds – all of us. Researchers and participants alike.

> *Wondering attention must be focused upon what de Certeau calls the particular. Attention to the particular is not easy. All our epistemological categories, de Certeau argues, are attuned to the abstracted generality but 'there remains so much to understand about the . . . "obscure heroes" of the ephemeral, those walking in the city, inhabitants of neighbourhoods, readers and dreamers' . . . He was filled with 'wonder' at the creativity of obscure women in kitchens and the humble and tenacious challenge their unnoted existence posed to dominant theories of social life.*
>
> (Walton, 2014, p. 182)

This understanding of culture, as a continuing process of creative making that involves us all, is one which has become increasingly important in social research recently (Walton, 2012). We live in very exciting times in which it is still possible to engage in traditional forms of empirical research to useful ends, but in which we can also employ the techniques more commonly associated with the creative arts to understand our social and spiritual worlds. This move has not yet received much attention in theological circles despite its huge potential. Arts-based research methodologies employ a whole range of creative techniques in order to generate knowledge. Attentiveness to the other is expressed in the process of research itself as much as in the outcomes. This open-ended, imaginative way of addressing the poetry of human existence lends itself to theological reflection in a fresh, challenging and generative way.

I remember listening to the gospel choir rehearsing in our rather uninspiring church hall in Birmingham and thinking, 'right here and now is sounding the music of all the spheres, the song that sung creation into being – if only we have ears to hear.' My vision for practical theological research is that it seeks to catch the echoes of this melody and to sing it well.

> *Why aren't the potentialities and problems of arts based or creative methodologies that are now becoming increasingly prominent in qualitative research being explored in practical theology? Clearly they are not empirical in the strict sense of the word but they are productive, political, engaging and transformative. They belong with our attempts to understand the depths of life and furthermore these newly emerging arts based methodologies offer us a particular challenge; they claim to be spiritually informed.*
>
> (Walton, 2015)

Seven theses about research in practical theology

You have now read four narratives of engagement about how the authors of this book got into, and understand practical theological research. You will have noticed differences and similarities in style and content between the four – we have not attempted to homogenise them – and you will have some sense of the different characters and preoccupations that contribute to our practical theological research. Practical theology is a spacious room; there is opportunity for different people with varying faith, life and intellectual commitments, using different methods and approaches, to enter and join the conversation and exploration that informs research.

We now want to provide a different perspective or 'take' on what we do by putting before you seven theses or propositions about what we believe is central to the practical theological research endeavour. This is, if you like, a kind of manifesto, a statement of commitments that we share in common. We think these characterise what is most important about the kind of practical theological research we are commending in this book. You have seen us talking diffusely and even past each other in our personal narratives. These did, in fact emerge from real conversations that we had to try and construct this book when we asked the question, 'Who are the people sitting round this table and why are we here?' Now we want to share with you what we think are the seven most important characteristics of practical theological research as we have come to understand it. The theses are presented in a very compressed form and the ideas in them will be expanded upon, directly and often indirectly, in the rest of the book; you might like to return to them later if they seem too dense and Delphic at the present juncture.

1   Practical theological research must start with the here and now

We (all of us) start from where we are, in the middle of life and experience; it is in the contemporary moment of embodied being that we choose to attend to particular things and direct our gaze in specific directions. Practical theological research affords priority to the 'texts' of contemporary experience and practice. There is no place or time but this present from which to start, nothing more important to explore and understand, nowhere else that divinity and the material order, including humanity, can be apprehended and responded to. Theological researchers, embodied, temporal, contextualised social beings, shaped by biology, the environment, society and the certainty of death, start their work in the present moment. The Christian tradition, the Bible, the community, and many other things inflected by the past deserve respect and attention. However, attending to, and indwelling the texts of contemporary experience deepens experience and understanding. It also provides better questions and insights for theological inquiry. If not here and now, where and when?

2   Nothing is sacred; everything is sacred

Practical theological researchers embrace the secular, 'what is of this age', as inseparable from the sacred. For practical theological research 'nothing is sacred'; everything is up for questioning and critical scrutiny, including the taken-for-granted processes, beliefs and thought-patterns of human societies, religious beliefs and practices, and theological constructions. Dialectically, however, 'everything is sacred'. The theologically disclosive may be found in the created and the quotidian, in the 'secular' as well as the 'sacred'. Practical theological research problematises the sacred/secular distinction. What we experience and name as sacred is 'of this age' as surely as what we experience and name, for example, as 'educative' or 'democratic'.

3 Careful attentiveness to the object of study has revelatory potential

Divine grace is found in everyday experiences. Thus revelation occurs through human experience as well as revealed tradition. Human action is redolent with meaning and expressive of deep values and action-guiding world-views: the material is suffused with signs of transcendence. This reaches beyond the useful to touch the tragic and sublime. Humanity's engagement in creation through the material and symbolic activities of world-building and meaning-making participates in God's continuing work of creation and redemption. This sacramental thinking and looking seeks the 'radiant immanence' of all things (Steiner, 1981, p. 1144). Transcendence is not the absence of the material or concrete, but its transformation. And, 'because the whole created order and the activity that constitute human history are potential disclosures of God to us, then all the human sciences, disciplines of learning, and ways of knowing are potential resources for our theologizing' (Groome, 1987, p. 61).

4 To be a practical theological researcher is to be a reflexive, critical and constructive inhabitant of an action-guiding world-view

There is no human world without world-views, chosen or assumed. All people on earth inhabit action-guiding world-views or cultures that seem unquestionably real and self-evident. Practical theological researchers try consciously to notice and explore the features of their own world-views, to become critically aware of the implications of the habits, objects, assumptions, beliefs and practices of the world-views that guide perception and action. This allows taking more responsibility for them, even challenging them, permitting different, more creative kinds of faithful action and engagement within that world-view. In this reflexive mode, researchers are changed by their own research as the form and content of what we believe we know is exposed to the critical scrutiny of evidence and arguments, of information gained and conceptualisations born.

5 Practical theological research is about moving and making, not mirroring

Theological reflection and reflective practice are essential to practical theological research, emphasising close observation. But 'seeing' risks descending into mimesis:

replicating, imitating, mirroring, reflecting back those elements that are important to researchers themselves and reinforcing customary patterns of professional behaviour and perception. A hallmark of a genuine epiphany is that the person who 'sees' must themselves make a move. The transforming effect that practical theological research facilitates should be that we start moving. Contemporary practical theological research rightly values clear vision – the kind of vision that shows the way to travel.

6   Knowledge arises within the reality and diversity of creative practice

Objective knowledge is a chimera. We understand the world as we engage with it. Observation cannot be divorced from participation. Truth is found through the making and shaping of material contexts, human lives and human history. This is understanding of truth as coming into being; truth in the process of formation; truth that is active in the world. Social research has also made a reflexive/participatory turn entailing a broadening of the understanding of research processes. Social researchers model the careful analysis of phenomena undertaken in the natural sciences, looking to the arts for understandings of what research entails. Creative artists make knowledge through practice. Meaning emerges in the making as something new comes into being that transforms how we comprehend what was previously present. This is easily comprehended on a grand scale with new understanding of humanity 'revealed' by Michelangelo's *David* or Rembrandt's reinterpretation of biblical scenes painted in the idiom of everyday life. More mundanely, when we make a home or plant a garden we create micro-cosmologies – visions of what we believe the world can and should be. In all creative work, it is within practice that knowing lies.

7   Process is as important as telos in practical theological research

The process and journey of practical theological research is as important as any final results, findings or insights. There is no finality in any kind of theological endeavour. Practical theological research consciously embraces the importance of the process of exploring practice/experience, theory and theology as having intrinsic value. Research leads to interim insights and judgements, to practical wisdom and creative imaginative possibilities. But these are staging posts on a journey that continues in the lives of faith groups, individuals and communities. Journeying is valuable and enlightening in itself in seeking to discern divinity in the incomplete complexity of the material and social world. The ongoing dynamic transformation of lives, practices and thinking accompanying practical theological research assists life to embrace and enhance life. This valuing of process is captured in the notion of praxis: action/understanding leading perpetually to new understanding/action that finds validation in performance. Concretely, this can be expressed in notions of continuous theological reflection emerging from and leading into practice. The research process itself creatively generates wisdom and continues beyond the point of production.

The theses outlined here do not exhaust the meaning, nature and priorities of practical theological research. They are intended sharply to capture some of our distinctive concerns and insights into the nature of this activity. Key nodes in our understanding of the field, they by no means exhaust the concerns and approaches that researchers bring to practical theology – as you will see below. They emerge from our own experiences and conversations – but different conversations and experiences might very well produce different theses. Perhaps you might like to write your own in response to ours?

Conclusion

In this chapter, we have tried to present a partial and complex picture of the nature, priorities and 'feel' of practical theological research from the very particular perspective of four researchers. Reflecting the diverse and pluriform nature of practical theological research itself, in approaches, outcomes and processes, we have attempted to locate ourselves and practical theological research within our own experiences of life and research. By presenting material in a variety of different ways, we hope that we will have given you a good sense of where we are coming from and what we believe research in practical theology can be and feel like. You may have felt moments of recognition or enticement in our various accounts, or moments of dis-identification and dissatisfaction. This is to be expected. Practical theological research involves a complex conversation about complicated things; we disclaim any Olympian viewpoint or superior wisdom in relation to this field. We have tried to articulate who we are and how and why we are implicated and involved in this complex, creative field. As you move through this book, you will hear the voices and experiences of others involved in practical theological research conversations and of their commitments, methods and learning experiences. This will provide confirming and contrasting perspectives with those outlined above as we now go on to explore further aspects and horizons of practical theological research, hoping to draw readers further into its rich complexity.

References

Bennett, Z., 2011. 'To see fearlessly, pitifully': What does John Ruskin have to offer to practical theology? *International Journal of Practical Theology*, 14, pp. 189–203.

Bennett, Z., 2013. *Using the Bible in practical theology: Historical and contemporary perspectives.* Farnham: Ashgate.

Bennett, Z., 2016. Finding a critical space: Scripture and experience in practical theology. In: A. Paddison, ed., *Theologians on scripture*. London: Bloomsbury T & T Clark. pp. 23–35.

Bennett, Z. and Rowland, C., 2016. *In a glass darkly: The Bible, reflection, and everyday life.* London: SCM Press.

Cahalan, K.A. and Mikoski, G.S., eds., 2014. *Opening the field of practical theology: An introduction.* Lanham: Rowman and Littlefield.

Carson, R., 1962. *Silent spring.* Harmondsworth: Penguin.

Dyson, A.O., 1983. Pastoral theology: Towards a new discipline. *Contact: The Interdisciplinary Journal of Pastoral Studies,* 78, pp. 2–8.

Eakin, P.J., 2004. *The ethics of life writing.* New York: Columbia University Press.

Graham, E., 1989. The pastoral needs of women. *Contact: The Interdisciplinary Journal of Pastoral Studies,* 100, pp. 23–25.

Graham, E., 1990. Feminism, pastoral theology and the future. *Contact: The Interdisciplinary Journal of Pastoral Studies,* 103, pp. 2–9.

Graham, E., 1995. *Making the difference: Gender, personhood and theology.* London: Mowbray.

Graham, E., 1996. *Transforming practice: Pastoral theology in an age of uncertainty.* London: Mowbray.

Graham, E., 2000. Pastoral theology as transforming practice. In: J.W. Woodward and S. Pattison, eds., *The Blackwell reader in pastoral and practical theology.* Oxford: Wiley-Blackwell. pp. 104–117.

Graham, E., Walton, H. and Ward, F., 2005. *Theological reflection: Methods.* London: SCM Press.

Groome, T.H., 1987. Theology on our feet: A revisionist pedagogy for healing the gap between academia and ecclesia. In: L.S. Mudge and J.N. Poling, eds., *Formation and reflection: The promise of practical theology.* Philadelphia: Fortress Press. pp. 55–78.

Pattison, S., 1997. *The faith of the managers: When management becomes religion.* London: Cassell.

Pattison, S., 2000a. *Shame: Theory, therapy, theology.* Cambridge: Cambridge University Press.

Pattison, S., 2000b. Some straw for the bricks: A basic introduction to theological reflection. In: J.W. Woodward and S. Pattison, eds., *The Blackwell reader in pastoral and practical theology.* Oxford: Wiley-Blackwell. pp. 135–145.

Pattison, S., 2007. *The challenge of practical theology.* London: Jessica Kingsley.

Plato, 1966. Plato in Twelve Volumes, Vol. 1 translated by Harold North Fowler; Introduction by W.R.M. Lamb. Cambridge, MA: Harvard University Press; London: William Heinemann Ltd. Available at: www.perseus.tufts.edu/hopper/text?doc=plat.+apol.+38a.

Rogers, C.R., 1969. *Freedom to learn: A view of what education might become.* Columbus, OH: Charles E. Merrill.

Steiner, G., 1981. The house of being, a review of Martin Heidegger's *Gesamtausgabe. Times Literary Supplement,* 4097, 9 October, pp. 1143–1144.

Stoddart, E., 2014. *Advancing practical theology: Critical discipleship for disturbing times.* London: SCM Press.

Walton, H., 1985. *A tree God planted: Black people in British methodism.* London: Methodist Publishing House.

Walton, H., 2012. Poetics. In: B.J. Miller-McLemore, ed., *The Wiley-Blackwell companion to practical theology.* Oxford: Wiley-Blackwell. pp. 173–182.

Walton, H., 2014. *Writing methods in theological reflection.* London: SCM Press.

Walton, H., 2015. Unpublished paper for TRS research seminar, University of Glasgow, October 2015.

2

REFLECTION, REFLEXIVITY AND THE RESEARCH JOURNEY

In the last chapter we presented narrative testimonies to our own commitments as practical theologians. They recorded how our perceptions have developed and changed. They describe moments of clarity and vision: the small epiphanies that shape lives and form faith. These stories were then reflected upon and refined into propositional statements about the nature of practical theology itself. The statements clarify and re-present approaches to practical theological understanding as alternatives to a more generalised or abstract form of knowledge.

The process outlined above is a common one. Indeed the drawing of close ties between developing perception – ways of seeing or apprehending – and the construction of knowledge – ways of knowing – is something so very familiar that we usually take for granted. In common sense terms we imagine people, from early infancy, growing in understanding as they observe the world around them and then reflect upon it. We grant profound respect to the sort of knowledge that appears grounded in the reality of what can be seen and shown. However, it is important to recognise that this way of 'thinking about knowing' does not simply describe the natural processes of human and reasoning. It is also profoundly culturally determined. Since this is a chapter that begins to focus our attention upon ways of knowing in practical theology we have work to do in interrogating our own reflective practices and placing them in a wider critical frame.

In this chapter, then, we will be inquiring further into the implications of these productive, but ambivalent, methods of knowing and understanding within practical theology, particularly as they have been manifest in our enthusiastic embrace of the techniques of reflective practice. The authors of this book have all taught and supervised through the paradigms of reflective practice for many years and we can all testify to the positive merits of this approach to academic enquiry and personal development. It encourages self-awareness, develops self-confidence and can be personally transformative – especially when it enables people to make strong links between their beliefs and their actions. However, we feel that it is now time that the same sort of critical scrutiny be applied to its use in practical theology as is now taking place within other disciplines, where serious challenges to its hegemony have emerged in recent years. There is a movement to the chapter which begins with practices of seeing the other well, then considers the need to see the self well, not as an end in itself, but as part of a movement back to the better seeing of the other.

Two key concepts, 'reflection' and 'reflexivity', will be interrogated, and their implications for the practical theological researcher examined. The meanings given to these terms in published work are not always consistent. Here, being reflective suggests looking thoughtfully at something – usually at some length, perhaps with the benefit of hindsight, and with a critical eye. Being 'reflexive' suggests additionally looking thoughtfully at one's own self – at what I am like, at how I see what is outside of myself, how I affect it, or how my seeing of it affects how I present it. We will be suggesting that it is important to acknowledge the limitations of the predominance of 'reflection' on practice within practical theology; to ask what biases it conceals, and what alternative modes of knowing and thinking about ourselves, the world and the divine might be available. Can practical theological researchers recognise and accept their own complicity as both subject and object of their own investigation? And is it possible to move beyond a naïve faith in the transparency of our own 'reflection on practice' to reach a more nuanced understanding of ourselves in relation to a complex field of knowledge and practice?

Reflection: observing the object

Reflective practice in practical theology is often associated with forms of personal and vocational formation in which it has been *the* dominant pedagogical approach for several decades (Graham, Walton and Ward, 2005; Thompson, Pattison and Thompson, 2008). This development is related to a larger movement in healthcare, education, social work training and beyond to re-evaluate how professionals learn, make decisions and develop competencies through practice.

It is, however, important to note that, as used within practical theology, this pedagogical model has at least four roots, and the goals and intentions of its use may vary considerably depending which explicitly or implicitly underlies the practice and research context.

> One root is in the educational tradition of experiential learning. This tradition emphasises that the way human beings learn is through their own experience, and through reflection on that experience. Other learning remains at a shallow or superficial level. A second root is in the professional tradition of the development of the reflective, therefore effective, practitioner . . . . . A third root is in the movement to return research and the development of theory and practice to the practitioners. This is has [sic] a strong tradition in the public service professions. Finally a [significant and familiar] root . . . is

liberation theology, which uses the Marxian concept of praxis to encourage reflection on practices in order to interrogate those practices, to inform action, and to facilitate change and transformation of society.

(Bennett, 2014, pp. 62–63)

A key thinker behind this influential reappraisal of professional expertise was Donald Schön. He was dismayed by what he understood as a reductive focus upon technical and instrumental competencies and deeply influenced by the theories of experiential learning which were gaining traction in liberal circles and informed educational practice from the 1960s onwards. He sought to understand how in complex and messy situations, in which pre-determined protocols were of little value, professionals shaped their practice through processes of 'reflection-on-action' and 'reflection-in-action'. Reflection-on-action is a retrospective reflective process. Reflection-in-action occurs when the professional, confronted by a new challenge, draws upon tacit wisdom and produces a new reflective response.

Schön came to believe that through recalling previous experience and improvising in response to the immediacy of new challenges:

> The practitioner allows himself [sic] to experience surprise, puzzlement, or confusion in a situation which he finds uncertain or unique. He reflects on the phenomenon before him, and on the prior understandings which have been implicit in his behaviour. He carries out an experiment which serves to generate both a new understanding of the phenomenon and a change in the situation.
>
> *(1983, p. 68)*

It is easy to understand the appeal of Schön's high view of the professional practitioner, creatively scanning the phenomenon before them and responding to the ambiguity and messiness of circumstances with transformative actions that, in turn, generate new understanding. His approach values people and their potential to problem-solve and shape change. In the contemporary context in which highly structured 'evidence-based practice' can appear to restrict the options available to practitioners, it appears to champion an affective, engaged *phronēsis* (practical wisdom) as an alternative or complementary virtue.

A rather different reason for the great popularity of reflective practice in vocational training is the apparently easy adaptability of Schön's thinking into pedagogical programmes. As stated, it has become the dominant paradigm guiding professional formation across a wide range of specialisms. Reflection, in Schön's understanding, is a dynamic and process-based activity. Furthermore, this process can be divided into distinct stages that seem more manageable to both the novice practitioner and the vocational tutor. Typically these stages might include:

- Description of an incident or experience that challenged the reflective practitioner.

- Analysis of their personal response.
- Theoretical linking. How does wider discipline-based knowledge resource reflection on this topic?
- Experimental thinking. Could the reflective practitioner have acted differently?
- Learning Assessment. How has the reflective practitioner's thinking changed?
- Ethical Assessment. How has the reflective process changed beliefs and values?
- Theological reflection. What faith resources are being brought to the situation?
- Action. What should be done with this new knowledge?
- Planning. How will future actions be congruent with new understandings?

(Adapted from Walton, 2014, p. 49)

The stages outlined above are not only commonly employed at the basic level of training in various forms of Christian ministry. They also shape research in practical theology. Frequently, the starting point for a research project is identified as a concrete dilemma that has arisen in practice and which the practitioner *as practical theologian* is seeking to comprehend and address through revised praxis. It is not a coincidence that Action Research flourishes in the same environments (social work, education, healthcare and ministry training) in which reflective practice is most highly regarded (Graham, 2013).

Some of the most exciting contemporary developments of Schön's thinking lie in the field of values-based reflective practice, such as that developed by Michael Paterson and Ewan Kelly, currently widely used in Scottish chaplaincy contexts. Their model proceeds from the presupposition that professionals for whom 'the tool of the trade are nothing less than the intentional use of the self' (Paterson and Kelly, 2013, p. 53), there is an integral link between ontology (professional and personal identity) and epistemology (the process by which one arrives at knowing how to act). Deeper levels of reflection are facilitated by means of encouraging participants to maintain a focus on person-centred care that is congruent with their core values and priorities amidst competing professional and organisational pressures.

Here the virtues which traditionally uphold professionalism find a contemporary and hopeful articulation. 'Maybe', writes Ghaye, 'reflective practices offer us a way of trying to make sense of the uncertainty in our workplaces and the courage to work competently and ethically on the edge of chaos' (Ghaye, 2000, p. 7). Kemmis echoes this when he defines *phronēsis* or practical wisdom as 'the disposition to act wisely in uncertain practical situations' (Kemmis, 2010, p. 422).

Beyond reflection

Many critics argue, however, that reflective practice encourages us to imagine a subject who observes an object with confidence that their observation will reveal the truth of a situation. Extending the visual metaphor, it is as if the process of reflection is merely a matter of holding up a mirror to experience without pausing to consider the problems inherent in giving an objective, transparent or comprehensive account of such a complex category:

> All attempts to privilege reflective knowledge are grounded in a binary divide of subject and object. The object is seen as something that is to be viewed and represented . . . [a] 'spectatorial' notion of knowledge.
>
> *(Canning, 2008, p. 11)*

The immediate implication of this focus is that reflection may become an individualised process based on a particularised view of an incident or experience without attending to the differential perspectives each circumstance contains. Too often the 'others' and the 'Other' in a situation are objectified in this process and this denies the reality of intersubjective ways of knowing (Kinsella, 2003).

Furthermore, because we have such a respect for 'eye-witnessing' in our culture we often fail to recognise that in a reflective account we are not dealing with an accurate representation of events but a construction that is designed (consciously or unconsciously) to serve the needs of its author. It is not simply a matter of simply 'seeing' but 'seeing well' (Bennett, 2010) and of attending consciously and self-critically to the ways in which one's own subjectivity is framed. John Ruskin, for whom seeing was 'the greatest thing a human soul ever does in this world' (in Cook and Wedderburn, 1903–1912, *Works* 5.333), claimed that: 'All true science begins in the love, not the dissection, of your fellow creatures; and it ends in the love, not the analysis, of God' (in Cook and Wedderburn, 1903–1912, *Works* 26.265–266).

If practical theologians are engaged in reading and interpreting a multiplicity of texts – biblical, phenomenological, narrative, theoretical – then there needs to be a way of reading and re-reading that both challenges entrenched understandings and inspires new action.

However, there is another, deeply worrying, aspect of our culture at work within the contemporary vogue for reflective practice. The trainee reflective practitioner is expected to be 'disciplined' and changed through the reflective process (Saltiel, 2010). Students are frequently required to display their intimate thoughts and feeling about a situation and publically confess their faults in a way that appears to be benign and self-directed but may, in fact, entail a gradual process of self-adjustment to dominant norms within their profession or educational context. Furthermore, the enlightenment which reflective accounts strive towards often eliminates the stubborn 'problematic residue' (Canning, 2008, p. 12) in an experience or situation. This residue refers to the elements of the situation that cannot be easily resolved within a typical reflective practice exercise. It includes such things as institutional power, the impossibility of acting innocently and unambiguously in highly complex situations as well as those hard to manage experiences such as desire, fear and irredeemable loss. Despite the supposed space they contain for honest self-questioning, 'successful' reflective accounts are too frequently expected to display a mastery, by the subject, of the objects under observation.

All of these factors may present serious problems when reflective practice is taken as a model for advanced research in practical theology. The structure of a thesis or a research project often uncritically applies the observation-to-knowledge models with which we are very familiar and many follow very closely the reflective practice stages outlined above. Of course, it could be argued that such ways of structuring research are infinitely preferable to the older models in which theology was simply 'applied' to living contexts. Nevertheless, it is important to complexify what is happening in apparently straightforward reflective processes if we are to create attentive and ethical research that acknowledges ambiguity and prescinds from premature closure in relation to the 'uncomfortable' residue with which theology must always wrestle.

Jaco Dreyer, for example, illustrates how his own identity as a practical theologian has radically shifted from early training in a scientific paradigm that privileged the neutrality and objectivity of the researcher, to an awareness of his own complicity with the 'colonial baggage' of apartheid South Africa. Despite his reservations that reflexivity is a recursive, self-referential activity which can never be adequately resolved, he recognises the loss of innocence inherent in the assertion that 'there are no unmediated knowledge claims' and he traces how the focus of his own sense of reflexivity and self-consciousness as a researcher has moved over time from the methodological and epistemological to the ontological (Dreyer, 2016, pp. 126, 130).

> The point is . . . that reflexivity cannot heal the 'epistemological wound' of researcher subjectivity, bias, and positionality. It could help researchers to better understand some of the factors that may influence the knowledge constructed, and it could make them more sensitive to the possible 'violence' in the act of representing others by means of research as well as the many ambiguities related to research practices. However, due to our existential 'situatedness,' our horizons of understanding, we will never be able to escape from our subjectivities . . . Just as we cannot see others from an 'objective' or 'God's eye view,' we cannot see ourselves from this vantage point. Reflecting on our reflexivity will thus continue indefinitely, with no possibility to reach a final point . . .
>
> *(Dreyer, 2016, p. 126)*

Being a privileged, white person confronts me and challenges me in my work as a practical theologian at a public university. How can I from my position as 'settler coloniser' . . . responsibly fulfill my duties as a practical theologian with a subjectivity tainted by colonialism and apartheid? . . . I cannot escape my colonial baggage in a postcolonial context. This colonial baggage is an important part of my subjectivity as researcher and colors every action that I take . . . My interest in the issue of researcher subjectivity and bias thus expanded from concerns primarily about research approaches and methods to concerns about ethical issues related to power and knowledge, whiteness, coloniality, and the knowledge system itself.

(Dreyer, 2016, pp. 132–133)

In the discussion so far, we have begun critically to interrogate reflection as a way of knowing that assumes it can record a true representation of things 'out there'. This often fails to acknowledge how far the reflective practitioner is implicated in the view they observe, and where they stand determines what they see. There is no place to observe the world from that will grant us a divine eye view of persons and events – we are all, already, part of the landscape that we seek to represent (Haraway, 1988).

Furthermore, we risk limiting our understanding of ourselves and others when our reflective processes tend towards over-emphasising the objective nature of the observer's account of what they see, without acknowledging the identity-constructing and performative nature of reflective accounts themselves. Similarly, reflective practice often fails to acknowledge the significance of intersubjectivity, or the understandings that occur through intuitive connections and purposeful conversations with others. By focusing on the professional competence and expertise of the subject, an over-instrumental approach to reflective practice may fail to acknowledge the 'otherness' of what is observed by seeking to incorporate it into the authoritative world-view of the observer. The process may inadvertently impose misleading coherence and intelligibility upon messy, disturbing or distressing encounters and events (Kinsella, 2003).

These are serious issues of concern. However, the forms of reflection discussed above, in which practical theology remains deeply invested, should not be dismissed as well-intentioned but deeply flawed practices. It is when we seriously engage with such reflective processes that we begin to understand both their uses and their limitations. The processes of reflection themselves have a powerful tendency to bring us to an acknowledgement of their limits and point us towards all sorts of significant entanglements – within ourselves, with others and in relation to the divine – that resist being unravelled. Thus they urge us towards ways of knowing that are stronger and more resilient and simultaneously more complex, ambivalent and challenging.

Reflexivity: attending to the subject/s

To be reflective does not demand an 'other' while to be reflexive demands both an other and some self-conscious awareness of the process of self-scrutiny

(Chiseri-Strater, quoted in Roulston, 2010, p. 116)

Reflexivity is the term used to describe an epistemological stance 'beyond reflection'. However, whilst reflexivity digs deeper and travels further than reflection it is important not to think of reflection and reflexivity as a binary or oppositional pairing. The two belong together in a fragile but unbroken continuum. Indeed, '[c]ritically reflective practice is underpinned by reflexivity . . . This is particularly important in research because, without reflexivity, we can fall into the trap of simply seeing what we expect to see, and our conclusions then become predictable' (Bassot, 2016, p. 130).

Reflexivity can offer a significant tool to practical theological researchers through autoethnography, as this account from a professional doctoral student illustrates.

REFLEXIVITY AS A TOOL OF RESEARCH: MINDFUL SELF-COMPASSION AND CONTEMPLATIVE ENQUIRY

Mary Younger, a Buddhist psychologist, used a highly self-reflexive approach in her professional doctoral research to explore the use of self-compassion in her personal and professional work.

My aim was to explore the cultivation of Self-compassion within my personal and professional contexts across a time span of one year. I needed to understand self-compassion from the inside out, and so I chose a qualitative methodology since I believed it would be the most appropriate way to explore and understand the complexity, contexts, meaning and richness of my experience. To account for the subjective, representational and contextual nature of my experience, I adopted an autoethnographic approach. Adopting an 'epistemology of insiderness' enabled me to access, reflect on and make sense of my experience. Underpinning my approach to autoethnography were four elements: a) contemplative inquiry, which involves Buddhist meditation and inquiry, b) Mindful Self-compassion practice and inquiry, c) critical reflexivity and d) journaling. All of these activities are contained within a model of 'Contemplative Practice', which encompasses the research processes and activities that are integral in exploring the cultivation of self-compassion.

Reflexivity and the construction of the self

We began this chapter by arguing that the principles of reflection appear easy to understand and confirm a common sense understanding of how we come to know the world. In contrast the language we have used to describe reflexivity (complex, ambivalent and challenging) already suggests the concept might be more difficult to grasp hold of. And indeed it is! This is partly because the word itself carries a number of related, but differing meanings, depending upon the context in which it is used. It can refer, for example, to the work of personal formation in postmodern cultures. In this context social theorist Anthony Giddens (1991) argues that contemporary individuals now engage in a 'reflexive project of the self' – that is a work of self-construction the aim of which is to demonstrate to others that they have attained personal 'actualisation' and 'authenticity' (become true to themselves) through an integration of values, lifestyle and achievements. Although this is an important use of the term, which emphasises the constructed nature of identity and its specular character, it is not the one which is our chief concern here.

Reflexivity as self-in-relation

Rather, we are more interested in the way social researchers use the word to refer to the processes through which they seek to become appropriately and self-consciously situated in relation to their research projects. Reflexivity begins when we start to ask some very basic questions:

- How does my personal history influence my approach to this topic?
- How does my social location (gender, class, ethnicity, sexual identity, religion, cultural location) impact upon my understanding?
- What is my own entanglement in what I am seeking to understand?
- Where do my allegiances lie and how do my religious and moral values and political commitments guide my inquiry?
- What can my body and my emotional responses contribute to my attempts to understand this subject?
- What are my responsibilities to the others involved in this research, whether participants, co-investigators or sponsors?
- What kind of knowledge do I want to create and who is it for?

Our identities are complex, multifaceted and always constructed in relation to others. A second way of understanding reflexivity places particular emphasis upon the ethical imperative to challenge both our self-understandings and our perceptions of the world in order to become accountable to those whose lives touch ours (Bochner and Ellis, 2002; Denzin, 2003). This kind of reflexivity is an attempt to understand the self-in-relation and is an acknowledgement of the profoundly political nature of knowledge creation. It is associated with the impact of critical movements such as feminism, queer theory and post-colonialism upon research paradigms. These movements challenged researchers to reconsider their claims to neutrality and lack of bias and forged a new awareness of the power dynamics that structure all research relationships. Thus reflexive researchers need to undertake a number of critical moves:

> The first is epistemological and asks 'what is knowledge and how is it acquired?' The second is political and inquires as to 'how knowledge is produced and by whom.' The third is dialogical and asks 'whose voices are heard and whose are silenced in the pursuit of knowledge?'
>
> *(Paterson and Kelly, 2013, p. 53)*

Social researchers vary in the degree to which they admit the legitimacy of the challenges represented by emancipatory political movements and critical cultural theories. For some, these are unhelpful distractions from their efforts to undertake serious empirical work. But many others have accepted that it is academic good practice to become present and accountable in research. It has become common for research studies of all kinds to contain a reflexive element in which the context, values and responsibilities of the researchers and their research project are addressed. This positive move addresses a number of the epistemological problems previously noted. However, it is important to question whether the reflexive turn has really provoked deep changes in the way social research is perceived and practised – or whether things continue to go on much as they did before.

Zoë Bennett and Chris Rowland have considered how the practices of seeing, reflection and discernment facilitate greater self-understanding, and especially awareness of how one's own social, economic, cultural, ideological locations are complicit in the construction of knowledge. 'We are bound to see and understand partially; it matters to know what the "parts" are that we are seeing, and how our *way* of seeing both reveals and distorts' (Bennett and Rowland, 2016, pp. 3–4).

They contrast the self-absorption of Narcissus with his own reflection in Caravaggio's famous painting with the more complex, fluid and multi-dimensional images occasioned by looking onto the surface of 'The Bean', a famous urban sculpture in down-town Chicago. Rather than assuming reflection to be a simple matter of holding up a mirror to experience, it is important to regard the process as one of seeing 'in a glass darkly':

> To see your own reflection is not necessarily to know the full "truth" about yourself; nor is seeking to see your own reflection always a safe practice . . . Furthermore, the image of looking into a pool of water, or a bedroom mirror, is too simple to denote the practice of reflexivity. Anyone who has visited Chicago and seen Anish Kapoor's "Cloud Gate", popularly known as "the Bean", will have seen a vastly more complex form of "self-reflection". In this massive sculpture with a highly reflective surface of seamless stainless steel plates, curved and shaped like a bean, your reflection is distorted by the curves and given a context within the also-distorted reflections of the crowd, the clouds and the skyscrapers of down downtown Chicago. As you move and look from another angle your own reflection changes. People take pictures of themselves taking pictures of themselves, taking pictures of themselves. The process of self-reflexivity is infinitely regressive. The more clarity the more mystery, leading to more clarity and thence to more mystery. This is the heart of the ongoing task of self-reflexivity.
>
> *(Bennett and Rowland, 2016, p. 152)*

After innocence

Before the values and social location of researchers became subject to such close scrutiny it was assumed that research was an undisputedly moral venture of better seeing, shedding light on what had lain in darkness. In our less confident, more critical, context there is nostalgia for such innocence; a desire to believe that research can still be undertaken in an ethical way and yet in a manner that acknowledges previous critiques. Pillow (2003) argues that many contemporary social researchers adopt a reflexive position out of a misplaced desire for purity. They preface the presentation of their research with a confession. They admit that they are privileged in class and social location, are frank about their own presuppositions and values, and discuss the importance of giving voice to research participants – whilst never presuming to have completely overcome the problems of power relations in research relationships. Like all confessions, the aim of these acknowledgements is the restoration of innocence.

> Prominent in much qualitative research is the idea that the researcher, through reflexivity can transcend her own subjectivity and cultural context in a way that releases her/him from the weight of (mis)representations. Self-reflexivity can perform a modernist seduction – promising release from your tension, voyeurism, ethnocentrism – a release from your discomfort with representation.
>
> *(Pillow, 2003, p. 186)*

Pillow is not arguing that reflexivity should be abandoned, but that it is not possible to conduct 'pure' ethical research in an unethical world. This is uncomfortable. Discomforting reflexivity enables us to proceed, painfully and with caution, in undertaking research which we know it is important to do, yet impossible to get completely right.

> I am advocating . . . the necessity of an ongoing critique of all our research attempts . . . with the realisation that many of us do engage in research where there is real work to be done even in the face of the impossibility of such a task. This is a move to use reflexivity in a way that would continue to challenge the representations we come to while at the same time acknowledging the political need to represent and find meaning.
>
> *(Pillow, 2003, p. 192)*

We concur with Pillow's thinking here. We are fully convinced that neither reflection nor reflexivity are neutral research stances. Nevertheless, we choose to adopt them because there is important work to be done and we are seeking the best possible ways to do it. This requires us to accept the ambivalence inherent in our actions. We cannot be relieved from our necessary discomfort in undertaking research through a privileged reversion to our primary theological vocation – as if, unlike secular academics, we have somewhere nice and safe to go home to. There is a tendency within some areas of practical theology to assume that the imperfections of research endeavours can somehow be overcome when these are subordinated to the magisterial influence of theology. As we have already argued, however, the processes of reflection that take place within theology are as limited and culturally determined as those which take place with any other epistemological frameworks.

Furthermore, those of us who seek to work reflexively *within* the theological tradition must become acutely aware that this also is a discourse of power containing the same processes of repression, forgetting, unsaying, marginalisation and control that are evident everywhere else. There is certainly glory and wonder in theology but it is not a peaceable place to dwell. But perhaps we are misguided if it is the security of home that we are seeking?

By contrast, Mary McClintock Fulkerson argues that to read a practical situation 'theologically' (in her case, an ethnographic congregational study of Good Samaritan Church, North Carolina) necessitates beginning from its 'worldly' character. Yet the initial task of describing a situation – even when characterising it as complex, dense and changing (Fulkerson, 2007, pp. 11–12) – also involves locating the researcher's pre-commitments and diagnoses of any given situation. That includes unmasking the societal and personal 'obliviousness' to structures and patterns of power, difference and exclusion. In Fulkerson's case, that was a matter of unearthing and acknowledging her discomfort with the disjunction between a discourse of inclusivity and the lived experiences of those in the congregation who were African-American or people with disabilities. For her, it arose out of an attentiveness to a proprioceptive, instinctive, awkwardness at entering a space where, as a white able-bodied academic, she felt 'out of place' and ill-at-ease:

> My feeling of strangeness in response to the unaccustomed "blackness" of the place and the presence of people with disabilities at that first visit suggests that my conscious commitments to inclusiveness were not completely correlated with my habituated sense of the normal. My posture "confessed" a disruption of the dominant world I inhabit, signaling an implicit break between my convictions and these perceptions. This tacit sense that surprised me when I became self-conscious of my whiteness and my able-bodiedness suggests forms of occlusion operating in my own internalised sense of the world . . . It is an unaccustomedness and obliviousness with widespread parallels, not only at Good Samaritan, but in the larger society as well. It is an obliviousness that comes with dominance, and it foreshadows fracture in the smooth veneer of welcome and Christly inclusivity in the church as well.
>
> *(Fulkerson, 2007, p. 15)*

Fulkerson's embodied reflexivity alerts her to the 'disjunctures' within her understanding, a sense 'of what is out of place, of what is broken and needs to be fixed, as well as . . . what is good and compels thanksgiving' (2007, p. 15). This fracturing represents the 'wound' from which creative thinking, and theological reflection, will emerge. (It is, of course, a profoundly Christological assertion to state that theology 'originates at the scene of a wound' (2007, p. 13).) From attending to the *body language* of her own reflexivity, Fulkerson is able to get in touch with the underlying dynamics and contradictions at the heart of Good Samaritan congregational life – including her own entanglements in that culture.

And the body?

Fulkerson's work reminds us that embodiment is an important feature of the literature on reflexivity (see also Leach and Paterson, 2015, pp. 143–164; Kinsella, 2007). Embodied encounters structure research relationships and are themselves sources of knowledge – and, crucially, by operating at different levels of consciousness, they are capable of disrupting, or troubling, other habituated or taken-for-granted ways of knowing.

The knowledge which emerges from attention to our own practices and processes of reflexivity resembles more a situated, context-rich practical wisdom than the knowledge engendered by the protocols of abstract rationality (Bass et al., 2016, p. 2; Leach, 2007)). In spite of her reservations regarding Donald Schön's theories, Elizabeth Kinsella contends that his departure from a professional epistemology premised on technical rationality inevitably commits him to an understanding of reflective practice as 'intelligence . . . revealed in ways that extend beyond propositional knowledge in such a way as to be embodied in the actions of persons' (Kinsella, 2007, p. 407). Similarly, a variety of arts-based methodologies and projects in research through creative practice are highlighting bodily wisdom in exciting new ways (Nelson, 2013; Tasker, McLeod-Boyle, and Bridges, 2011).

BODY AND MUSIC IN REFLECTION AND RESEARCH

Eleanor Richards is a psychotherapist and music therapist, investigating understandings of interpersonal events within psychotherapeutic practice from her perspective as a student of Zen in the context of her professional doctorate.

I can only research with my whole self, whether or not I am aware of it. Fundamental to my research is the recognition that much that is significant is felt and processed initially at an unconscious level and is not articulated in words or, in subsequent reflection, framed in conceptual thought.

In the context of research which is concerned with contemplative practice and psychotherapy, the places of language and conceptualisation are continually challenging to consider. Both Zen and psychanalytic thought emphasise experience outside the frame of language as a primary source of learning and understanding, and place faith in the proposal that new perceptions and transformations need not always be put into words. Further, both recognise that most of the emotional energy and impulses that drive our thoughts and feelings are, at first at least, unconscious. Both are also concerned with process itself, rather than with practice as a means to an identified end. As a researcher, with all the anxieties that involvement in that can bring, it feels immensely important for me to find a means of reflection which has immediacy and which involves, as all activity does, my whole self.

I am a musician by background, so part of my reflective/reflexive process is to improvise alone, usually using the piano. I might do that after a session with a patient, after a period of reading or writing, or just when the impulse arises. That could be seen simply as means of some emotional release, but its value for me rests beyond that in the business of moment by moment unfolding of sounds, without any real idea of what is to come, reflecting my continuing unconscious involvement in events. It engages feeling and, through physical action and aural sensation, the body.

There will be many points in this book where these topics are raised and discussed in more depth. We want to place the body in such a theological framework and understand it not only as the place where knowledge begins but to where faith eventually arrives after a long journey.

Knowing ourselves

Self-awareness is an indispensable part of any reflexive research process. Similarly, spiritual direction nominates self-awareness as the *sine qua non* of any process of spiritual growth. Becoming self-aware is not about conducting a skills audit or categorising ourselves according to some basic personality type (interesting and illuminating as these processes can be). Nor is it about the quest for an 'authentic' identity (as in the 'reflexive project of the self' mentioned above). It requires recognising that selfhood is complex and multi-faceted. We are 'many-selved'; it is in the assemblage of these diverse aspects that we find character and create coherence.

There is no quick way to become reflexively self-aware in this extended way. It is a demanding and long-term practice, rather like a spiritual discipline. If we are to flourish in this endeavour, we must become more conscious of the many selves that form us. There will be the dominant ones often related to significant roles we play: colleague, partner, parent, consumer, carer and so on. There are those we repress, such as the frightened child or passionate lover, which may intrude into and disrupt these conventional roles. Perhaps less easy to discern are the aspiring selves and the secret selves we long to nourish. They exercise powerful and sometimes puzzling influence upon our choices causing us to act in ways that we find hard to account for.

DISRUPTIVE SELF-KNOWLEDGE

Clare Herbert has completed research for a professional doctorate on the theological meanings of civil partnership. Listening to her body proved a route to giving herself permission to create her own queer theology of marriage.

> *As I began writing a chapter about the theology of same-sex marriage, before completing it, I took a serious fall. Fainting at the kitchen sink, I hit my head so hard that I was concussed for a month and could not write. At the time, I made no connection between this incident and my attempt to write this chapter. But as I tried to return to the writing, I experienced the strange, overwhelming psychological power of resistance, and knew that I must examine this experience for the chapter to be authentic.*
>
> *I realised on reflection that my resistance to the alignment of civil partnership and marriage stemmed from painful roots. The Bishops of the Church of England had been very cautious about clergy like me entering civil partnerships, but it was not forbidden. To enter a same-sex civil marriage was, by contrast, forbidden, and if I were to do so, I would run the risk of losing my licence to minister. The House of Bishops Pastoral Statement written in response to the same-sex marriage legislation clearly states that clergy are not to enter same-sex marriage, not to bless the same, nor to use church building to do so. The official prohibition is therefore clear and emphatic. Since writing well involves the assimilation and consideration of others' ideas, writing about civil partnership understood by my research participants to be marriage would entail either my inner, possibly dishonest, denial of the appeal and importance of such ideas, or my envisaging for this group something of value which I myself cannot have. Writing necessitated confronting my decision to place my priesthood within the Church of England before my partnership, something I had managed successfully to avoid so far.*
>
> *To write this chapter was to be aware of pain and to find ways of reflecting safely about that pain. It is no wonder, perhaps, that I fell, vomiting up that which was indigestible, broke my head, and injured my brain, since to go on using my brain was possibly too painful to contemplate for a while. I needed time for reflection.*

An important way to gain understanding of our many-selved identity is to attend to our emotions – as is recommended in many spiritual disciplines and in particular the Ignatian exercises. Strong feelings often seem to come from nowhere and can be very threatening. But if accepted gently and attentively held they can often contain important messages that cannot be delivered any other way.

Our multiple, permeable and connected selves are also selves in transition. The work of Van Gennep (1960 [1909]) on rites of passage, and its revision and adaptions through the work of Victor Turner (1969) and others, has encouraged us to pay attention to the process through which people move through different stages of life, careers, relationships and so on. The process of leaving behind one stage of life and entering another is not a simple progression from A to B. Between the place we leave and the destination we arrive at is a liminal (threshold) space where the old has been left behind and the new has not yet been achieved. For example, practitioners who become researchers initially find themselves suspended between identities and no longer certain of either. The process of becoming a practitioner-researcher not only involves academic transitions but a significant shift in self-image, often entailing the shedding of deeply-entrenched anxieties regarding one's own competence to enter the field of advanced research (Wall, 2015):

> Practitioner-researchers step through a doorway from practice to research, and in doing so begin a process of self-examination in order to determine their existing assumptions in preparation for the research project ahead. Individually, such reflection necessarily has a destabilising effect on the person concerned . . . A liminal journey makes the self a stranger: it stretches and sometimes severs the ties of meaning that link us with the everyday life to which we were accustomed.
>
> *(Deegan and Hill, 1991, p. 330)*

Undertaking research can often propel even the seasoned researcher into a lost or liminal state. We prepare ourselves as best we may but 'entering the field' is always entering an unknown world where much of what we have assumed and known is challenged. This will often be an uncomfortable process and involve confronting the difficult personal and ethical issues discussed above. However, what we have found most difficult to prepare our research students to expect is the heightened intensity of feeling and the fascination that they will encounter as they enter this stage of the research journey. In sometimes small but often quite significant ways the vivid encounters of the liminal phase provoke lasting changes in the researcher.

For Bruce Moore, enrolling on a professional doctorate set off a process of enquiry into the unspoken dynamics and assumptions informing his own practice and revealed the dysfunctions within his organisation in ways that eventually made his professional position untenable. He describes it in quasi-biblical terms, as a loss of innocence: from dwelling in paradise, to eating the forbidden fruit of self-reflexive knowledge, to Fall and banishment. Rather than enhancing professional competence, the adoption of reflexive, insider research only exposed uncomfortable truths:

> Until I made the commitment to undertake insider research, I had always been too busy and task oriented to notice or consider the assumptions and norms of behaviour implicit in my day to day interactions which were shaping my perceptions and sense of identity. I found that professional codes and protocols did not encourage the asking of seemingly awkward questions and social bonds of loyalty and my desire to fit in meant I had held off from critically evaluating or challenging the way the organisation worked.
>
> It was only when I recognised and embraced the subjectivity of my own special position and perspectives as an inside researcher that my studies started to have any real meaning or personal consequence . . .
>
> Rather than shining the light of truth outwards onto others, insider research was turning the spotlight of scrutiny back onto me to consider the perceptions and insights that were hidden within me and my psyche . . . .

The sin I committed by undertaking insider research was to bring to light and start to taste my guiding assumptions and preferences so that I could appreciate and distinguish my position and feelings from the dominant views and values that held sway within the board.

Doing anything that raised doubts about the fundamental assumptions upon which the board of the organisation based its definition and legitimacy, however, could be seen to be tantamount to a treasonable act.

(Moore, 2007, pp. 30–31)

The concept of liminality offers a way of speaking about the surprising range of passionate and vivid encounters that characterise advanced research in practical theology. Research entails unexpected encounters and revelations. Developing a research project is like preparing for a journey – a necessary first step but something quite unable to prepare us for the demands of the expedition itself. In the planning stage it is easy to imagine research subjects or co-researching participants as moving in orderly ways according to our expectations. Yet the reality is always very different. We are quickly brought to acknowledge not only the deep emotional attachments that may arise but also our dependency and our obligations to wider networks and stakeholders.

Furthermore, it is essential to become aware of our connectivity; to give active consideration to those ties which anchor our humanity – or, more prosaically, give us the will to live. There will be important personal relationships with family and friends and meaningful ties to institutions, interest groups and movements. Connectivity is also about the stories that we use to make sense of things, the values we espouse and the beliefs we hold. In the emerging pastoral discipline of spiritual care, connectivity is now frequently taken as *the* key to understanding a person's particular spiritual framework. Interestingly, this has provoked recognition of how very important the apparently mundane connections of everyday living can be and how our small and local narratives connect us into larger frames. The inquiry 'what do you believe in?' frequently reveals far less than the questions 'what connections matter most to you?' or 'what would you most hate to lose?' These two questions can also tell us a great deal about the reason we are undertaking research as well as about the manner in which we are seeking to approach it (Pattison, 2010).

The kind of connectivity characterised by alienated objectification and exploitation of marginalised research subjects is emphatically not a form of relation the reflexive researcher is seeking. But we must be aware of the constant pressure to establish our own credentials as 'knowers' by 'othering' participants as the unconscious bearers of the knowledge we seek. We may, consciously or unconsciously, subordinate their way of knowing in order to establish our own. Reflexive awareness challenges us to wrestle with this uncomfortable problem and in the process move towards a reassessment of an epistemological dominance dependent upon the construction of supposedly unknowing subjects. A way forward that has its origin in feminist thinking but has now become accepted within reflexive research more broadly, is to recognise and revalue the situated nature of all knowledge.

Feminist theorists wrestling with this issue came to believe that the whole concept of objective knowledge (supposedly unbiased, rational, disembodied, based upon the God's-eye view of things) had to be subject to critique. Standpoint epistemology emerged as a way of affirming that seeing from a particular place and position (for example from a woman's body, from a particular social class or geographical location and even from an ideological or committed stance) was a more valid way of knowing than methods denying location and laying claim to general authority. No God's-eye view is actually available to us and the partial understandings generated from acknowledged positions are at least accountable for their perspective and can be judged as such. Harding (1991) developed this approach further by claiming that those most affected by a particular problem or circumstance were not only possessed of knowledge but the best 'knowers' – only those who wear the shoe really understand where it pinches. In the past their valuable understandings might have been dismissed as biased or emotionally compromised. However, Harding argued, these should now be given priority in epistemological conversations.

The word 'conversation' is important here. Whilst reflexive researchers may have found new ways of acknowledging that they are indeed dependent upon their research subjects and embedded in particular contexts and perspectives, the necessary counterpoint to standpoint epistemology is that knowledge must be formed from the shared work of those whose vantage-points may be completely different – including researchers, research participants and research readers. Making knowledge should be participatory and dialogical to the core. Donna Haraway has made this clear:

> Feminists don't need a doctrine of objectivity that promises transcendence . . . but we do need an earth-wide network of connections, including the ability to partially translate knowledges among very different power differentiated communities. We need the power of modern critical theories of how bodies and meaning get made, not in order to deny meanings and bodies, but in order to build meanings and bodies that have a chance for life . . . Feminist objectivity means quite simply situated knowledge.
>
> *(Haraway, 1988, pp. 579–80)*

Reflexive researchers who are becoming aware of their multifaceted, and at times ambivalent, dependence upon research subjects and co-participants have a particular responsibility to ensure that the knowledge they generate displays this dialogical character. This is not easy to achieve. Practical ways must be found to build the researcher's accountability to research subjects into the research design itself. This requirement arises partly from the obligation to generate the best research possible, the best knowledge we can. It also comes from a fundamental obligation of respect for the other which is both an epistemological and a spiritual stance.

WRITING MYSELF: REFLEXIVITY AND PARTICIPATION

Elizabeth Jordan, a graduate of the professional doctorate programme at Anglia Ruskin University, here discusses the various types of learning that emerged from an approach going beyond reflexivity in analyzing data and presenting findings. Her thesis, 'Friends, family or foe? Fostering good relationships between lay leaders and the newly-appointed ordained leaders of Anglican congregations', can be found at http://arro.anglia.ac.uk/605485/1/ COMPLETE%20THESIS.pdf

I have recognised that it is necessary to do more than conclude research with reflections about the effect of my own pre-conceptions and behaviour on the subjects of research, the analysis of data and the recommendations I make. I found that my own identity and practice was itself the object of research. The conversation between theological sociological perspectives, integral to the practice of practical theology, needed to make space for reflection on how I was formed through interaction with them. As I realised that knowledge about the churches and congregations that I was studying was gained when I made connections between their theological identities, their sociological influences and my own allegiances, I developed a relational epistemology. Personal and professional integrity required, therefore, that I named my own identity within the research.

The key word was 'participation'. Rather than being an observer who was aiming to be objective or even fully reflexive, I was present in the research situation as a participant in the practices and beliefs of the church members with whom I was meeting. A relationship based on shared faith enabled knowledge of the situations I was researching. The result of discovering myself in the research proved to be of value to its theoretical framework, to the research process and to the proposals for changed practice that I made.

First, while writing myself into the triangular framework of theology, sociology and self I noted the value of examining the interactions between these perspectives. The influence of biblical and liturgical descriptions of the Church as the new family of God and of Family Systems Theory on my own identity proved an effective lens for analysing the dynamic relationships of lay and ordained leaders in each place.

Second, locating myself in this framework affected the research process. As one in relationship with those researched I aimed to conduct research for their benefit. The doctoral research examined a process for the development of fruitful relationships between the newly arrived priest and the lay leaders and at the end of each meeting we prayed together for this. I used the tools of narrative and conversation analysis to give me the best chance of listening to the participants' own words. I treated each church as a distinctive community, examining the transcripts of each meeting in its context rather than by thematising words or phrases.

> *The recommendations that I have made as an outcome of this research have resulted from awareness of the importance of discerning my own identity in relation to the local churches. All who work with and in a congregation must pay attention to its structure of emotional and theological relationships of which they are an integral part.*

Research as spiritual journey towards the 'other'

To be provoked into new encounters with what is unfamiliar and strange using reflective/reflexive approaches can be a profoundly enriching experience. It might even be described as being in some ways like a spiritual journey if we are willing to embrace the discomforting aspects of reflexive approach to the self, to others and to the Other. It then also becomes a theological quest, not because it rests upon the firm foundations of established traditions, but because it desires and seeks that deeper engagement with the Other for which theological traditions provoke a longing and to which they point.

One of the most profound thinkers on this topic is Emmanuel Levinas, whose work has been particularly embraced by theologians seeking a connection between human encounters with human 'others' and the encounter with the divine 'Other'. Levinas offers an arresting image of how an awareness of 'the face of the other' calls forth not just a feeling of solidarity, but a recognition of difference, becoming the basis of an ethics that take us beyond moral convention into a realm of responsibility and integral relation (Pattison, 2013, pp. 79–84).

Drawing upon Judaic roots, Levinas characterises this in prophetic terms. The encounter with the widow, stranger or orphan is simultaneously a human ethical relation and an intrusion of a hidden/revealed Other who always/only comes through this sacred, proximate encounter:

> The Justice rendered to the Other, to my neighbour, gives me an unsurpassable proximity to God . . . One follows the Most High God, above all by drawing near to one's neighbour, and showing concern for 'the widow, the orphan, the stranger and the beggar'.
>
> *(Levinas, 1990, cited in Veling, 1999, pp. 291–292)*

This completely inverts any idea that the securely established subject is the sovereign observer of the world. It asks us to imagine instead that we only become capable of first loving and then understanding anything because of the force of an encounter with something we are incapable of incorporating or assimilating into ourselves and which will also ultimately remain mysterious to us. Even though we can only begin from where we are, with ourselves, the search for knowledge must not be circumscribed by the limits of our own self-interest. Rather, this is reflexivity as demanding a kenotic loss of ego.

> Our *search* for truth can all too easily be tempted by the need to *possess* truth, to make it my *own*, something I can now claim that I *know* as a truth *belonging to me*. In other words, the search for truth is often tamed or domesticated – no longer infinite in its horizon – but reduced to my own horizon of knowing. Truth is scaled down to coincide with myself, such that anything strange or different or other is now secured, safely incorporated into my own world of knowing, brought home to me and made comfortably 'the same.' Knowledge becomes *self-knowledge*, rather than a response to the call of the other, and it is this movement in philosophy that worries Levinas, the movement toward knowledge that assimilates and appropriates truth to our own familiar designs and frameworks.
>
> *(Veling, 2005, p. 79)*

In a sense, this turns the practice of reflexivity as a demonstration of professional competence and self-possession on its head. It offers a clear challenge to rethink our expectations of research as a process of classification and control and to admit the possibility that it might be seen in an entirely different light as an encounter with what is strange and compelling, indeed potentially divine.

Conclusion

In this chapter we have considered some of the possibilities, strengths and weaknesses of reflective and reflexive approaches in practical theological research. While recognising the promise and utility of these approaches, and the close relationship between them, we have also noted problems and issues arising from their employment. Two key issues explored in the chapter have been that of the partial and contextual nature of observation and the objectification of others. We have observed that the quest for innocence and purity in the usage of these approaches is not possible – all research is impure and imperfect. Nonetheless, there are important, creative possibilities here, not least the potential for theological insight and spiritual growth arising out of deep learning encounters with others and otherness. The research journey may be rewarding on many levels, but it is often not easy. In the next chapter, we turn to the importance of practice, the locus from which reflection and reflexivity emerge and in which they find their context and end.

References

Bass, D., Cahalan, K., Miller-McLemore, B.M., Nieman, J. and Scharen, C., 2016. *Christian practical wisdom: What it is and why it matters*. Grand Rapids: Wm. B. Eerdmans.

Bassot, B., 2016. *The reflective practice guide*. London: Routledge.

Bennett, Z., 2010. 'To see fearlessly, pitifully': What does John Ruskin have to offer to practical theology? *International Journal of Practical Theology*, 14(2), pp. 189–203.

Bennett, Z., 2014. *Your MA in Theology: A study skills handbook*. London: SCM Press.

Bennett, Z. and Rowland, C., 2016. *In a glass darkly: The Bible, reflection and everyday life*. London: SCM Press.

Bochner, A.P. and Ellis, C., 2002. *Ethnographically speaking: Autoethnography, lietrature, and aesthetics.* New York: Alta Mira Press.

Canning, R., 2008. *Reflecting on the reflective practitioner: Muddled thinking and poor educational practices.* [Online] Available at: https://dspace.stir.ac.uk/bitstream/1893/566/2/reflective%20 practice.pdf [Accessed 25 October 2016].

Cook, E.T. and Wedderburn, A., eds., 1903–1912. *The works of John Ruskin.* 39 vols. London: George Allen (referred to as *Works*, volume and page number).

Deegan, M.J. and Hill, M.R., 1991. Doctoral dissertations as liminal journeys of the self: Betwixt and between in graduate sociology programs. *Teaching Sociology*, pp. 322–332.

Denzin, N., 2003. *Performance ethnography: Critical pedagogy and the politics of culture.* London: Sage.

Dreyer, J., 2016. Knowledge, subjectivity, (de)coloniality, and the conundrum of reflexivity. In: B.M. Miller-McLemore and J.A. Mercer, eds., *Conundrums in practical theology.* Leuven: Brill.

Fulkerson, M.M., 2007. *Places of redemption: Theology for a worldly church.* Oxford and New York: Oxford University Press.

Ghaye, T., 2000. Into the reflective mode: Bridging the stagnant moat. *Reflective Practice*, 1(1), pp. 5–9.

Giddens, A., 1991. *Modernity and self identity: Self and society in the late modern age.* Cambridge: Polity Press.

Graham, E., 2013. Is practical theology a form of action research? *International Journal of Practical Theology*, 17(1), pp. 148–178.

Graham, E., Walton, H. and Ward, F., 2005. *Theological reflection: Methods.* London: SCM Press.

Haraway, D., 1988. Situated knowledges: The science question in feminism and the privilege of partial perspective. *Feminist Studies*, 14(3), pp. 575–599.

Harding, S.H., 1991. *Whose science? Whose knowledge? Thinking from women's lives.* Ithaca, NY: Cornell University Press.

Kahn, A., ed. 2005. *Georg Lukcas: Writer and critic and other essays.* iUniverse.

Kemmis, S., 2010. What is to be done? The place of action research. *Educational Action Research*, 18(4), pp. 417–427.

Kinsella, E.A., 2003. *Toward understanding: Critiques of reflective practice and possibilities for dialogue.* [Online] Available at: www.casae-aceea.ca/~casae/sites/casae/archives/cnf2003/ . . . / rt-annekinsellaCAS03.pdf

Kinsella, E.A., 2007. Embodied reflection and the epistemology of reflective practice. *Journal of the Philosophy of Education*, 41(3), pp. 395–409.

Leach, J., 2007. Pastoral theology as attention. *Contact: The Interdisciplinary Journal of Pastoral Studies*, 153, pp. 19–32.

Leach, J. and Paterson, M., 2015. *Pastoral supervision: A handbook.* 2nd ed. London: SCM Press.

Moore, B., 2007. Original sin and insider research. *Action Research*, 5(1), pp. 27–39.

Nelson, R., ed., 2013. *Practice as research in the arts: Principles, protocols, pedagogies, resistances.* London: Palgrave Macmillan.

Paterson, M. and Kelly, E., 2013. Values-based reflective practice: A method developed in Scotland for spiritual care practitioners. *Practical Theology*, 6(1), pp. 51–68.

Pattison, S., 2010. Spirituality and spiritual care made simple. *Practical Theology*, 3(3), pp. 351–366.

Pattison, S., 2013. *Saving face: Enfacement, shame, theology.* Farnham: Ashgate.

Pillow, W., 2003. Confession, catharsis, or cure? Rethinking the uses of reflexivity as methodological power in qualitative research. *International Journal of Qualitative Studies in Education*, 16(2), pp. 175–196.

Roulston, K., 2010. *Reflective interviewing: A guide to theory and practice.* London: Sage.

Saltiel, D., 2010. *Judgement, narrative and discourse: A critique of reflective practice.* [Online] Available at: www.researchgate.net/publication/255650391_Judgement_narrative_and_discourse_critiquing_reflective_practice

Schön, D., 1983. *The reflective practitioner.* New York: Basic Books.

Tasker, D., McLeod-Boyle, A. and Bridges, D., 2011. From practice to research and back again: Living transformations. In: J. Higgs, A. Tichen, D. Horsfall and D. Bridges, eds., *Creative spaces for qualitative researching: Living research.* Rotterdam: Sense Publishing. pp. 291–300.

Thompson, J., Pattison, S. and Thompson, R., 2008. *The SCM study guide to theological reflection.* London: SCM Press.

Turner, V., 1969. *The ritual process: Structure and anti-structure.* New York: Aldine de Gruyter.

van Gennep, A., 1909. *The rites of passage.* 1960 ed. London: Routledge and Kegan Paul.

Veling, T., 1999. In the name of who? Levinas and the other side of theology. *Pacifica*, 12, pp. 275–292.

Veling, T., 2005. *Practical theology: On earth as it is in heaven.* Maryknoll: Orbis.

Wall, T., 2015. Turning practitioners into practitioner-researchers. In: R. Hinton and A. Minton, eds., *Facilitating work-based learning: A handbook for tutors.* London: Palgrave Macmillan. pp. 114–133.

Walton, H., 2014. *Writing methods in theological reflection.* London: SCM Press.

3
RESEARCHING RELIGIOUS PRACTICE AND PERFORMANCE

For outsiders to practical theology, the discipline's self-designation can sound like a contradiction in terms. Theology may popularly be assumed to be about the extraordinary, supernatural, unreal, eternal and unworldly, that which cannot be sensed, while the realm of the practical is supposed to be that of the everyday, temporal, ordinary, unexceptional, embodied and material. The two may seem divided by an unbridgeable gulf.

However, we want to challenge this distorting division, in many ways a function of Enlightenment dualistic thinking which arbitrarily exalts thought and cognition as modes of knowledge and perception over more embodied kinds of knowing and being. Instead, we would argue that practice and theology belong integrally together, and that practice is a privileged locus for undertaking theological research and enquiry. Practices are absolutely central to practical theology in a variety of different ways. Our strong claim is that practical theology and practical theological research begins, proceeds by, and ends – in practice.

This chapter will discuss the nature of practice and practices, arguing that these are constitutive of our spiritual, theoretical and material worlds, whether understood overtly theologically or not. It is practices that make and maintain the 'really real' of everyday and theological realities. Here, we will develop the vital centrality of practice in practical theological activity and research using five theses to anchor and develop discussion.

The theses are:

1   The *theology* of practical theology is instantiated within action, praxis, performance and practice.
2   Practices build worlds, both symbolic and material.
3   Religion is more than 'belief'.

4 **Practices are value-laden and revelatory – as practices build worlds, so they (and we) perform our truths.**
5 **Researching practice requires particular skills.**

If systematic theology is perceived as the study of 'the ordering of beliefs about God, the church, or classic texts' (Miller-McLemore, 2012, p. 14), practical theology finds an alternative focus in the primary study of the theology of practice and the practice of theology. It is thoroughly committed to the theological nature of practice, whether those are explicit practices of faith, or the routines and rituals of everyday life; whether they are Christian, non-or post-Christian; institutionalised or spontaneous and informal. Rather than being the poor relation to the pure pursuits of disembodied reason, then, practice is an essential *locus* and dynamo for highly sophisticated questioning and theoretical contributions. These may be more motivating and prompt better, more urgent and more diligent research and practical outcomes.

HOW PRACTICE 'TROUBLES' THEORY AND THEOLOGY AND LEADS TO STRONG, TRANSFORMATIVE OUTCOMES IN RESEARCH

Trevor Adams, a researching professional who undertook a professional doctoral programme, here shows how engaging with vital, fundamental questions arising from practice and experience really leads to insight and transformation in theory, theology and practice. See further Trevor Adams' thesis, 'The Black hero's journey' submitted in 2014 (http://arro.anglia.ac.uk/583105/).

At the start of my doctoral journey, I was a pastor and educator working to raise the aspiration and attainment of Black boys and young men, disaffected with, and underperforming at, school, at risk of exclusion and being drawn to the streets and gang life.

My research, about bringing a fresh approach to my professional practice, originated out of assumptions arising from a combination of interconnected events. First, there was a critical incident that occurred in the course of my daily practice. I was asked by one of the boys, during the aspiration and attainment raising workshop I was conducting, 'Are you a genius, Sir?' This unexpected question affected me emotionally and caused me to become conscious of an unresolved disparity between my personal life and professional practice. I could see the boys' potential to advance at school, as well as to be exceptional in their future careers. However, I could not see my own. Embarrassed about my lack of educational attainment at their age, I remained silent about my subsequent accomplishments.

Until questioned, I was unaware that my silence hid an inconsistency between what I believed about others, but not about myself. I believed that my academic ability was fixed, not those of the boys who I worked with, in my practice, to inspire.

> *Learning to engage in theological conversation as part of the doctoral pro-gramme challenged me to make conscious some of the assumptions that I held about my life and practice. Unconsciously, I believed that my failure at school made me a hypocrite and less effective, as a practitioner, to inspire the Black young males. After all, how could someone who left school with low grades really inspire the boys to succeed in their schooling?*
>
> *Together, the critical incident, the reflective process, doctoral supervision and my struggles to put my thoughts in textual form, then made me recognise that I had questions about my life and practice that needed answering. Why did I underperform at school? How did I complete a master's degree if I did not have the academic potential? Why did I feel guilty about being on a doctoral programme? How does it feel to be a 'problem' personally and educationally? I held a negative view of my life, based on my past educational experiences, that I thought was a foregone conclusion. However, my assumptions underpinning my viewpoint had never been tested. Therefore, the conclusion that I had drawn about my past life situation and current practice was suspect and possibly outdated.*
>
> *My research concluded that I made a positive impact on the learning and devel-opment of Black young males in my practice. This has resolved my doubt about my educational past and the legitimacy of my practice. My use of a Black metaphori-cal theological perspective and theological theme of redemption, arising from my experiences, to reinterpret my past and practice, made this difference. Creating an autoethnography, a study that exploits the narratives of self and others, evidenced this change. It also showed that I had generated a fresh understanding of existing issues. Whilst I cannot change my past experiences, I can reinterpret them anew, in the light of theological insights of God's redemptive act, to continuously bring a new work into existence that inspires others. This has added new insights to the literature that focuses on the successful educational development of Black young males. The production of my autoethnographic work, using text, pictures, music and video, now provides 'show and tell' access to insights that underpin my approach to profes-sional practice. It also answers why, within the field of practical theology, the cre-ation of a human document, for reflection, is possible beyond the use of text alone.*
>
> *By reflecting and using my own autoethnographic work, I am now able to better model, as practical theologian, for colleagues and disaffected Black young males in my practice, why and how we can create and tell our own education success stories.*

Practices both perform and create worlds and world-views. It is possible, there-fore, to infer the shape of theological worlds from the practices of religious adherents in analytical terms. Generalised, formally articulated theologies and theories of practice arise from specific practices and experiences. They both reflect and refract them, as well as potentially critiquing them. In this context, the task of practical theological research is to unearth, articulate and enrich the nature of, and relations between, action-guiding theories and performances. Research allows those engaged in performances of all kinds to articulate and critique what they are doing and therefore to do, and perhaps to think and to act, differently. It enables groups and individuals to preach, to analyse, and to creatively enrich what they practise in much the same way that players' analysis of their performances in sport might help them to do differently or better.

Of course, the methods and practices of research themselves have theological and theoretical underpinnings, so there is potentially an infinitely recursive, reflexive task here. We discuss the value- and world-view-laden nature of research approaches and methods in later chapters of this book (see especially Chapters 5 and 7). Here our focus lies on the importance of non-research practices themselves and their importance for life, theory and theology.

Before advancing to the main text of the chapter, it is worth saying that although much of the chapter is concerned explicitly with a dialogue with Christian theology, the 'lake' from which practical theology flows, the critical points and arguments can also be applied to any action-guiding world-views and ideologies (Pattison, 1997, 2007). The apparent gulf between undergirding theoretical knowledge and principles and practices is not confined to the disciplinary sphere of theology.

The nature and importance of practice

Practices are ubiquitous, essential and extraordinarily various and diverse, ranging from the highly conscious, unique and significant (the thesis viva, or wedding) to the assumed, trivial and unnoticed (using the bus, or car, to go to town). As you read this text, wherever you are, whatever technology you are using – printed paper, electronic reading device or even audiobook – you are engaged in a practice. This involves particular conventions, and may be shaped by your own special preferences: a cup of coffee to hand, music (or silence) in the background, in a library, in a private office, taking notes, underlining or highlighting passages, and so on. If you are blind, reading a version of this book in Braille, then your reading practice may be different again – more tactile than visual, alerting us to some of the bodily and physical dimensions of practice.

You are probably not reading this aloud, either to yourself alone or to a group of others, although in other cultures and historical periods apart from Western modernity these, too, have been established reading practices. The closest you may get to that is if you attend a religious retreat at which mealtimes are accompanied by the public reading of a spiritual text. You might pause to ask yourself what difference those variations in reading practice – alone, silent, actively annotating and commenting, or corporately, aurally, even meditatively – might make, and what is significant about the particular practices that mediate a certain text to you?

Similarly, as we write what you now read – writers writing for a reader we may never meet (except through the text), across unknown spaces of distance and time – we, too, are engaged in a practice. And for you, a wider public, to have access to what we write now will entail many other kinds of practice: some intellectual (correcting and revising a first draft; publisher's reviewers commenting and evaluating);

some more technical, requiring particular skills or expertise (copy-editing, indexing, marketing); others more practical still (packing and shipping – rarer now in the days of print-on-demand, although *someone* has to drive the delivery van or maintain the fibre-optic cables that transmit your eBook to you).

Western academic culture is dominated by these practices of reading and writing. Taken together, we group these activities under the umbrella term of 'research', but nevertheless it is bound by specific kinds of practices: not just manual or intellectual skills but broader webs of convention and meaning by which discrete actions or repetitions are regulated.

It is important to recognise the ubiquity of practice in everyday life and in research because it is such practices that construct and maintain reality. In *Laboratory Life*, Woolgar and Latour (1979, p. 40) observed the myriad, often highly routine ways in which 'the daily activities of working scientists lead to the construction of scientific facts'. They described scientific theories as essentially elaborate narratives, encrypted via the various writing practices of 'coding, marking, altering, correcting, reading, and writing' (Woolgar and Latour, 1979, pp. 48–49). The terms on which hypotheses and recorded data were discussed and interpreted were not self-evident, but dependent upon 'the social construction of scientific facts'. What we call 'science', argued Latour and Woolgar, is socially constructed according to conventions of verification and exemplification. *Laboratory Life*, based on the tradition of the 'naïve' participant observer who suspends taken-for-granted assumptions about the society around them, challenged presuppositions about the objective and factual nature of particular social phenomena to reveal their basis in activities of meaning-making and interpretation. From this perspective, science is not a body of hard facts but a series of culturally contingent practices and social relationships. How much more so the ordinary 'soft' practices and facts of everyday life?

'Practice' is a complex and culturally freighted term. It is also absolutely fundamental in thinking critically about how it is we know what we know, and how we make sense of living. What is 'practice'? What is *a* 'practice'? And how might practice be theologically significant? What is it about (a) practice that enables people to glimpse, and participate in, divine action? What are the implications of these kinds of perspectives for the way research is conducted (practised) in a discipline that claims to be 'practical', rooted in and oriented towards 'practice'? And what makes the study of practice(s) necessarily theological? What is it about our world-creating and sustaining practices that we want to deal with and focus on in practical theology?

EDUCATIONAL ACTIVITY AS A PRACTICE PRODUCES IMPORTANT RESEARCH QUESTIONS

Eric Stoddart, a university teacher at St Andrews University, here reflects on the way in which teaching and working with church groups has lead him into working on the highly topical issue of social surveillance. You can see more of his practical theological work on this theme in Stoddart (2011).

To trace my interest in surveillance, I'd go back to the run-up [to] the UK General Election in 1987. I was Associate Minister of a Baptist church in Aberdeen. One of my responsibilities was to organise the house-based weekly bible study and fellowship groups. I often wrote the study notes and for a four-week period asked the study group leaders to help their group members discuss the election manifestos of the major parties, in the light of Scripture. Most of the groups either humoured me or leapt at the opportunity. One group leader however declined. In his opinion, this was not what a bible study group was for. This sowed the seed for me of the importance of lay adult theological education that connects with contemporary concerns rather than turned inwards to 'spiritual' issues.

Completing my PhD in the early 2000s, I started working at the Scottish Churches Open College, an ecumenical distance learning adult theological institution. I designed a four-year undergraduate degree for university validation, following themes including health, economics and the workplace. Each module was developed as one cycle of Groome's model of shared praxis. The whole programme was basically a degree in practical theology engaging lay people with the world.

A module on citizenship found new life when I offered it whilst teaching at Aberdeen University in 2004. One small section was on electronic citizenship (e-voting, and government's use of technology to deliver services). Revising this as a module at the University of St Andrews I stumbled across an article by sociologist David Lyon containing a footnote reference to Miroslav Volf. Tracking that down, and discovering Lyon's Christian faith and interest in how surveillance impacts concerns for human flourishing started my long engagement with the topic.

My ambivalence to how power is practised (in the church and more widely) gave me considerable impetus to unpack surveillance. I've always suspected that hard-won human and civil rights are more a veneer than a thoroughly embedded seam in western public life. Recent turns towards nativist far-right populism suggest there's good reason for my suspicion. We must understand surveillance and engage it theologically because, as a social and technological phenomenon, it could undermine – but perhaps also bolster – human and civil rights.

Thesis 1: the theology of practical theology is instantiated within action, praxis, performance and practice

Practical theologians maintain the primacy of practice both as fundamental human activity and as the means by which we inhabit the life of God. Practical theology is a practice-oriented discourse that describes, regulates and stimulates committed practice towards those ends. It emerges out of, and is orientated towards, questions of life. Contemporary practical theological research is committed to inductive models of knowledge and reflection, beginning with context/experience/practice;

moving to correlate with elements of tradition; leading to new understandings generated that inform practical strategies of action. Practical concerns inform all kinds of understanding; practical knowledge inhabits institutions, bodies, spaces and social conventions.

In the last part of the twentieth century, practical theology underwent a seachange in its self-understanding. The assumption that authentic, normative faith was enshrined in authoritative texts such as Scripture or in the presuppositions of doctrine, a body of cognitive knowledge that was 'applied' into everyday life, was axiomatic for understanding what it meant to do practical theology. Furthermore, there was a general (unspoken?) consensus that the locus of practical theology should be the activities of ordained ministry, exemplified by Seward Hiltner's designation of the field as one of 'shepherding', 'communicating' and 'organising' (Hiltner, 1958). Behind that lay Schleiermacher's understanding of practical theology as the discipline concerned with the management and discipline of the Church (Schleiermacher, 1966).

This is helpful insofar as it attends to the tangible outworking of philosophical and historical enquiry, but still problematic in its assumption of what was later termed the 'clerical paradigm' (Farley, 1983), as well as its unexamined premise that practice is secondary to, and derivative of theory. Theory – *epistemē* or *theoria* – is held to be the highest, purest form of knowledge. More recently however, scholars have challenged this notion of knowledge as internal to the processes of the mind and disembodied cognition (Ralston Saul, 1993). The Cartesian legacy in Western philosophy established hierarchy of theory over practice, assuming that *epistemē* (propositional knowledge) underpins all else. This 'Cartesian heresy' has been displaced by alternatives stressing the integration of mind, affect, embodiment, materiality and social relationships (Lakoff and Johnson, 1999).

The turn to practice within practical theology clearly owes much to Alasdair MacIntyre's work, which will be discussed in more detail later. Human activity is rule-governed, contextually-grounded, and – after MacIntyre – capable of embodying and giving rise to social goods, or virtues. The value-laden, aims-oriented nature of practice thus became adopted within practical theology as a way of overthrowing the primacy of 'mind over matter' (Miller-McLemore, 2016, p. 175). An understanding of theological reasoning emerged which resisted the separation of doctrine from its 'application', regarding the practice(s) of faith as denoting the 'embodied expression of particular kinds of knowledge' (Cahalan, 2014, p. 3). Thus, practical theology 'becomes theological reflection on and for the sake of practice' (Smith, 2012, p. 250).

This works itself out within practical theology in a number of ways. First, the emphasis on practice foregrounds *the significance of the human context and the realities of lived experience* as the domain in which Christian ministry or action takes place. In work Heather and Elaine did with Frances Ward in the early 2000s, their aim was not so much to produce a handbook for exercises in theological reflection as to re-contextualise the history of Christian doctrine and put forward just such a manifesto for regarding all theology as practical – from start to finish. So they argued that theological discourse begins (and ends) in practice: theology itself is engendered by the imperatives of discipleship and lived experience (Graham, Walton and Ward, 2005).

Historically, certain key practical challenges and tasks prompted the need to construct a Christian world-view:

- Initiation and nurture, or the formation of character
- Circumscribing the boundaries of belief, or building communities of faith
- Communicating the gospel to the wider world

(Graham, Walton and Ward, 2005, pp. 10–11)

This is also why practical theology has come to differentiate itself from anything approaching 'applied' theology, because theology does not simply end in practice, but starts there, too. It means, at an elementary level, that practical theology is essentially problem-centred: how should Christians conduct their lives? How does the community of faith order its affairs? What does the revelation of God in the life, death and resurrection of Jesus Christ actually mean for Christians today? As Stephen is wont to say, practical theologians are thus 'critical inhabitants of action-guiding world-views' (Pattison, 2007, p. 7); they seek to *interrogate* and interpret how beliefs and values facilitate faithful practice (Bennett, 2009, pp. 338–339).

That takes us to a second dimension of why theology is practical. Theology is *practical*, but practice is also *'theological'* – 'practice is taken to be theologically significant' (Beaudoin, 2016, p. 9), since it is the bearer of the implicit values that will engender virtue. No theologian is going to admit to their theological study as being 'impractical' in the sense of having no practical bearing; but what really differentiates practical theology is this second turn to practice as the bearer – one might say sacrament – of theological understanding:

> [T]heology [is] a practical discipline. It is the intellectual reflection on the faith we share as the believing community within a specific cultural context. But it has as its goal the application of our faith commitment to living as the people of God in our world.
>
> *(Grenz, 1993, pp. 17–18)*

However, this consolidates further (as Elaine began to do in *Transforming Practice*, first published in 1996), into a sense that these lived experiences and faith practices actually constitute a kind of 'performativity' in respect of theological truth-claims. This is the third movement of practical theology: not just to say that theological adequacy is tested in practice or as it translates into action, but that theology is primarily performative and enacted, and only secondarily or derivatively written down and systematised. Here, the influence of postmodern and liberationist thinking is notable: theology is practised as *orthopraxis* first, and systematised as *orthodoxy* second (Graham, 1996, 2000).

> The aim of theology is not to work out a system that is enduring so much as to meet everyday experiences with faith – and to express that faith in terms

of everyday experience. Theology is an ongoing process. It is the *habitus* of praying Christians, of reflective ministers, and believing communities.

(Bevans, 2014, p. 49)

Trying to understand human action and thought and the meanings inherent in practice – including their theological bearings – requires sophisticated methods of enquiry and interpretation. In turn, how these meanings constitute 'action-guiding world-views' for their actors – and whether one rests with a descriptive account or moves into normative and transformative mode – draws one back to the world of actions and practices. So whilst most practical theologians would affirm Browning's (1991) characterisation of 'practice-theory-practice', it is not straightforward. We need to see how practices are always theory-laden, and theory, or concepts, or doctrines, are themselves forms of meaning-making that serve practice.

Practical theologians' engagement with theologies of liberation has been another clear influence in the emphasis on the primacy of practice – everyday and religious – as the source of reflection and research, indeed, the primary *locus theologicus*. In particular, liberation theologies have emphasised *orthopraxis* (right action) rather than *orthodoxy* (right believing) as the test of theological truth-claims (Gutièrrez, 1974, p. 10). This reverses the flow of logic from theory to practice. Orthodoxy, the expression of doctrinal statements or propositions of belief, is an inadequate way of framing theological understanding since it over-looks the necessity of divine incarnation within the particular, immediate and concrete. A more symbiotic relationship between theory and practice is expressed in the notion of *praxis*, value-guided action, in which meaning and purpose are interwoven into practice itself.

In classical Aristotelian and Marxist thought, the concept of *praxis* denotes the dialectic of action and theory. Liberation theology's elevation of *orthopraxis* as the criterion of theological authenticity appropriates the Marxist dictum that whilst the acme of philosophical endeavour may be to understand the world, the goal of the truly engaged intellectuals is to change it (Bottomore and Rubel, 1963, pp. 82–84). Thus it is to the transformation of culture that the efforts of people of faith must be directed, fuelled by an analysis that transcends mere materialist accounts of history in 'openness to the spiritual roots of creative energies' (Holland, 1990, p. xv). More radically, *praxis* is the primary criterion of truth. Theology is disciplined and critical reflection on the exercise of faith in which action, and *the practice of the gospel*, has primacy:

> Theology is reflection, a critical attitude. The commitment of love, of service, comes first. Theology *follows*: it is the second step . . . The pastoral activity of the church does not flow as a conclusion from theological premises. Theology does not generate a pastoral approach; rather it reflects upon it . . . The life, preaching, and historical commitment of the church will be a privileged *locus theologicus* for understanding the faith.
>
> *(Gutiérrez, 1974, pp. 11–12)*

So, whereas 'practice' may denote something quite routinised and unreflective, the term '*praxis*' points towards something more reflexive that is both value-directed and value-laden. It is the meanings we bring to practice and the meaning-making associated with our actions. This attests to the insight that theology is essentially embodied in and mediated by forms of 'primary, performative religious activity that happen[s] in and through ordinary adherents, and often by means of their practices' (Nieman, 2002, p. 202).

Contemporary practical theology strives for 'the intelligence within practice . . . a kind of theological knowing that arises within practice and makes good practice possible' (Miller-McLemore, 2016, p. 173). It seeks to find ways of researching, understanding and analysing the practices that constitute faith, as well as considering whether that is a descriptive or normative task. A more radical approach, then, is to insist that one must begin with the practices of faith, and read them *inductively* for what they reveal as enactments of theological worlds or truth-claims. In some respects, this perspective turns Schleiermacher on his head, inverting the logic of historical-philosophical-practical into 'the hermeneutics of lived religion' (Ganzevoort and Roeland, 2014).

Practice, then, is the 'Alpha and Omega' of theological discourse. Theological traditions (codified practices of believing and behaving) have a guiding and formative role, but their function is to facilitate practical following of the way. This requires a degree of both performance and improvisation. Thus we participate in and inhabit traditions – a matter of embodied 'dwelling' rather than cognitively 'believing'.

> One of the things I learned from the rabbinic tradition was that as the rabbis searched for the meaning of a text, they were always drawn to finding its *ethical* message. Even when the ethical message was not immediately apparent to them, they would stay with the text, 'turning it and turning it,' until its ethical import twisted free. The meaning of a text was primarily about *the way one should live*. God's word, the Torah, is something *to live, to do*, and such was the purpose of study and prayer, to bring our lives into alignment with the teachings and commandments of Torah.
>
> *(Veling, 2005, p. 91)*

Some doctrinal theologians argue that all theology has to be 'recontextualised' to reconnect with the essentially practical questions that gave rise to theological reflection in the first place (Charry, 1997; Graham, Walton and Ward, 2005). In turn, however, theology that emerges from practical questions also returns to practice, as theological understanding leads to further action. This is embodied in many standard introductions to practical theology that refer to the hermeneutical circle or pastoral cycle (Segundo, 1976; Ballard and Pritchard, 2006).

This is not to say that practical theologians are cavalier towards texts, such as those contained within Scripture and Christian tradition. As authors of this book we strongly contest the accusation that in being responsive to lived experience and seeking to address meaningfully and intelligibly contemporary context, we are somehow neglectful of or 'unfaithful' to the received tradition. Rather, we are simply asserting that the process of practical theological interpretation, or hermeneutics (Bennett, 2009, p. 339) must engage both with the 'context' of lived experience and practice and the 'texts' of received tradition. And of course, where else does 'tradition' originate but from practice?

Thesis 2: practices build worlds, both symbolic and material

Practices are the activities by which we 'build worlds' (Paden, 1994) of meaning, and which enable us to communicate with and mediate the sacred. All human understanding is practical; no conceptual and theoretical thinking is context-free; all action is always already theory-laden and interpretative, thus a hermeneutical act (Browning, 1991). Practice is a set of actions that instantiate knowledge, meaning and understanding; action is always socially embedded, habitual and embodied. This overturns the dualism/hierarchy of theory and practice, whereby action is an 'application' of some ideal philosophical system of pure reason.

The notion that human practices are the basis upon which worlds of meaning and social relations are constructed has proved influential across many academic disciplines. For example, feminist scholars have insisted on the embodied, proprioceptive nature of acquiring gender identity via social practices. We learn to inhabit culture, social identities and environments through the practices of our bodies – but in truly reflexive style, these cultural practices already inhabit *us* from the moment we are born (Wildman, 2010). So, for example, the philosopher Judith Butler has famously argued that gender identity is not the expression of some inner, core 'self' but rather the manifestation of 'stylised repetition of acts' (Butler, 1990, p. 78) – a performance we are continually engaged in enacting, or rehearsing. This mimesis of gender is what passes for gendered personhood. Identity is thus acquired and maintained via social, cultural, embodied and linguistic practices. Iris Marion Young (1990) has argued, similarly, that from a young age, children are conditioned to regard their bodily abilities – through things such as play, sport and so on – as gendered. Thus, some aspects of bodily deportment are deemed more or less 'masculine' or 'feminine'. In time, this becomes a self-fulfilling prophecy as internalised gendered expectations are translated into actual physical capabilities – girls 'throw like a girl' not by virtue of innate nature, but because societal pressures have conditioned their bodies to act in certain ways (Young, 1990).

Similarly, Elaine's work in practical theology has attempted to put to rest once and for all a model of the discipline as 'applied' doctrine. Instead, her model of theology as 'practical all the way down' (Korsgaard, 2003, p. 112) represents a conviction that there is no external or transcendent referent of truth beyond the values embedded in the enacted performances of faith – just as New Testament writers insist that Christian love is incarnational and performative, not simply an abstract principle or theoretical matter (1 John 4.8; James 1.18–26). The incarnational practices of love-in-action are systematised into words, not the other way around.

To regard theology as 'performative' is to say that theology in its primary form is a language of practice: enacted and embodied in the liturgical, evangelistic, sacramental and practical/caring actions of faithful communities. Christians 'talk about God' quintessentially in their everyday activities of offering worship to God, in their secular lives and livelihoods and in their care for others. Thus theology takes place most authentically in the very practices of transformative faith-in-action.

> What is normative and authentic for the Christian community is enacted and embodied in praxis. It is these diverse pastoral practices that reveal, and construct, the dominant frameworks of meaning and truth. The activities of fostering moral ways of life, story-telling, promoting human development, and pursuing gender equality are undertaken because the community has inherited, and inhabits, a particular set of truth-claims. These claims are fundamentally theological; Christian pastoral practice has particular aims and ends because of what Christians proclaim and experience concerning God. However . . . the theological values of practice are only manifested in the concrete praxis of the community in a given context . . .
>
> Therefore, the focus for principled and theologically-informed pastoral practice rests upon the ordering of the life of the faith-community, but must be an analysis which resists appeal to ultimate values enshrined beyond the praxis of the same community. The task of the pastoral theologian . . . is therefore . . . to construct a . . . critical phenomenology, studying a living and acting faith-community . . . to excavate and examine the norms which inhabit faithful praxis.
>
> *(Graham, 1996, pp. 139–140)*

Practice is not so much the outworking of a rational will, therefore, as an embodied *habitus* that springs from our embeddness in the world. Habitus can be understood as a 'system of structured, structuring dispositions, which is constituted in practice and is always orientated towards practical functions' (Bourdieu, 1997, pp. 78–79). Dispositions are ways of acting that are part of our social world:

> . . . systems of durable, transposable dispositions . . . predisposed to function . . . as principles which generate and organise practices and representations that can be objectively adapted to their outcomes without presupposing a conscious aiming at ends or an express mastery of the operations necessary in order to attain them.
>
> *(Bourdieu, 1990, p. 53)*

Via practices of 'regulated improvisation' the self is constituted through the internalisation of social conventions and embodied social relations. Social relations are 'written on the body'. 'What is "learned by body" is not something that one has, like knowledge that can be brandished, but something that one is' (Bourdieu, 1990,

p. 73). However, human action and interaction is not just mimesis or dull repetition. It is rather a synthesis or dialectic of 'preoccupied, active presence in the world' which is constantly – cybernetically – processing contextual information alongside 'the incorporated products of historical practice' (Bourdieu, 1990, p. 52). These serve to structure presuppositions concerning the nature of the social world. Insofar as these conventions are rule-governed, collective, instantiated in tangible, verifiable outcomes, and not simply instinctive actions, they are practices.

The philosopher Alasdair MacIntyre's work has influenced practical theology's turn to practice from a moral and ethical perspective. He argues that in the face of postmodern fragmentation there is no over-riding moral authority (MacIntyre, 1987). Notions of virtue and good can no longer be metaphysically grounded; instead they are realised through practices of excellence. Virtue enables us to attain the goods to which we strive. Goods are achieved through cultivation of practices that are directed towards intrinsic criteria of excellence, i.e. culturally determined not transcendentally experienced. In this context, a 'practice' is

> . . . any coherent and complex form of socially established cooperative human activity through which goods internal to that form of activity are realised in the course of trying to achieve those standards of excellence which are appropriate to, and partially definitive of, that form of activity, with the result that human powers to achieve excellence, and human conceptions of the ends and goods involved, are systematically extended.
>
> *(MacIntyre, 1987, p. 187)*

Practices shape character. They cultivate a particular way of being that becomes aligned with, and governed by, a vision of excellence. People of faith imbibe and manifest a particular vision by inhabiting traditions in particular practices. The more one practises, the more one becomes attuned to norms and aspirations. Knowing, being and acting are indivisible. Practices of faith are the activities that induct and sustain individuals in particular communities whose norms and values are intrinsic to the very conventions of the practices themselves.

Derived from this strand of thinking is the contemporary recovery of an ancient terminology of *phronēsis, prudentia,* or practical wisdom. Such practical moral and theological reasoning is more complex than the application of generic theories to human cases. It attends to the particularities of a situation, and requires judgement as to the best way of achieving moral ends in the light of contingency. This is does not require abstract reasoning but rather skills of attention to the situation and the exercise of discernment in the face of changing circumstances.

Practical wisdom is the kind of reasoning that promotes virtue and best practice. It represents a unity of 'knowledge of truth and reason with a concern for action related to human goods' (Bass et al., 2016, p. 5). As we will argue in Chapter 4, such wisdom is perhaps best framed as a form of moral inquiry in the context of communities of practice (Vokey and Kerr, 2011, pp. 73–75). It is relational (in terms of promoting justice and virtue) and embodied. Traditions are embedded in and communicated by the *habitus* of practice exercised by and within communities of practitioners rather than via textual or doctrinal media. Religious practices enact inherited values and in the process reiterate them performatively. Thus, 'practices *bring-into-practice* their intrinsic goods and values' (Immink, 2014, p. 131).

Practical theology therefore regards practice as significant in a number of ways. First, it foregrounds the significance of the human context and the phenomenological realities of lived experience as the domain in which Christian action takes place. Secondly, and more crucially, practice is theologically significant (Beaudoin, 2016). Practical theology must deal with practices non-reductively, regarding them as expressions of truth claims about the world: theology is *in practice*. This moves us beyond understandings of religion itself as 'belief in' something and more towards practice/s as phenomena that mediate and communicate the sacred through activities such as communication, intercession, praise, invocation.

FROM ACADEMIC INTEREST TO EMBODIED, PRACTICE-FOCUSSED ENGAGEMENT IN RESEARCH

Leah Robinson teaches practical theology at Edinburgh University. Here she describes how her initially theoretical interest in reconciliation evolved into something intensely practical and practice-focused. Her thesis, 'The influence of social context on a theology of reconciliation: case studies in Northern Ireland' can be found at www.era.lib.ed.ac.uk/bitstream/handle/1842/5993/Robinson2011.pdf?sequence=2

My research in Northern Ireland is on the interplay of theological belief and practices of peace building and reconciliation, and how they inform one another.

I had a grandiose idea of what it would be like to drop into a foreign country and be something of a journalist getting the next big story. What I found is that I was almost immediately put to work amongst those who were doing reconciliation work locally. I learned by working alongside those who were long time committed advocates of peace in Northern Ireland; my days were often long and tiring and not altogether academic. I realised that my research questions were beginning to emerge in overheard conversations in the tea breaks, in the laughter and occasional tears of casual conversation, in the trust that was gained by mutual commitment to a cause.

Through this, a practical theology began to emerge from those who had devoted their lives to healing their country. It wasn't always extraordinary by ivory tower standards, but it was always uniquely profound in the context.

> *In the meantime, I was challenged by a continuous question asked by those who I worked alongside: What is your interest in this? It confirmed in me that the days of standoffish ethnography, at least in the field of practical theology, is not a research methodology fit for purpose. I was now a part of this story that I was researching. Accepting that, and learning from it, made me a better peacebuilder, a better theologian, and thankfully an adopted daughter of a country of beloved people who never cease to amaze me with their love and hospitality. They taught me something that theologians have been wrestling with for many years-the true meaning of an embodied theology of reconciliation.*

Thesis 3: religion is more than belief

Religion is not merely a matter of cognition or 'belief' (Harvey, 2013; McGuire, 2008; Orsi, 2005). It is a complex system (or world) constituted by the *practices* of belonging, believing and behaving. The turn to practice reconstrues religion as a form of 'lived experience'. Thus the study of the 'living human document' in context is preferred as a more holistic and authentic representation of faith than the study of religious ideas and texts (Boisen, 1936). It is practices – embodied, liturgical, administrative, deliberate or unintentional – that constitute the living human expressions of faith.

Regrettably, modern Western study of religion – including and especially academic Christian theology – has been dominated by a philosophical, idealist and cognitive paradigm, which emphasises that thought – which itself has been decontextualised, removed from the conditions of its production and stripped of any vestiges of thought as itself also a practice – is more important than deeds. This logocentric emphasis represents a kind of contempt for craft, embodied experience, and the material world and a negation of Christianity as essentially an incarnational religion (Pattison, 2007).

To say that religion is about practice, then, is neither reductionist nor inconsequential. Recently, scholars of religion have questioned the predominant norm – largely inherited from Western Protestantism – that religion is primarily a cognitive phenomenon structured around propositional belief (Orsi, 2005). Similarly, they have problematised assumptions that the proper sphere of the study of religion lies in textual hermeneutics, rather than firmly embedded in lived experience to place more emphasis on analysis of the material and symbolic practices that comprise inhabited cultural 'worlds'. So, for example, religion can be studied as a system of material, symbolic or ritual attachments to a range of significant sacred others: human, non-human, natural or supernatural, all mediated through the media of bodies, practices and space (Pattison, 2007, 2010; Vasquez, 2011, p. 11). Values are always mediated by means of artefacts: texts, rituals, images, material culture, anecdotes and common wisdom, etc. All actors in a complex network are both bearers of meaning and creative agents of it (Kaufman, 2016, pp. 155–158).

In this context, theology cannot be reduced into a body of abstract premises or propositions. Christian theology has over-emphasised the cognitive and unseen over against the non-cognitive, relational and practical, which are then seen as a kind of after-thought for the uneducated. But what matters about Christianity and the life of the church is not what is contained in books or statements, but what is embodied in its practices:

> . . . the church does not speak only in its sermons, episcopal statements, papal encyclicals, working party reports, and theological tomes It also speaks in the manner of its being . . . The Christian church *shows* its vision of things quite as much as it *states* it.
>
> *(Biggar, 2011, p. 80)*

Thesis 4: practices are value-laden and revelatory – as practices build worlds, so they (and we) perform our truths

One of the reasons why the 'turn to practice' in so many disciplines has occurred is due to a crisis of meaning. It is frequently argued that in the face of postmodern fragmentation, it is impossible to speak of any kind of over-riding moral authority (MacIntyre, 1987). If notions of virtue and good cannot be metaphysically or ontologically grounded, however, they may instead be realised in and through practice, and specifically, the regular habits by which we orientate ourselves towards the good and the virtuous. Flourishing as individuals and as persons is attained through the cultivation of practices that are directed towards intrinsic criteria of excellence; that is, culturally determined rather than transcendentally experienced.

This, in turn, roots the practical theological researcher in the lived experience and faith practices of their subjects. It underlines the importance of focusing on the 'performativity' of theological truth-claims. Theological adequacy is not just tested in practice or as it translates into action. It is evaluated as 'embodied, situated knowing-in-action' (Bass et al., 2016, p. 2):

> the specific practices by which we respond to God's grace – practices such as prayer, forgiveness, and hospitality – bear knowledge of God, ourselves and the world that cannot be reduced to words, even though words are often important in helping us to learn and participate faithfully in them. Such practices embody certain kinds of wisdom and foster certain kinds of intelligence when engaged in serious and critical ways.
>
> *(Bass and Dykstra, 2008, p. 358)*

A core motif within practical theology that continues to stimulate thinking is Anton Boisen's characterisation of the discipline as directed towards the 'living human document' (revised by Miller-McLemore (1996) into the 'living human web'). This privileges a strong sense of the incarnational, storied individual as bearer of profound insights into the human condition. The major criticism of such a term is its implicit idealism: its assumption that meanings, values and beliefs constitute culture, to the detriment of material culture, artefacts, structures and embodied practices. However, if we reconceive the 'living human document' not simply as a semiotic, meaning-making self or self-in-relation, but an embodied, situated actor in a network of material and structural relationships and social practices, then 'practice' as constitutive of identity and meaning acquires new dimensions of significance for understandings of culture itself.

If everything is a practice, then texts are the records of historic and sedimented practices. Biblical texts and traditions were themselves generated in and from practice. Reading the Bible, too, is a practice. To read the Bible from the practice-focused perspective advanced here is part of the process of recontextualising Christian tradition, restoring the practices that are at its root.

Christian practice is always already theological insofar as it is informed by received, performed tradition: 'The meanings of the word "God" are to be discovered by watching what this community does' (Williams, 2000, p. xii). Theological enquiry always begins in the middle of things, amidst practices that are themselves already formed by traditions and interpretations that have expressed and embodied convictions about the nature of God.

This renders practical theology (or divinity in practice) a prime site for the communication and cultural circulation of Christianity – or the performance of Christian values and assumptions. Even 'tradition' as something related to, or normative for, practice exposes the extent to which the continuity of tradition is itself constructed in and through a range of textual, moral, discursive practices. These practices are the things that place one inside, outside, or at the margins or centre of a particular community of faith. Certain practices are ways of laying claim to a continuity with a particular past that is constructed as more or less authentic.

However, as Michel Foucault's work reminds us, practices are always already freighted with institutional patterns of power and knowledge, however innocuous (Foucault, 1979). Is the process of interpreting certain practices as theological, spiritual, religious by reference to particular modes of performance, styles of reading definitive texts, finding connections and affinities, also, then, one of 'disciplining' and even censoring? Habits and routines become congealed in words and texts and thereby become canonised into authoritative, even ideological knowledge. They perform a normative function, exercising social control or enforcing particular understandings of how to 'perform'. Drawing on Daniel Boyarin's work, Tom Beaudoin has characterised the perpetuation of what he terms 'christianicity', such that 'Christianity is always a rhetorical invocation intended to establish and manage the border between what is . . . and what is not Christian' (Beaudoin, 2016, p. 19). This should alert us to the hidden presuppositions inherent not only within the conduct of practice, but within the critical enquiry into the very *logic* of such practices.

'Worldly theology': from systematic to practical theological research

In *Places of Redemption*, Mary McClintock Fulkerson relates how she came to undertake research as a participant observer alongside the congregation of the Good Samaritan church in South Carolina. In the midst of an ethnically diverse, socially mixed community which contained a substantial number of members with disabilities, Fulkerson became acutely aware of her own status as a white, middle-class, able-bodied woman. She quickly realised that an 'applied' model of theological research which privileged beliefs over practices would fail to do justice to the myriad dilemmas of power, difference and representation that confronted her. She chose instead to adopt the methods and sensibilities of a practical theologian as the best way of capturing the complexity of life at Good Samaritan. An adequate theological reading – and one, not least, that acknowledged the danger that her own preconceptions and biases might perform exactly the kind of Foucauldian 'disciplining' function alluded to above – necessitated a more 'worldly' and ethnographic immersion in the practices and everyday dynamics of the life of the congregation.

Significant is Fulkerson's use at one stage of the terminology of 'representation': meaning not simply how she recorded or depicted her engagement with the people of Good Samaritan, but also its more political resonances: who speaks for whom? Who becomes the public 'representative' – the mouthpiece, the visible face or advocate – of such a heterogeneous community? Can such a 'representation' ever tell the whole truth?

> To do theological justice to this community will be to write about its people, about its habits and idiosyncracies, its mistakes and its blindness, as well as its moments of honesty and grace. That requires attention to the markers of difference, the role of bodies, and visceral responses. These are as much a part of the ambiguity and grace – the 'worldliness' of this faith community – as the Bible studies and the preaching. All this is crucial to making theological sense of the community.
>
> Success at this kind of theological representation is no small challenge. Theological framing can easily miss or obscure this worldliness. From overly cognitive and orthodox definitions of Christian faithfulness to concepts of practice that ignore the contribution of bodies and desire, prominent theological options risk overlooking both the worldly way that communities live out their faith and the worldly way that God is among us . . .
>
> By such a 'worldly theology', of course I do not mean an empirical, 'objective' analysis of this community . . . Instead I propose an inquiry for a theological frame that will be adequate to the full-bodied reality that is Good Samaritan, one capable of displaying its ambiguity, its implication in the banal and opaque realities of ordinary existence, even as it allows for testimony to God's redemptive activity . . . Attention to the worldly, situational character of Christian faith directs me to the task of practical theology.
>
> *(Fulkerson, 2007, pp. 6–7)*

Thesis 5: researching practice requires particular skills

Just as there are skills to be learned in handling texts or translations in advanced academic research, so there are particular methods and approaches to enable those researching their own practice to examine its theological, ethical and strategic significance. Enquiry into practice, our own and other people's, is a particular kind of research that calls for certain kinds of skills and sensibilities (Loftus, Higgs and Trede, 2011). To consider practical theology as in some degree a 'problem-centred' or enquiry-based discipline introduces the idea that research begins when the assumptions of practice no longer fit the situation, when, for example:

- Research addresses questions that cannot be answered simply by appeals to common sense;
- Research troubles the taken-for-granted – the implicit knowledge or worldview underpinning a practice is disrupted by illness or similar crisis
  (cf. Frank, 1995);
- When the tradition in which one has been rooted no longer makes sense and no longer offers adequate sources and resources to sustain one;
- What is perhaps more difficult are the practices that are not even acknowledged as problematic that must be interrogated;
- A practice – singing hymns or saying the creed – suddenly becomes problematic and dissonant due to other kinds of cognitive shifts, such as adoption of feminist insights (Fiorenza, 1983);
- The introduction of a new paradigm troubles the naturalism and taken-for-grantedness of prior experience.

Such a turn to practice is then reflected in the methods and methodologies of practical theology, as the discipline has looked at strategies of gathering and analysing lived experience. It has asked what representations and manifestations of the practices at the heart of practical theology might constitute legitimate data (Fulkerson, 2012). In response, there has been a proliferation of methodological debate and innovation: practice is brought to centre-stage, but there remain a host of questions as to what it actually constitutes, and how it might properly be examined.

This realisation is at the root of terminology that is standard fare within many branches of professional education, such as health care, teaching, clinical sciences such as psychotherapy and counselling, the creative and performing arts, not to mention many 'technical' subjects such as engineering, which is that of the 'reflective practitioner' (Schön, 1983). Learning emerges from practice and not the other way around – or perhaps more precisely, it happens in a cyclical or dialectical movement, although never as a straightforward 'application' of theory into practice. Where does the theory come from in the first place if not from lived experience and the practical questions engendered by the tasks of making, doing, building, caring and performing? Similarly, the practitioner may be reflective – stepping back from the routines and pressures of practice in order to throw a critical lens back onto themselves – but they are always already embedded in and advancing their own practice.

Another task might be to 'excavate' the levels of meaning that comprise the world-views that underpin people's taken-for-granted beliefs and practices. These always imply an underlying epistemology, which may even contradict people's professed opinions. For example, ethnographic studies of congregations will not be truly comprehensive if they simply focus on descriptive accounts of practices without placing those in a wider perspective – against sociological, cultural and historical analysis – or challenging the community's own self-description (Healy, 2012, p. 183). So there needs to be a way of valuing the integrity of phenomenological experience whilst holding any account (however 'thick', in Clifford Geertz's terms) up to a critical mirror (Geertz, 1973).

The *habitus* of research entails an enculturation into the practices and conventions of selectivity, accountability, responsibility, verifiability. It also requires the deployment of a variety of tools and approaches which themselves are embodiments of practice. These include reading; data gathering; data analysis; writing; discussing; journalling; arguing; and publishing. As we work through the remainder of this book, we will continue to consider the nature, values and significance of research practices from a variety of critical perspectives. These, too, create as well as well as bearing witness to the worlds that they seek to explore.

> This critical interrogation of practices and of values, in which the world we live in and the traditions we are shaped by, the book of the Bible as well as the book of life, are set side by side, is not fundamentally a practice of making connections but of seeing connections. In practical theology, in the engagement of the Bible with the book of life, we need to pay less attention to the hunt for a transferable and generalisable model of making connections, and more attention to the discipline of seeing well those individual minute particulars that lie before us: critically, imaginatively and courageously, as well as analogically and comparatively.
>
> *(Bennett, 2013, p. 134)*

HOW RESEARCH ARISES FROM PRACTICE AND FEEDS BACK INTO THEORY, THEOLOGY AND PRACTICE USING A PLURALITY OF RESEARCH METHODS

Mark Pryce, Anglican minister, poet and Diocesan Continuing Ministerial Education Adviser, researched for a professional doctorate by undertaking a sustained, evaluative theological reflection on his practice as an adult theological educator and poet working in the field of professional development among clergy in the Church of England. His 2015 thesis, 'The poetry of priesthood: a study of the contribution of poetry to the continuing ministerial education of clergy in the Church of England' (available at: http://etheses. bham.ac.uk/5772/3/Pryce15DPT_Redacted.pdf), forms the basis for a book (Pryce, forthcoming). Here, he explains how his research emerged from and affected his practice.

Participating in the professional doctorate provided a framework and forum for critical reflection on practice which enabled me to identify issues and questions in ministerial formation and development of clergy which I wished to pursue in deeper, more intentional and systematic ways.

Using a case study as a means of critical reflection on practice enabled me to problematise the way in which I drew on a poem in a clergy training session, and this developed into an understanding of using poetry as a distinctive approach in Continuing Ministerial Development (CMD) which deserved further analysis and development.

Reflection on my own practice enabled me to identify that I brought a distinctive approach to clergy CMD through use of poetry as a means of reflective practice. The professional enabled me to examine this practice as a methodology within reflective practice, to locate it within an inter-professional context, and to illuminate the method with literature about poetry and language in practical theology.

The research helped me to become more intentional in my work – for example in the ethical framework in which I operate alongside clergy colleagues, and in a more critical and intentional use of poetry as a means of reflection in Clergy CMD. Doctoral work in practical theology has instilled in me an informed confidence, rooted in reflexivity, and sustained with the skills for critical reflection on practice.

The critical analysis of the Poetry Reflection Groups I studied has enabled other practitioners to make use of this method in utlising poetry in clergy professional development, e.g., a poetry session introduced into the Women in Leadership programme.

Beyond the strictly practical, my research identified the wide use of poetry in practical theology, and that this is an unresearched usage which is often deployed uncritically. I identified the poetical discourse in practical theology, developed a taxonomy of this approach and the need for a more critical and appreciative deployment of poetry as a reflexive resource.

The development of poetry as reflexive method in PT Qualitative Research has been a particular interest for researchers, and I have been asked to speak and teach about poetry as a dimension of auto-ethnographic method as well as to write about research methodology.

Conclusion

Theology is thoroughly practical, or practice-oriented. Practice is the living resource by which Christians become the bearers of inherited tradition through the out-workings of everyday discipleship. Theological discourse is the guardian and critic of faithful practice; a rich repository of stories, rules of life, values and visions by which people can faithfully order their lives (individually, collectively) under God. In terms of advanced research into the theology of or practices, we will need firstly 'a comprehensive and coherent model of human action' (Mager, 2012, p. 260) that takes account of its 'conditions, dimensions, and dynamics' of behaviour, including a theological horizon.

Theology in general, and practical theology in particular, are, or should be, essentially orientated towards different kinds of practice: specifically, the practices that constitute the performances of faith, of discernment, of transformation; of the practices that cultivate an sensitivity to the signs of the sacred in the here and now; of the practices that aspire to draw nearer into the presence of the sacred and to find truer, better ways of inhabiting a reality suffused by the transcendent.

References

Ballard, P.H. and Pritchard, J.L., 2006. *Practical theology in action: Christian thinking in the service of church and society.* London: SPCK.

Bass, D.C., Cahalan, K.A., Miller-McLemore, B.J., Nieman, J.R. and Scharen, C.B., 2016. Engaging the intelligence of practice. In: D.C. Bass, K.A. Cahalan, B.J. Miller-McLemore, J.R. Nieman and C.B. Scharen, eds., *Christian practical wisdom: What it is, why it matters.* Grand Rapids, MN: Wm. B. Eerdmans. pp. 1–18.

Bass, D.C. and Dykstra, C., 2008. In anticipation. In: D.C. Bass and G. Dykstra, eds., *For life abundant: Practical theology, theological education, and Christian ministry.* Grand Rapids, MN: Wm. B. Eerdmans. pp. 355–360.

Beaudoin, T., 2016. Why does practice matter theologically? In: B.J. Miller-McLemore and J.A. Mercer, eds., *Conundrums in practical theology.* Leuven: Brill. pp. 8–32.

Bennett, Z., 2009. Theology and the researching professional. *Theology,* 112(869), pp. 333–342.

Bennett, Z., 2013. *Using the Bible in practical theology.* Farnham: Ashgate.

Bevans, S., 2014. Contextual theology as practical theology. In: K. Cahalan and G. Mikoski, eds., *Opening the Field of Practical Theology: an Introduction.* New York: Rowman & Littlefield. pp. 45–59.

Biggar, N., 2011. *Behaving in public: How to do Christian ethics.* Grand Rapids, MN: William B. Eerdmans.

Boisen, A.T., 1936. *The exploration of the inner world. A study of mental disorder and religious experience.* Chicago: Willett, Clark & Co.

Bottomore, T. and Rubel, M., 1963. *Karl Marx: Selected writings in sociology and social philosophy.* Harmondsworth, Middlesex: Penguin.

Bourdieu, P., 1990. *The logic of practice.* Translated from the French by R. Nice. Cambridge: Polity Press.

Bourdieu, P., 1997. *Outline of a theory of practice.* Translated from the French by R. Nice. Cambridge: Cambridge University Press.

Browning, D., 1991. *A fundamental practical theology.* Minneapolis, MN: Fortress Press.

Butler, J., 1990. *Gender trouble: Feminism and the subversion of identity.* New York: Routledge (2nd Edition, 2002).

Cahalan, K.A., 2014. Introduction. In: K.A. Cahalan and G.S. Mikoski, eds., *Opening the field of practical theology: An introduction.* New York: Rowman and Littlefield. pp. 1–10.

Charry, E.T., 1997. *By the renewing of your minds: The pastoral function of Christian doctrine.* New York: Oxford University Press.

Farley, E., 1983. *Theologia: Fragmentation and unity in theological education.* Philadelphia, PA: Fortress Press.

Fiorenza, E.S., 1983. *In memory of her: A feminist theological reconstruction of Christian origins.* London: SCM Press.

Foucault, M., 1979. *The history of sexuality, vol. 1: An introduction.* Translated by R. Harley. London: Penguin.

Frank, A., 1995. *The wounded storyteller: Bodies, illness, and ethics.* Chicago, IL: University of Chicago Press.

Fulkerson, M.M., 2007. *Places of redemption: Theology for a worldly church.* Oxford: Oxford University Press.

Fulkerson, M.M., 2012. Interpreting a situation: When is 'empirical' also 'theological'? In: P. Ward, ed., *Perspectives on ecclesiology and ethnography.* Grand Rapids, MN: Wm. B. Eerdmans. pp. 124–144.

Ganzevoort, R. and Roeland, J., 2014. Lived religion: The praxis of practical theology. *International Journal of Practical Theology*, 18(1), pp. 91–101.

Geertz, C., 1973. Thick description: Towards an interpretive theory of culture. In: C. Geertz, ed., *The interpretation of cultures: Selected essays.* New York: Basic Books. pp. 3–30.

Graham, E., 1996. *Transforming practice: Pastoral theology in an age of uncertainty.* London: Mowbray.

Graham, E., 2000. Practical theology as transforming practice. In: J.W. Woodward and S. Pattison, eds., *The Blackwell reader in pastoral and practical theology.* Oxford: Wiley-Blackwell. pp. 104–117.

Graham, E., Walton, H. and Ward, F., 2005. *Theological reflection: Methods.* London: SCM Press.

Grenz, S.J., 1993. *Revisioning evangelical theology: A fresh agenda for the 21st century.* Downers Grove, IL: Inter-Varsity Press.

Gutiérrez, G., 1974. *A theology of liberation.* London: SCM Press.

Harvey, G., 2013. *Food, sex and strangers: Understanding religion as everyday life.* Abingdon: Routledge.

Healy, N.M., 2012. Ecclesiology, ethnography, and God: An interplay of reality descriptions. In: P. Ward, ed., *Perspectives on ecclesiology and ethnography.* Grand Rapids, MN: Wm. B. Eerdmans. pp. 182–199.

Hiltner, S., 1958. *Preface to pastoral theology.* Nashville, TN: Abingdon.

Holland, J., 1990. Preface. In: J. Holland and P. Henriot, eds., *Social analysis: Linking faith and justice.* 2nd ed., Maryknoll, NY: Orbis. pp. xii–xxii.

Immink, G., 2014. Theological analysis of religious practices. *International Journal of Practical Theology*, 18(1), pp. 127–138.

Kaufman, T.S., 2016. From the outside, within, or in between? Normativity at work in empirical practical theology. In: B.J. Miller-McLemore and J.A. Mercer, eds., *Conundrums in practical theology.* Leuven: Brill. pp. 134–162.

Korsgaard, C.M., 2003. Realism and constructivism in twentieth century moral philosophy. *Journal of Philosophical Research*, 28(Supplement), pp. 99–122.

Lakoff, G. and Johnson, M., 1999. *Philosophy in the flesh: The embodied mind and the challenge to western thought.* New York: Basic Books.

Loftus, S., Higgs, J. and Trede, F., 2011. Researching living practices. In: J. Higgs, A. Titchen, D. Horsfall and D. Bridges, eds., *Creative spaces for qualitative researching: Living research.* Rotterdam: Sense Publications. pp. 3–12.

MacIntyre, A., 1987. *After virtue: A study in moral theory.* 2nd ed. London: Duckworth.

Mager, R., 2012. Action theories. In: B.J. Miller-McLemore, ed., *The Wiley-Blackwell companion to practical theology.* Oxford: Wiley-Blackwell. pp. 255–265.

McGuire, M., 2008. *Lived religion: Faith and practice in everyday life.* New York: Oxford University Press.

Miller-McLemore, B.J., 1996. The living human web: Pastoral theology at the turn of the century. In: J. Stevenson-Moessner, ed., *Through the eyes of a woman: Insights for pastoral care*. Minneapolis, MN: Fortress Press. pp. 9–26.

Miller-McLemore, B.J., ed., 2012. *The Wiley-Blackwell companion to practical theology*. Oxford: Wiley-Blackwell.

Miller-McLemore, B.J., 2016. Academic theology and practical knowledge. In: D.C. Bass, K.A. Cahalan, B.J. Miller-McLemore, J.R. Nieman and C.B. Scharen, eds., *Christian practical wisdom: What it is, why it matters* (pp. 173–229). Grand Rapids, MN: Wm. B. Eerdmans. pp. 173–229.

Nieman, J., 2002. Attending locally: Theologies in congregations. *International Journal of Practical Theology*, 6(2), pp. 198–225.

Orsi, R., 2005. *Between heaven and earth: The religious worlds people make and the scholars who study them*. Princeton, NJ: Princeton University Press.

Paden, W., 1994. *Religious worlds*. Boston, MA: Beacon Press.

Pattison, S., 1997. *The faith of the managers: When management becomes religion*. London: Cassell.

Pattison, S., 2007. *Seeing things: Deepening relations with visual artefacts*. London: SCM Press.

Pattison, S., 2010. Spirituality and spiritual care made simple. *Practical Theology*, 3(3), 351–366.

Pryce, M., forthcoming. *Practical theology, poetry and reflective practice*. Abingdon: Taylor & Francis.

Ralston Saul, J., 1993. *Voltaire's bastards: The dictatorship of reason in the West*. New York: Vintage Books.

Schleiermacher, F., 1966. *Brief outline of the study of theology*. Translated from the German by T. Tice. Richmond, VA: John Knox Press.

Schön, D., 1983. *The reflective practitioner*. New York: Basic Books.

Segundo, J.-L., 1976. *The liberation of theology*. Translated from the Spanish by J. Drury. Maryknoll, NY: Orbis.

Smith, T.A., 2012. Theories of practice. In: B.J. Miller-McLemore, ed., *The Wiley-Blackwell companion to practical theology*. Oxford: Wiley-Blackwell. pp. 244–254.

Stoddart, E., 2011. *Theological perspectives on a surveillance society: Watching and being watched*. Farnham: Ashgate.

Vasquez, M., 2011. *More than belief: A materialist theory of religion*. Oxford: Oxford University Press.

Veling, T., 2005. *Practical theology: On earth as it is in heaven*. Maryknoll, NY: Orbis.

Vokey, D. and Kerr, J., 2011. Intuition and professional wisdom: Can we teach moral discernment? In: L. Bondi, D. Carr, C. Clark and C. Clegg, eds., *Towards professional wisdom: Practical deliberation in the people professions*. Farnham: Ashgate. pp. 63–80.

Wildman, W., 2010. Distributed identity: Human beings as walking, thinking ecologies in the Microbial World. In: N.M. Knight, ed., *Human identity at the intersection of science, technology and religion*. London: Ashgate.

Williams, R., 2000. *On Christian theology*. Oxford: Wiley-Blackwell.

Woolgar, S. and Latour, B., 1979. *Laboratory life*. Beverley Hills, CA: Sage.

Young, I.M., 1990. *Throwing like a girl and other philosophical essays*. Bloomington, IN: Indiana University Press.

4

COMMUNITIES OF PRACTICE

When a group of us gathered together to discuss our work at an international conference in practical theology in Manchester in 2003, we little realised where those conversations would lead. But as we have documented elsewhere (Bennett, 2007; Graham, 2006) the issue we began to identify there – of teaching master's level postgraduates who had evident ability to progress to doctoral research but were discouraged from advancing further due to lack of professional and institutional support – became the catalyst for a subsequent major venture within the discipline in the UK. That was the creation of a part-time, portfolio-based professional doctorate in practical theology. One of the most significant considerations in designing this innovative and unique venture was to avoid the solitariness of the PhD process. So a keynote feature of the programme was the premium it placed on the formation of peer group cohorts. These comprised what, subsequently, we have come to identify as 'communities of practice' and 'communities of learning'.

We are passionately convinced that the concept and reality of 'communities of practice' are appropriate to the discipline of practical theology, and enhance practical theological research. This rich concept has encouraged us to think of the practice of research in a particular way: as emerging from specific contexts and prompted by particular pragmatic needs; as developing collaboratively and iteratively; and as valuing process as much as product. These features are strongly apparent when we come to think of the 'added value' of doing research as part of a community of practice and learning.

Practical theology places itself within an understanding of *phronēsis*, or practical wisdom (Miller-McLemore, 2016). Several elements of this concept can be related directly to communities of practice: an epistemology of the generation of knowledge and understanding through action and practice; the centrality of community for the generation of understanding and wisdom; and the performative element of wisdom. Such practical theology resonates with the characterisation of scholarship around communities of practice as emphasising 'context, process, social interaction, material practices, ambiguity, disagreement – in short the frequently idiosyncratic and always performative nature of learning' (Amin and Roberts, 2008, p. 353). We will return, therefore, to some of the affinities between communities of practice, and practical theology and theological method at the end of the chapter. In microcosm, the life of an effective community of practice embodies the dynamics of lost, changed, rooted and claimed. It is about a willingness to take the risk of making oneself vulnerable to, and being transformed by, the needs and gifts of others; and it is about creating relationships of trust in shared endeavour and reaping the 'dividends' of such collaborative networking.

Communities of practice in context

We bring to the discussion of communities of practice three sets of experiences on which to reflect and from which to learn. First, there is the community of practice we have belonged to as we have designed and implemented the professional doctorate in practical theology. Secondly, there are the communities of practice which have been an integral part of the doctoral learning cohorts which constitute this programme. And finally, there is the community of practice which we have become over the last few years as we have co-authored this book. We all belong to other communities of practice, too, but these are the ones we have shared and upon which we reflect together.

The professional doctorate, currently delivered in all the universities for which we work, constitutes a specific instantiation of a community of practice in practical theological research. This is a *research* community; the candidates on this programme are not pursuing taught modules but are engaged in practices of advanced enquiry in relation to their professional research question from day one. Whilst these practitioners enjoy a high degree of autonomy in pursuing independent research projects, they are also involved in a collaborative and interactive community, with tangible benefits.

It is intriguing to look back over the process of initial conception and design of that programme. First, as we worked on the curriculum together, we were in many respects working as a community of practice ourselves, theological educators striving to bring something new and innovative to birth. We relied on one another's expertise and institutional contacts. We drew strength and strategic support from the knowledge that we were not alone in our experiences as supervisors in encountering a significant mismatch between the standard model of a postgraduate doctoral researcher – a junior scholar, probably full-time, in receipt of funding, with aspirations to gain entry to an academic career – and the experience of most of our most able practitioners: mid-career, part-time, already embedded in a professional trajectory outside Higher Education.

Secondly, as our plans for the professional doctorate took shape, and as we explored the wider literature, we were able to place theories and concepts alongside our own anecdotal experience. They furnished us with concepts and language to describe what prior to that had been much more intuitive, and helped further to shape and direct our thinking. So, we learned to differentiate between 'the professional researcher' and 'the researching professional' (Bourner, Bowden and Laing, 2001). We realised that supervision of professional candidates required different skills and aptitudes on our part because of their specific needs and prior learning (Morley, 2005). We gained a sense of the quite distinctive pedagogical challenges and opportunities offered by a strongly practice-based, enquiry-led methodology, in which the professional contexts and experiences of participants represented a baseline of primary research data (Fulton et al., 2013). These realisations, in turn, helped us to design a curriculum that was fit for purpose for the needs of these particular communities.

And thirdly, as we reflected on that process – and continue to do so in this volume – we realise that what we stumbled on, almost by accident, not only has wider theoretical cadence, but has also borne fruit in our own, and our practitioners' journeys. The communities of learning embodied by our respective professional doctoral programmes have proved vital to our developing understanding of what advanced research in practical theology is really all about. In this chapter, then, we begin to unpack what the significance of these 'communities of learning' – for our own research and that of others – in practical theology.

Wenger-Trayner and Wenger-Trayner (2015, p. 1) define communities of practice as 'groups of people who share a concern or a passion for something they do and learn how to do it better as they interact regularly'. Communities of practice are characterised by relationality, problem-centred and enquiry-based activity, and knowing-in-action (Amin and Roberts, 2008). In this chapter, we will be addressing the following questions: what difference does it make to ground advanced research in communities of practice? How do such communities work? What do they tell us about the process and practice of doing theology, and of practical theological research in particular?

Relationality: the key to communities of practice

Communities of practice are not task-oriented in the sense of an extrinsic goal (such as the completion of a project), or the creation of technical outputs (Wenger-Trayner, 2006). They are defined by the shared outcome of enhanced learning:

> The community of practice may engage in certain tasks, but it doesn't end there. What brings value in a community of practice is its members' shared learning . . . what brings them together is the exchange of ideas, best practices and new knowledge that allows them to return to their teams and do their jobs better.
>
> *(de Cagna, 2001, p. 7)*

A community of practice emerges (or is intentionally formed) by bringing a group together (with shared or convergent interests) to address a common activity.

Communities of practice work at advancing the breadth, scope and quality of expertise pertinent to their profession; but crucially, this is knowledge advancement from the perspective of the practitioners themselves (Wenger-Trayner, 2006). The hub of communities of practice is, effectively, the creation of rich networks of learning that are vital for organisational and professional development. At their heart is a shared undertaking of the 'communal activity of coming to know' (Kameen cited in Fillery-Travis, 2014, p. 617).

The process of building those networks of learning, in turn, hinges on the driving force of relationship and collaboration. Successful communities of practice – those which produce innovative or creative learning in some respect – depend on qualities such as trust, mutuality, shared purpose and common goals (Amin and Roberts, 2008). Functioning communities are realised through the discursive activity of their members, in terms of the types of knowledge used and produced, the nature of the social interactions taking place, the kind of innovation and organisational dynamic. Knowledge transfer within the community tends to be tacit, person-centred, relational, incremental and performative.

> Communities of practice build upon the characteristics of a working team or group, i.e. members of people able to interact with one another, psychologically aware of each other, and who perceive and are perceived as being members of a team or group.
>
> *(Shacham, 2009, p. 280)*

One of the key characteristics of communities of practice is the 'proximity' of its members, whether that is ideological, physical, virtual or organisational (Amin and Roberts, 2008, p. 353). This enables the formation of strong networks into which members bring extant skills, knowledge, values and experience – the resources of 'social capital' – which effectively oil the wheels of common purpose and collaborative working. It is as if the investment of time and energy that goes into forging working relationships subsequently begins to pay dividends in the form of mutual support and common purpose. But these communities cannot be engineered, since communities are engendered organically, through practices and social relations, rather than rendered theoretically or designed by external mandate. 'One learns how to be in community as one engages in social relations with others' (Calderwood, 2000, p. 18).

SUPPORTIVE RELATIONSHIPS WITHIN A COMMUNITY OF PRACTICE

Sally Buck, a theological educator who conducted research on the poetic nature of ministry of the Word through a professional doctorate, reflects on how the network of relationships with her cohort constitutes an ongoing critical friend within the day-to-day conduct of her research practice. (For further, see Buck, 2016.)

Being part of a cohort has contributed a number of qualities to the doctoral experience for me. On nights when I would happily light a fire and watch a film the thought of colleagues working on their research has motivated me to turn on the computer.

The cohort has offered support (listening to my struggles in the balancing of family, work and study commitments); it has provided encouragement through the shared motivation to relate theory to practice in a way that has academic credibility; it has been challenging ('what do you mean by . . . . ?', 'have you read . . . . . . ', 'how are you going to evidence that?') and it has given me a necessary level of competition (if they can finish that paper I'm jolly well going to!).

Most importantly, though, being part of a cohort has set the doctoral process in a collaborative environment with people who understand me when others respond with blank looks when I say things like 'I think I'm drowning in my own mind' or 'I'm so excited – I just explained my research topic and it only took one sentence'! Without the cohort I would probably be lighting lots of fires and watching too many films.

(Quoted in Bennett and Lyall, 2014, p. 193)

Communities of practice may be gathered or dispersed. Participants experience the benefits of being part of a community of practice even when they are not physically present to one another. Sally Buck identifies motivation, support and a deep level of mutual understanding which forges a virtual network of support that enables its members to undertake the demanding intellectual work of practical theological research. The work that goes into forming and maintaining a viable community will thus have a significant impact on the quality of its interactions and long-term sustainability. Another member of Sally's cohort writes that the group 'confirm(s) the value of theoretical work'; and yet another speaks of its 'intellectual impact'. Other members identify the social capital within an academic community – realised in shared wisdom, and in shared eating and drinking (Bennett and Lyall, 2014). These themes underline the importance of communities of practice as embodying 'thick' values of trust, mutual accountability, critical friendship and shared purpose (Amin and Roberts, 2008; McNiff, 2017, pp. 205–215).

Communities of practice sharpen the mind. They hold their members to account and constitute a critical benchmark. As Sally's account shows, a community of practice offers both support and challenge across affective and cognitive domains of learning, sharpening conceptual thinking and enhancing emotional support in the process of the quest or research.

Research reveals that communities of practice serve and expand their members' cognitive and affective development (Shacham and Od-Cohen, 2009). An emphasis on learning in a cohort fosters a climate of consultation on core research skills such as content, design, methodology, structuring and presenting an argument. Over time, effective communities of practice become forums for sharing ideas, concepts and resources. They help with sharpening communication and critical thinking, becoming safe spaces in which members can hold one another to account and be open to critique. There may be an element of bench-marking, as well – especially in an extended programme such as a part-time research degree – as members can compare relative rates of progress and hold one another to deadlines. Communities of practice also become sites of emotional support and evolving coping strategies, as Sally's testimony also shows.

Pedagogies of learning

Communities of practice are, then, to a greater or lesser degree, essentially communities of learning: about and towards intrinsic tasks or goals, but also as sites of gathering and nurturing transferable skills and qualities (Leshem, 2007). They represent very particular styles and approaches to learning, regarding knowledge not as something to be imparted or hierarchically handed down, but rather to be developed collaboratively:

> The path to expertise in any craft, discipline, profession or field is one of gradual initiation into the shared beliefs, attitudes, interests, norms and priorities that define members of that particular community of practitioners and are embodied in its activities. By definition, full membership in such a community means being able to contribute to the ongoing development of its explicit and implicit standards of assessment.
>
> *(Vokey and Kerr, 2011, pp. 71–72)*

Communities of practice locate learning as relational, within contracted networks of practitioners. This implies a very particular set of assumptions about pedagogy and epistemology. In one of our early meetings designing the professional doctorate we were challenged by our institutions to offer 'a clear alternative philosophy of pedagogy appropriate to our discipline'; the formation of a community of practice has been central in our response to this (Bennett, 2007, p. 75). Such assumptions include that of practice as a location of knowledge and understanding; knowledge as cognitive, affective and relational; the belief that robust collective support and challenge proves effective at fostering the deep self-confidence required in autonomous learning. Such communities will flourish and function if members feel they have beliefs, identity, goals and values in common; there are focal points and occasions when community is celebrated; competent membership of community is regarded as something to be earned; and differences and tensions within the group are acknowledged and explored (Calderwood, 2000, pp. 1–18).

Matching literature on communities of practice against that of life-long learning and 'andragogy' (Robinson, 2011) develops this sense of the embedded and contingent nature of learning within a community of practice. It reveals some interesting correlations. In both, learning is contextual and inductive; the emphasis is on a model of pedagogy premised as much on dialogue and accompaniment as instruction or hierarchy; and the focus is on 'doing and being' as much as on knowledge-or skills-acquisition (Robinson, 2011, p. 213).

This is something also echoed in literature on formation for the professions as directed towards the cultivation of wisdom (Vokey and Kerr, 2011). In parallel, communities of practice exhibit a high degree of 'collective responsibility' and a certain latitude within the group itself for defining what kinds of knowledge (and what repertoires) are fit for purpose (Wenger-Trayner, 2006). There is also a strong performative element to the knowledge generated by communities of practice, which are, by definition, embedded in the contexts into which new learning will be transferred (Wenger-Trayner, 2006, p. 4).

The practitioner-researcher

An increasing number of researchers in practical theology are practitioner-researchers whose area of research concerns the actual practice in which they are engaged. This is certainly true of the professional doctorate candidates enrolled on the programmes we, the authors, direct and administer. By definition, they are members of two distinct communities of practice: in the workplace and in the academy. They may at times feel as if they live in the cracks between both, exploiting spaces and never quite fitting. The experience of living between two worlds may be disorienting, rather like the turning of the coloured pieces within a kaleidoscope, where shapes are constantly forming only to dissolve as rapidly as they appeared. It may involve experiencing a sense of rootedness and belonging simultaneously with feelings of displacement and loss (see Chapter 1).

Learning to be a practitioner-researcher certainly brings technical challenges. For example, it entails the acquisition of new skills, such as interviewing, research design, or data analysis. However, first and foremost, the researcher develops by becoming a full member in at least two functioning communities of practice. This is similar to the way in which a professional acquires a sense of mature moral discernment. Knowledge is less a transaction or exchange of information than 'participation in . . . a community's ways of life', embracing 'perceptual, affective, intuitive, deliberative, volitional and communicative competencies' (Vokey and Kerr, 2011, p. 72). Practitioner-researchers in intentional communities of practice are essentially modelling these qualities for one another – or learning to demonstrate them for one another – in a shared enterprise of cultivating the virtues of practitioner-research.

This is consistent with Vokey and Kerr's thesis that professionalism is a matter of moral and practical wisdom. Communities of practice are also engaged in activities of moral enquiry, in which the capacity for *discernment* is primary as the sensibility best suited to managing situations of complexity. The professional doctorate cohort is one significant place where a new community of practice is formed which learns the discernment and wisdom to do this. Those who are experts in their (professional) practice have learned these skills in relation to the one community of practice. The practitioner-researcher must then transpose that learning into a different context, that of the research community of practice. If successful, the outcome will be something that will create a bridge between these two communities with which they have engaged.

Bridging the gap

There are issues here, however, about identity – even, fundamentally, about belonging. If communities of practice thrive on affinity, common purpose and 'proximity', might that not lead to a kind of narrowing of horizons? In valuing the mutuality of peer support, might a community of practitioner-researchers avoid asking the most difficult questions about the very legitimacy of their professional priorities? Is it possible for a practitioner-researcher who is embedded in a particular context to achieve an appropriate degree of critical distance from their organisation, their colleagues, or from the tacit practices and routines into which they have been socialised? Might situations be envisaged in which members of a group collude, consciously or unconsciously, in evading difficult questions? Ideally, a healthy community of practice will not involve mutual reinforcement of prejudice and habit, but will embody forms of questioning and critique which come from the opening of critical spaces and perspectives through difference and disagreement.

Similarly, practitioners conducting 'insider research' face a complex task. Their knowledge base is not from one single source but from a dynamic set of different domains: professional, academic and organisational. Learning from, and speaking into, these different constituencies, is a challenging process. These may not correspond with established methodological conventions. Even the polarity of 'insider/ outsider' may not capture the 'multiple integrities' (Drake and Heath, 2011, p. 5) and the complex negotiations necessary to manage the research process.

A researcher-practitioner's embeddedness in their own organisation is, potentially, then, both opportunity and risk. It represents a richness of affinity and common purpose, but may inhibit critical distance. Do communities of practice therefore need strategies of estrangement as much as orientation in the cultivation of critical reflexivity?

A PRACTITIONER-RESEARCHER REFLECTS ON OVERLAPPING COMMUNITIES OF PRACTICE AND THE CRITICAL ROLE OF SUPERVISION

Linda Robinson's research, for a professional doctorate and beyond, investigates the roles which supervision plays in research practices, with their complex interactions between communities of practice (Robinson, 2011).

My ability to conduct my research was entirely dependent upon my membership of various communities of practice which I described as a Venn diagram type structure of circles that overlapped the common member, me. Each community gave a distinctive voice and perspective as I sought to answer my research question. Peculiar to my research were voices from adult learning theory and my choice of a theological partner, and perhaps most significantly, my own unique voice grounded in my personal and professional experiences which coloured my apprehension of all that spoke into my research.

My supervisory relationships and the specific learning community of my cohort were means of helping to manage a potential cacophony of sound. The cohort community modelled and, indeed, embodied the principles and practices of a community of practice. Empirically, this community demonstrated that learning transformatively is fuelled and driven in relationship with others who have an orientation towards learning and who develop a common identity glued around a shared value and belief system.

The more secure our relationships within the group, the more we felt able to test our ideas. It was of no consequence that our research areas were all different. Indeed, this might well have been a strength as we committed to peer supervision that became more attentive and challenging. We developed our capacity to ask open coaching type questions that did not require us to be experts in each other's fields. Collaboration and interdependence socialised the power dynamic.

Likewise, my one-to-one supervision reflected two persons coming together, each with her own complex layers and overlapping 'Venn' diagram of communities of practice. One of my research participants described supervision as where 'two ontologies meet'. In this way I think it could be argued that even a one to one supervisory relationship could be regarded as a community of practice.

I found the relationship could be one of mutual and reciprocal learning. Throw into this mix a heady combination of a workplace supervisor and academic supervisor and watch the learning crackle!

I was privileged in both my supervisory and cohort communities to be blessed with such learning relationships. Underpinning the processes and structures to achieve the academic purpose of my doctorate, was a set of beliefs and values which were committed to human flourishing beyond that of assessment. This went a long way in balancing the inevitable power dynamics that exist in what I have described since my graduation as the love triangle of a professional doctorate, a force field of student, academy and workplace.

In theological terms it could be argued that the embodiment of a community of practice is to be found in the perichoresis of the Trinity, its common identity and purpose, mutual flow and energy.

Collusion and critique

We might ask, therefore, does a community of practice encourage its members into conformity with 'tacit' knowledge and rules, or can it genuinely allow for innovation and dissent? If communities of practice deal in part with the tacit knowledge of its members, in what ways, and to what ends, do its learning activities interrogate and challenge that knowledge?

For communities of practice in practical theological research two particular questions of diversity arise, both of which are signalled in the recent publication from the context of the USA *Conundrums in Practical Theology*, namely 'christian-centrism' or 'christianicity' (Beaudoin, 2016) and the 'racialised zoo of practical theology' (Goto, 2016). While Beaudoin (2016, p. 12) argues that practical theology in the USA (and we would echo this of our experience in the UK) has been 'too untroubled in its Christian confidence', Goto (2016, p. 121) examines the 'lack of critical awareness' that 'allows practical theologians . . . to base assumptions about the collective "we" on white experiences' (Goto, 2016, p. 121).

Effective and sustainable communities of practice should be able to facilitate a greater clarity towards one's own preconceptions and the value of the 'research capital' one brings into the community and its work. A community of practice should not simply reinforce theoretical, professional, theological or performative assumptions but embody *critical* enquiry. For example, literature on professional doctorates stresses the value of communities of learning as places not only to gain new cognitive skills and understandings, and not only to experience moral support, but precisely to embody diversity and plurality of perspectives, within the common overall aim of acquiring a higher degree (Fulton et al., 2013, pp. 22–24). Thus a community of practice is not merely a support group. Embedded in its procedures should be practices of mutual critique as well as strategies for moving beyond the descriptive to engage with theoretical/conceptual frameworks which may question existing knowledge and practice.

Being open to the danger of collusion and mutual reinforcement of our own blinkered vision may offer communities of practice resources for exactly the opposite of this: the encouragement of critical thinking. Two important ways in which this is done are through the diversity of the community and through the encouragement to reflexivity. The perspectives brought by others in the community of practice challenge taken-for-granted ways of seeing by furnishing a view from another place and by offering comparative viewpoints. Theory does not have to be built by abstraction, but may be built by comparison and analogy.

DISTURBING THE CANONS AND NORMS OF OUR NATIVE 'TRIBES'

Stephen reflects on his learning from working with others in an interdisciplinary, inter-professional community of practice. See Gilliat-Ray, Ali and Pattison (2013).

There are many communities of practice in research. An important one, especially on funded projects, is the interdisciplinary, inter-professional research team. The last such team I belonged to on a three year government funded research project consisted of a social scientist principal investigator, a Muslim theologian/ field researcher, and me, a Christian practical theologian as co-investigator. There was a greater community around this of consultants and Muslim chaplains in the UK, the subject of the study. All of these people needed to be integrally involved. We worked together for four years.

I learned a lot about Islamic practice, institutions and thought from my Muslim colleagues, as well as about the state of contemporary chaplaincy across British public institutions – that was the aim of the project. I had to get my head round qualitative research data gathering methods such as interviewing and shadowing and then, dauntingly, to become competent in interrogating and analysing the data base via NVivo programmes. I also learned a lot about my colleagues' perspectives on the subject matter and on research.

We each brought different concerns and perspectives, one as a Muslim professional 'insider' new to field based research, one as an 'outsider' religious studies social scientist and my own perspective as a Christian insider and former chaplain. The perspectives mostly complemented each other and allowed us each to read and interpret data differently, then discuss it together. This allowed a richer, if more problematic analysis to occur that would have been possible if we'd worked alone and followed the canons and norms of our native religious and academic 'tribes'.

The experience of working together is taxing. Do not do unto others as you would they do unto you – they are different! You have to explain your familiar world to others carefully and be prepared to learn slowly from them, too.

People work at different speeds and in different ways; you can disagree on everything from timetable to interpretation and representation of data. Inevitably in a people-focussed project where collaborators have different demands on their time and varying strengths and weaknesses, things don't always get done at the time and in the way any individual might prefer.

Working together takes time, trust and empathy, not only with interviewees but also with all-too-human colleagues with lives, commitments and families. Just because you are the oldest and most senior person, a white bloke at that, and used to preaching and lecturing, does not mean that you know most or have least to learn. I needed to be careful to keep my mouth appropriately shut and my ears open. And it is sometimes difficult to see your way of doing and expressing things being moved over and relegated.

So a good and fruitful experience that produced a better project than any of us could have produced individually. But a demanding one, too.

Forming and inhabiting communities of practice

As we have been arguing, research is itself a practice. It is a practice which at its best in the discipline of practical theology has an intention to generate practical wisdom through truer knowledge and better understanding. It is unsurprising, therefore, that research in practical theology is often conducted through communities of practice. These may well take forms shared by other disciplines and research communities, but their contours will be shaped by the nature of the subject researched and by the particular nature of the discipline of practical theology. This may take one or more of several forms. Mentioned already have been joint research projects, doctoral research cohorts, peer-related and other forms of supervision. Research in which participants have a more or less collaborative role offer possibilities for rather different forms of communities of practice. One recently developed and influential research practice is Theological Action Research (Cameron et al., 2010).

THEOLOGICAL ACTION RESEARCH: PRACTICAL THEOLOGY THROUGH, WITH AND FOR COMMUNITIES OFPRACTICE

Clare Watkins, a lecturer at the University of Roehampton, is one of the team who developed Theological Action Research (TAR) and continues to work with and advocate it. Here she explains its fundamental rootedness in communities of practice. For more on TAR see, e.g., Cameron et al. (2010); Watkins (2018) and www.theologyandactionresearch.net.

It is, perhaps, one of the most pressing challenges for practical theology: how to 'research' practices of faith in ways which avoid undue distortions of those practices, either through a lack of critical distance, or through an adoption of a quasi-social scientific 'objectivity'. In either case, the authentic nature of these practices as essentially interpersonal, communal, faith-full is obscured, as the mysterious reality of praxis as both particular and the embodiment of something universal and transcendent, is over simplified to suit the paradigms of research and its narration. Too often, practices become 'objects of study', which are then reported on to the communities who live them, often with alienating effects. This limits the effectiveness of the research for the practice communities themselves, and fails to be true to Christian theological insights concerning the movement of the Spirit, and the locating of wisdom and of grace.

Theological action research adopts insights from participative action research to develop ways of practical theological learning in which practitioners, theologians and other 'experts' work together to design, discern and disseminate research and thinking around practices. The research process itself depends on the creation of communities of reflective practice, as the lone researcher model is rejected in favour of practices of research conversation, in practitioner and academic reflector groups.

As co-designed and co-discerned, the processes of theological action research bear fruit in ways which build learning, insight and renewed practice through a shared learning. Communities that have worked with theological action research processes are better able 'own' these points of learning and transformation, as they have been arrived at through a common journey, rather than presented from someone else's learning.

This approach is not only a practical theological learning from action research; it is also a response to a fundamental theological conviction about the nature of God's self-revelation in the world. For, if theology is faith seeking understanding, and if its 'authority' comes from attending faithfully to the 'ways God speaks', then it is compelled to attend not only to normative traditions, and academic theology and its interdisciplinary partners; it must also attend to what God is doing and saying in the here and now of faith-full practices. This theological conviction informs the conversation and essentially communal learning of theological action research. It is a formative sense that 'truth' is being discerned communally and across communities, for the sake of increasingly God-ward orientated practice and learning.

With action research methodologies a wide variety of different possibilities exist for co-operative and collaborative work (see, for example, Reason, 1994; Reason and Bradbury, 2006; McNiff, 2017). The choice of such methods often stems from value commitments such as the democratisation of research, a desire not to treat participants as 'objects' of research, or an appreciation of the importance of communal approaches to human flourishing. Sometimes the use of co-operative methodologies might be related to optimising possibilities for change, or maximising possibilities of understanding. Whatever the motivation, co-operative and participatory methodologies require complex inhabiting of communities of practice, in which the power-positioning of various members of those communities becomes an important object of reflexivity.

POWER AND COLLABORATION IN ACTION RESEARCH: THE NAKED RESEARCHER?

Jason Boyd, Minister of Witney Congregational Church, teaches for the Congregational Institute of Practical Theology and the Nazarene Theological College, Manchester. He reflects on the mutual vulnerability of himself and his participants in his collaborative research project. See Boyd (2018).

'What happens in that space between me and the congregation when I preach a sermon?', I asked during a postgraduate seminar. My question coincided with my first encounter with practical theology, action research and the Ignatian spiritual exercises. Through my inquiry emerged ART: action research as a way of doing theology.

I decided to 'answer' my question through action research. I came to realise that action research is not a 'tool' in the social science box of methods. It is an orientation. My definition is that 'Action research is a **whole-life** quality of attention to self-in-relation-to-others-in-the-world acting, reflecting, planning and renewing action through dialogue which includes the unique contribution of each person in generating knowledge that works and transforms.' It is not done 'on' or 'for', but 'with' others.

I asked my congregation if my question mattered to them. It did. Collaborative planning meetings eventuated in the creation of Word Café: ten services of worship followed by a light lunch as the congregation explored, 'What happened to you as you listened to the sermon today?'

I discovered I was both the naked preacher and the naked researcher: I was directly involved in the practice into which I was inquiring. What if people were bored with my sermons? What if my involvement rendered me unable to analyse my practice? I wrestled with the myth of the 'objective observer' and embraced my vantage point and place within the nexus of power.

My congregation was vulnerable. How dare they say what they thought about my preaching? What if I dismissed their views? The lengthy process of collaboration built trust. Here are three examples of growing confidence:

1   'A couple of us had said after their first experience of "Word Café" they would not come and yet they are still coming and have learned to enjoy it. They thought their views did not matter, but they now know they are understood and contribute.'
2   At the start, a participant with special educational needs was nervous about being a part of the Word Café. At the end of 9 months, this person was not only contributing to conversations, they acted as host and scribe.
3   A participant who described that they were not 'very good at small talk' 'felt that the Word Café was conversation with a purpose'. This person went on to report that they 'had spoken with more people in the church today about meaningful things than [they] had ever done in [their] whole time as part of the church . . . '

Word Café opened a communicative space in which we confronted our mutual nakedness thus discovering new insights transforming a practice of preaching.

Communities of practice are more than accidental insofar as they embody a common commitment to remain embedded in the various contexts from which their members are drawn. There is something significant here, not just about the nature of the knowledge engendered by communities of practice, but about the nature of those who participate in the learning and researching practices of those communities. For example, it is likely, that by virtue of their problem-centred, enquiry-based and situated knowledge production, learning and innovation – embodying learning-in-action – communities of *practice* will value these qualities for their own research outcomes. Similarly, as a community of *practitioners* who value collaborative, reflexive and context-rich research, researchers have a strong investment not only in a successful outcome for their own doctoral research but that of others.

This has affinities with the kind of model of action research expounded by Kemmis. One of the primary objectives of such activity is 'to create the conditions for public discourse in public spheres' (Kemmis, 2010, p. 424): In other words, this contributes towards the formation of a Habermasian ideal-speech situation in which research engenders positive, ethical and transformative outcomes for the sake of a greater common good:

> It aims to model democratic relations between people in which there is recognition and respect for difference, and in which people strive to reach understandings and agreements on the basis of the arguments 'on the table' about issues and states of affairs in the world.
>
> *(Kemmis, 2010, p. 424)*

Finally, we should not forget that collaborative authorship is also a community of practice. We reflect on our own experience of this with amazement and delight in our conclusion below. Mercer and Miller-McLemore also write of 'a solidarity which allowed us to persist' within the community which wrote *Conundrums* of the beginnings of the book 'in conversation and community', and of the way in which vulnerability was evident not just within the process of research but the process of scholarly writing: 'the work was hard and laid bare questions about our scholarly identity and vocation' (Miller-McLemore, 2016, p. 6). Collaboration in authorship has the potential to offer critical space in which reflexivity is heightened by the taking seriously of the perspective of others/another. Zoë describes this in relation to the co-authoring of a book with Christopher Rowland on 'the Bible, reflection and everyday life'.

WRITING COLLABORATIVELY: DIALOGUE, ACCOUNTABILITY, MUTUALITY

The act of writing collaboratively is a much-needed antidote to our shortcomings and fallibility, though there is no guarantee that collaboration will not turn into a collusion that will mask these from us. The process is dialogical and mutual, one offering a suggestion – an alternative way of saying or organising things – and the other responding. From this process clarity of meaning and a coherence of presentation emerges which would not have come to one of us working alone. It is that kind of interchange at the practical level, added to the dialectic over the thesis of the book and the shape of its chapters, which has given the book the shape it has, and helped us to find some measure of critical space within the process. What started as a disparate set of pieces, directed in one way or another to our

> concerns, slowly evolved into a more coherent narrative as the result of the ongoing exchange about the nature and purpose of the book.
>
> It would be presumptuous to write that we intended to model what we have written about in the book in terms of critical reflexivity, though we hope we have begun to do that. In retrospect, however, this method has been an ever-evolving process of critical reflexivity considerably facilitated by joint authorship. We don't think of ourselves as pioneers, but we do testify to the importance to the development of a critical perspective that joint authorship brings. JonathanWolff (2016) wrote sympathetically about joint authorship and its relative rarity in humanities research and writing. We have valued the fact that 'one's ego gets submerged when writing with another person.' In a sense what collaboration does is ensure that peer review is a diachronic process throughout the genesis and gestation of the book not a discrete moment in its assessment.
>
> (Bennett and Rowland, 2016, pp. 204–205)

A theology of communities of practice

Many of the aspects of communities of practice that we have been highlighting in this chapter embody our essential vision of practical theological research as collaborative, conversational and grounded. Insofar as communities of practice and learning are enquiry-driven and task-based, that should come as no surprise. It is, however, their interactive and dialogical nature, and the extent to which in the course of an extended research project, members accompany one another on a journey of both intellectual and personal discovery that stands out at this stage. For all the talk of 'proximity' and 'affinity' within functioning communities of practice, there is also a necessary recognition of difference and an encounter with the 'alterity' of fellow practitioners or community members without which no growth, no learning, no new understandings will take place.

As one doctoral student, quoting Australian practical theologian Terry Veling, states:

> [Veling] recognises that 'living theologically' demands active listening to the voice of the other, stating that if all of our listening 'will only lead back to me' (2005, p. 60), we might as well not be in dialogue at all. The critical factor for Veling is to enter into relationships that understand a voice other than their own, through inclusive conversation.
>
> *(cited in Bennett and Lyall, 2014, p. 7)*

The risk of surrendering given certainties and acknowledging the value of others' perspectives is essential for the life of communities of practice. This goes beyond the functional to confront us with new insights regarding the process of learning and discovery.

In her doctoral research into the nature of the supervisory relationship on professional doctorates, Linda Robinson (2011, p. 213) has speculated about the potential of the human interaction in that context to embody a glimpse of a divine 'I-Thou' encounter. This transcends an understanding of supervision as a transaction, towards seeing it as an ontological process: as profoundly transformative in its capacity not only to engender new understandings, but also new ways of being and becoming. For many, this will be an understanding of what it means to be human that is rooted in divine reality. So in community, we enter into a fuller humanity. Thus, for Robinson, the activities of supervision embody and prefigure a deeper exchange of mutual trust, reflection and enquiry that is at the heart of what it means to be in *imago Dei*.

'Trust' is not a word that has appeared very much in this chapter so far, but it may serve to encapsulate much of what we have been saying about the nature of communities of practice. So, just as Veling alerts us to the fact that authentic humanity – and equally, the research process – cannot be effected solipsistically, so our testimonies of the risk and reward of journeying through a programme of advanced research with one's fellow-travellers reveals a similar thread of necessary vulnerability and openness to the Other.

Communities of practice ultimately thrive on rich repositories of 'social capital', in which members commit resources of intellectual resources, energy and relationships in pursuit of shared goals and objectives. However, we should not underestimate the extent to which these investments of human, physical and material capital – which pay dividends in the shape of strong networks – have to be 'paid forward' and committed in advance of any undertaking. In other words, we have to invest our *trust* – first and foremost – in the integrity of a community of practice well before we see any tangible benefits, to ourselves or others.

Once more, then, we return to themes of risk, loss and openness to change (see Chapter 1). The research endeavour can be disturbing, intellectually and emotionally. It calls us into new bonds of affinity, but not, perhaps, without first requiring us to leave old certainties, secure and taken-for-granted affiliations or identities, to enter into new ways of relating, being and knowing.

Much of the literature of the New Testament which relates the formation of the first Christian communities reflects a similar dynamic of the loss of particular certainties – perhaps rooted in certain kinds of ethnic or religious identities – in favour of a gradual recognition that the gospel of Jesus Christ transcends ordinary human divisions. Material, embodied practices of hospitality, focused on a Eucharistic table fellowship, became a central expression of that new and radical unity. In reflecting on the practices of group supervision and the tasks of building effective working communities of practice, Leach and Paterson (2015, p. 217) develop this sacramental motif of 'being met and fed in community' to reflect on the tension between our own needs and priorities as individuals and professionals, and those of others.

They relate experiences, both from the lives of Jesus' disciples and their own practice, in which being present for others – often in the face of one's own pressing need for attention – becomes, paradoxically, the source of greatest support. In Mark 6:30–37, the disciples are commanded to find food for the crowd when they feel most hunger; but as meagre supplies of food are shared, they discover 'there is enough for all to be fed and more' (Leach and Paterson, 2015, p. 218). Similarly, in a community of practice with a high degree of mutual trust, a commitment to the needs of the other generates a kind of 'communion' in which all can be nurtured by being 'fully present . . . to one another and so be fed in the community' (Leach and Paterson, 2015, p. 219).

There are powerful themes here about solidarity through mutual vulnerability; a willingness to invest in the common good rather than one's own immediate demands: 'the courage to be fully present ourselves and invite others to take that risk and so be met and fed' (Leach and Paterson, 2015, p. 219).

Elsewhere in the New Testament, the Pauline image of the Body of Christ as diverse and yet united and interdependent (Rom 12: 4–8; 1 Cor 12) may also have important resonances. Whilst communities of practice may not have a common faith-commitment around which to gather, the extent to which shared values serve to generate significant levels of trust and mutual solidarity must surely be at the heart of building and maintaining their lives. Here, there may be something of a dialectic between communities of practice as forged from the tension between 'proximity' and shared objectives, and 'difference'. In theological terms, this might be considered in terms of the interplay of the specificity of context and the 'catholicity' of wider global or historical traditions (Bevans, 2014; Schreiter, 1985). How does 'the word made flesh' incarnate in the particularities of human history relate to a Divine Creator who transcends all time and contingency?

As Schreiter (1985) and Bevans (2014) both argue in their respective work on local and contextual theologies, it is the creative tension between the specific and the universal, or the local and the global, which give rise to a deeper appreciation of cultural diversity. Yet such encounters with forms of *alterity*, whilst superficially appearing to pose a threat to one's own identity or values, does not have to lead to relativism or to the corrosion of one's own stance. Rather, they release one from the pretensions towards universality, resist the temptation to insist on Christianity as a master narrative, embracing instead the realisation that the dynamic of destabilisation and of being pushed beyond the boundaries of one's certainty are at the very heart of what Christian theology proclaims as the gospel.

Similarly, Jesus himself can be seen as 'the very paradigm of the open narrative' (Boeve, 2003, p. 119). As 'God's interrupter', Jesus' life and ministry is all about the fracturing of closed systems and narratives. By challenging the law, forgiving sins, reaching out to the marginalised and preaching the Kingdom, he signals both the interruption and the indwelling of God in human affairs. The resurrection is the ultimate *praxis* of the open narrative.

> The God of Jesus of Nazareth is the God of the interruptive (grace) event, the God who calls us beyond harsh inflexibility and closedness . . . Indeed, it would seem possible to maintain theologically that the Christian narrative can only be authentic when it structures itself as an open narrative: a narrative

that allows itself to be interrupted time and again by a God who gets involved in history but does not let Godself be captured by it.

(Boeve, 2003, pp. 106–107)

In their mutual journeyings after knowledge, similarly, communities of practice (especially within practical theology) might learn something from contemporary theologies of mission. These are no longer premised on activities of entering a place of ignorance or abjection in order to 'rescue' souls but one of mutual discovery and dialogue, in a shared quest for a Truth that ultimately transcends any one culture or human imagination. An evocative set of images comes from Bevans and Schroeder (2011), who not only characterise mission as essentially dialogical and contextual, but deploy the motifs of treasure hunter, guest, stranger and garden visitor to describe those who undertake it. All four reprise elements of our discussion in this chapter already: the nature of communities of enquiry and practice as collaborative, open and rooted in a shared endeavour of discovery.

Thus, the 'treasure hunter' does not come already bearing a precious object, but engages in a process of local searching which will necessarily involve learning the landscape, customs and wisdom of their adopted land. The treasure, is, of course, already buried in that place, and it is as much the journey of preparation as the unearthing of the 'treasure' that brings enrichment to everyone. As 'guest', a missionary must respect and learn the ways of their hosts, just as in our discussion we have been stressing the nature of communities of practice as spaces of mutual hospitality, of giving and receiving. Being and remaining, to some extent, a 'stranger', resonates with the earlier discussion of elements of vulnerability and risk within communities of learning: a willingness to be 'lost' and to subject oneself to the critical gaze of the Other. Even though the price may be uncertainty or apparent weakness, only by acknowledging the limits of one's own knowledge – and the reality that as a stranger one can never be fully 'at home' – can one hope truly to listen, learn and be changed.

Finally, Bevans and Schroeder talk of mission as 'entering into someone else's garden' (2011, pp. 33–34). This evocative image has clear relevance for undertaking a research journey in the company of others.[1] (There is also probably a whole other book to be written between the four of us about how much we love our respective gardens!) For a start, it is an aesthetic experience: gardens are places of beauty, and one can simply appreciate another's achievements or habitat in their own right, and for their own intrinsic qualities. Yet on another level, gardeners are always on the look-out for hints about soil, or pests, or new plants: not to transplant another's achievements up by the roots but to observe, appreciate and learn.

For Bevans and Schroeder, as contextual theologians writing about global Christian mission, the metaphor of visiting another's garden speaks to them of ' . . . how God is already present and nurturing them, the seeds of the word of God, or . . . the treasure buried in the ground' (2011, p. 34). For us as practical theologians, it also speaks of the significance (and privilege) wrought by belonging to a community of practice: of inhabiting the work and world of another, of knowing that their climate or terrain may not be identical to our own, but of finding wisdom and insight neverthe-less. Researchers can draw from gardeners the qualities of patience and of respecting the ebb and flow of the seasons. Like a garden, good research may take many years of careful attention to come to fruition; like gardening, doing research well entails many painstaking skills of tilling, sowing, planting and pruning as well as harvesting!

Can communities of practice survive on pragmatic goals, then, or are they reli-ant for their flourishing on 'thicker' values and visions of the good? Perhaps here we might return to that notion of *phronēsis*, practical wisdom, so influential within practical theology recently, and remind ourselves that it rests on deeper traditions of Aristotelian virtue ethics. Within this tradition, which also owes a great deal to the work of Alasdair MacIntyre (1981), communities of practice are themselves repositories, and schools, of wisdom. They are critical spaces in which we grow and learn in virtue and acquire moral – as well as professional – maturity. Induction into a community of practice is thus also an invitation into a community of moral reasoning, with corresponding norms of human flourishing as well as professional competence (Vokey and Kerr, 2011, p. 72). *Phronēsis* is thus related to *prudentia*: it embodies the kind of reasoning that will promote virtue and wisdom. In that respect, it seeks to promote 'best practice': or, perhaps more accurately, the practice that does not simply pursue good outcomes, but is grounded in a clear discernment and apprehension of moral goods:

> . . . a kind of knowing that is morally attuned, rooted in a tradition that affirms the good, and driven toward aims that seek the good. It is not a package of pre-planned rules but stays open and adaptive to new situations. It is nimble and at times self-critical. Most of all this knowledge is practical, grounded in ordinary experience, and learned over time in the company of others and for the sake of others.
>
> *(Bass et al., 2016, p. 5)*

This might serve well as a model for the necessary intellectual and emotional intel-ligence required to undertake advanced research, but also as a manifesto for the kind of practical theological knowing we are seeking to promote in our own communi-ties of practice.

Note

1 Etienne Wenger also speaks about 'tending the garden of knowledge' in connection with building communities of practice (de Cagna, 2001).

References

Amin, A. and Roberts, J., 2008. Knowing in action: Beyond communities of practice. *Research Policy*, 37(2), pp. 353–369.

Bass, D.C. et al., 2016. Engaging the intelligence of practice. In: D.C. Bass, K. Cahalan, B. J. Miller-McLemore, J. Nieman and C. Scharen, eds., *Christian practical wisdom: What it is, why it matters*. Grand Rapids, MN: Wm. B. Eerdmans. pp. 1–18.

Beaudoin, T., 2016. Why does practice matter theologically? In: J.A. Mercer and B.J. Miller-McLemore, eds., *Conundrums in practical theology*. Leiden: Brill. pp. 8–32.

Bennett, Z., 2007. Evaluating the feasibility of a cross-institutional doctorate in practical theology: A report. *Discourse*, 6(2), pp. 63–94.

Bennett, Z. and Lyall, D., 2014. The professional doctorate in practical theology: A new model of doctoral research in the UK. *Reflective Practice: Formation and Supervision in Ministry*, 34, pp. 190–203.

Bennett, Z. and Rowland, C., 2016. *In a glass darkly: The Bible, reflection and everyday life*. London: SCM Press.

Bevans, S., 2014. Contextual theology as practical theology. In: K. Cahalan and G. Mikoski, eds., *Opening the field of practical theology: An introduction*. New York: Rowman & Littlefield. pp. 45–59.

Bevans, S. and Schroeder, R., 2011. *Prophetic dialogue: Reflections on Christian mission today*. New York: Orbis.

Boeve, L., 2003. *Interrupting tradition: An essay on Christian faith in a postmodern context*. Leuven: Peeters.

Bourner, T., Bowden, R. and Laing, S., 2001. Professional doctorates in England. *Studies in Higher Education*, 26(1), pp. 65–83.

Boyd, J., 2018. *The naked preacher: A practice of preaching and action research as a way of doing theology*. London: SCM Press.

Buck, S., 2016. Ministers of word. In: P. Tovey, S. Buck and G. Dodd, eds., *Instruments of Christ's love: The ministry of Readers*. London: SCM Press. pp. 1–29.

Calderwood, P., 2000. *Learning community: Finding common ground in difference*. New York: Teachers' College Press.

Cameron, H., Bhatti, D., Duce, C., Sweeney, J. and Watkins, C., 2010. *Talking about God in practice: Theological action research and practical theology*. London: SCM Press.

de Cagna, J., 2001. Interview: Tending the garden of knowledge: An interview with Etienne Wenger. *Information Outlook*, July, pp. 6–12.

Drake, P. and Heath, L., 2011. *Practitioner research at doctoral level*. London: Routledge.

Fillery-Travis, A., 2014. The framework of a generic DProf programme: A reflection on its design, the relational dimension for candidates and advisors and the potential for knowledge co-creation. *Studies in Higher Education*, 39(4), pp. 608–620.

Fulton, J., Kuit, J., Sanders, G. and Smith, P., 2013. *The professional doctorate: A practical guide*. London: Palgrave Macmillan.

Gilliat-Ray, S., Ali, M. and Pattison, S., 2013. *Understanding Muslim chaplaincy*. Farnham: Ashgate.

Goto, C., 2016. Writing in compliance with the racialised 'zoo' of practical theology. In: J.A. Mercer and B.J. Miller-McLemore, eds., *Conundrums in practical theology*. Leiden: Brill. pp. 110–133.

Graham, E., 2006. The professional doctorate in practical theology: An idea whose time has come? *International Journal of Practical Theology*, 10(1), pp. 293–311.

Kemmis, S., 2010. What is to be done? The place of action research. *Educational Action Research*, 18(4), pp. 417–427.

Leach, J. and Paterson, M., 2015. *Pastoral supervision: A handbook*. 2nd ed. London: SCM Press.

Leshem, S., 2007. Conceptual frameworks in a research community of practice: A case of a doctoral programme. *Innovations in Education and Teaching International*, 44(3), pp. 287–299.

MacIntyre, A., 1981. *After virtue: A study in moral theory*. London: Duckworth.

McNiff, J., 2017. *Action research: All you need to know*. London: Sage.

Miller-McLemore, B.J., 2016. Academic theology and practical knowledge. In: D.C. Bass, K. Cahalan, B.J. Miller-McLemore, J. Nieman and C. Scharen, eds., *Christian practical wisdom: What it is, why it matters*. Grand Rapids, MN: Wm. B. Eerdmans. pp. 173–229.

Morley, C., 2005. Supervising professional doctorate research is different. In: *Supervising postgraduate research: Contexts and processes, theories and practices.* Melbourne: RMIT University Press. pp. 106–122.

Reason, P., ed., 1994. *Participation in human inquiry.* London: Sage.

Reason, P. and Bradbury, H., eds., 2006. *The handbook of action research.* 2nd Concise ed. London: Sage.

Robinson, L., 2011. Supervision: A meeting of minds and hearts: A coach and facilitator of adult learning reflect on the experience of engaging in supervision as a professional doctoral student in practical theology. *Work-Based Learning e-Journal International,* 2(1), pp. 212–238.

Schreiter, R., 1985. *Constructing local theologies.* London: SCM Press.

Shacham, M. and Od-Cohen, Y., 2009. Rethinking PhD learning incorporating communities of practice. *Innovations in Education and Teaching International,* 46(3), pp. 279–292.

Veling, T., 2005. *Practical theology: On earth as it is in heaven.* New York: Orbis.

Vokey, D. and Kerr, J., 2011. Intuition and professional wisdom: Can we teach moral discernment? In: L. Bondi, D. Carr, C. Clark and C. Clegg, eds., *Towards professional wisdom: Practical deliberation in the people professions.* Farnham: Ashgate. pp. 63–80.

Watkins, C., 2018. *Disclosing church: Generating ecclesiology through conversations in practice.* London: Routledge.

Wenger-Trayner, E., 2006. *Communities of practice: A brief introduction.* [Online] Available at: http://wenger-trayner.com/resources/ [Accessed 7 April 2015].

Wenger-Trayner, E. and Wenger-Trayner, B., 2015. *Communities of practice: A brief introduction.* [Online] Available at: http://wenger-trayner.com/resources/ [Accessed 30 June 2017].

Wolff, J., 2016. Why my philosophy practitioners will be working together for a change. *The Guardian,* 18 January.

5

FINDING A CRITICAL SPACE

Interpreting and inhabiting traditions

The place of (T/t)radition(s) in practical theological research is controversial. What we are attempting to do in this chapter is to show how tradition plays a part in practical theological research by problematising it, not in order to dispense with it (both impossible and undesirable), but to show how it plays a part in locating us as researchers, and in the very act of research itself and the interpretation of that research. As we indicated in Chapter 1, even though we are committed to a fundamentally experientialist and practice-oriented form of practical theology, we take respectfully and seriously the traditions, communities and sacred texts (the Bible in our case) as absolutely crucial in practical theological research. They have shaped us as researchers, and they inform our work at the deepest level.

Our exploration of the complexity of tradition, and how it informs research in practical theology, starts with 'home' and finishes with contrasting examples of how two of us are wrestling with 'home' and tradition within our research. In between this beginning and end we will outline some influential streams of thought about tradition, discuss implications for the researcher in practical theology, and offer a tentative typology of the ways researchers in practical theology find a critical space in relation to traditions. The prior theological framework of belief and commitment, formed by traditions, provides a critical perspective on experience and practice; likewise the interrogation of experience and practice provides a critical perspective on the 'taken-for-granted' of our theological framework of belief and commitment.

'Home'

To the communities of practice we explored in the last chapter we all bring a prior framework, which is already there within us, in which we 'live, and move, and have our being' (Acts 17: 28). This is 'home' for us; a home which dwells in us, and a home in which we dwell. But our lives are constantly on the move, as is the world around us; the ancient philosopher Heraclitus noted that everything is always in flux and it is impossible to step into a river which is identical to one we stepped into even a few seconds ago. The novelist Ursula Le Guin expresses this poignantly in relation to the idea of 'home':

> You shall not go down twice to the same river, nor can you go home again. That he knew; indeed it was the basis of his view of the world. Yet from that acceptance of transience he evolved his vast theory, wherein what is most changeable is shown to be fullest of eternity, and your relationship to the river, and the river's relationship to you and to itself, turns out to be at once more complex and more reassuring than a mere lack of identity. You *can* go home again . . . so long as you understand that home is a place where you have never been.
>
> *(LeGuin, 1975, p. 52)*

All understanding is historically conditioned (Gadamer, 1985, p. 270). Out of this prior framework, this world-view, this 'preunderstanding' – shaped by our context, upbringing, education, historical and geographical location – we negotiate and renegotiate the rapids and the shallows of new discoveries, contested meanings, and unexpected self-understandings which threaten to submerge or strand us in our research and our communities of practice. We say communities in the plural because no researcher has only one community of practice; the patterns of our professional, academic, family and religious commitments and loyalties criss-cross bewilderingly and the undertow may feel at times unbearable. 'Home', or being 'at home' is not a straightforward concept.

> *Wo* ist man daheim? Wo man geboren wurde oder wo man zu sterben wunscht?
>> *(Where are we at home? Where we were born or where we hope to die?)*

Opening his autobiography with these words, Carl Zuckmayer (1966) indicates both the fundamental nature of home to human beings, and also the way in which what we understand as 'home' both changes throughout our lives, and is, in part at least, open to the constructions we put on it. His work moves through the times and the places in which he has lived, constructing a story of which he is the product as much as the producer – his title: *Als wär's ein Stück von mir,* 'as if it were a part of myself'. Bring rooted and being changed are in a constant movement and dialectic throughout life, for which the buildings which have been a literal home are, in Zuckmayer's work, a vivid metaphor.

We are all embedded in a network of traditions and commitments: theological/ religious, philosophical, political, ethical, emotional, pragmatic. We breathe them in with our first breath. But traditions are living, and grow and move, and so do we. So in the course of our lives neither the tradition which we knew as our first home, nor we ourselves in relation to that living tradition, will stay in one place, immoveable. It is open to us to reflect on our autobiography, our home(s), and to construct a story which we inhabit. This story will weave in and out of 'traditions' in a dialectical relationship. Our journeys involve a tension between finding or recognising, being claimed by 'home', and searching for a critical space by seeking to conceptualise and reflect on places in which we have found ourselves. In Chapter 1 Elaine tells a story of being claimed 'by the world and its woes' but not yet having 'some kind of larger cause or community that would help me make sense of [that] world'; of looking for a home and finding at an SCM conference a critical space which turned upside down her 'conventional middle-class assumptions'. Likewise Heather's experience of being plunged into a critical space far from home – 'I was white'; 'You must immerse yourself in the life of multi-racial congregations, hang out with young Black people' – started her journey to a home as a university professor with particular commitments to the task of an academic researcher. Our home of tradition(s) and commitments affects the epistemology we embrace, the kind of knowledge we seek, and the research methodologies which we use. Without a critical interrogation of such 'homes' our work remains ideologically imprisoned.

The word 'home' here indicates several things of importance about our relationship to religious and other traditions: recognition, belonging, emotional investment, ambiguity of feeling and of relationship, the dialectic of leave-taking and return, a 'house of being' whose legitimating function we do not question, as the plausibility of the world-view within which it contains us is communally reinforced. Zoë has tried to reflect on some of the complexity of this in her own journey:

> The intellectual journey within which [my] professional attainment is situated has involved a tension between finding or recognising 'home', and searching for a critical space by seeking to conceptualise and reflect on places in which I have found myself.
>
> Three quite different places have been my intellectual and theological 'home'. The first I found with my parents and in my schooldays – a humanist home of English and European literature, Latin and Greek classics, and a political and social morality which was residually Christian and explicitly socialist. The second, I found in my student and early adult life in Anglican Evangelical Christianity. This was open to other Christian traditions and to social concerns, though very narrow in its intellectual understanding and human sympathies compared with the home I had known. Nevertheless, I embraced it with uncritical fervour until the twin 'catastrophes' of divorce and postgraduate study of theology turned it upside down. The third home I found at Westcott House where I worked from 1990 to 2000, a manifestly Christian place in which, however, intellectual and theological questions might be explored with openness.
>
> But more than one home inevitably means the end of unquestioned 'home', and the beginning of finding a critical space. The view is always from somewhere and thus perspectival, and, crucially, is known to be such.
>
> *(PhD critical commentary, http://arro.anglia.ac.uk/313911/)*

Paradosis

'Tradition' is a key religious word. It is an ambiguous word: carrying etymologically the meaning of 'handing on' but also of 'handing over' – passing on or betraying: '*traditio*' in Latin, '*paradosis*' in Greek. Paul hands on the witness he has received to the death and resurrection of Jesus (1 Corinthians 15.3) and to the Last Supper (I Corinthians 11.23); Judas hands over Jesus to the authorities (Matthew 26.45–6). Thus in Christian faith it is fundamentally stories and persons who are handed on or handed over, though our traditions may be enshrined also in laws, in buildings, in texts and in institutions. Stephen Prickett (2009) locates the origins of the word in an oral and face-to-face 'handing over' (*paradosis*) and brings out the double-edged nature of the process. The handing over of knowledge, crucially, may challenge the conventional wisdom of the time. Indicating its origins in the Socratic dialogues of Plato's Academy, where teacher and pupil engaged in a face-to-face dialectic which sought to question and disturb the *status quo* of knowledge and understanding (Prickett, 2009, p. 10), he goes on to instance Matthew 11.27 as a striking example of *paradosis* in this sense: 'All things have been handed over to me by my Father; and no one knows the Son except the Father, and no one knows the Father except the Son and anyone to whom the Son chooses to reveal him'. Here Jesus hands over orally, in a face-to-face encounter, the deep wisdom – based in relationship and displayed in infants – which challenges the 'wisdom' of the greatest religious and secular powers of his day.

There is therefore an uneasy balance between commitment and challenge as well as a dialectic of continuity and discontinuity in human inhabiting and interpreting of the traditions they have received. Furthermore, traditions may be invented, and legitimised by reference to the past, and traditions may also be contested.

What is 'tradition'?

WHAT IS TRADITION? SHIFTING AND STABLE

Mark Cartledge is Professor of Practical Theology at Regent University School of Divinity, Virginia Beach, Virginia, USA. In a recent book (Cartledge, 2015), he attempts to bring together Pentecostal studies and practical theology, intending to 'provoke thought, provide new insights, and engage fairly committed and stable academic identities, perhaps opening up a pathway of enquiry, or shifting a boundary line of knowledge'.

I assume that 'religious tradition' is the expression of a spirituality that is 'handed on', or socialised from one generation to the next, or from those on the inside to those embracing the spirituality from the outside. It is living and evolving, inextricably embedded in a communal life that contains narratives, symbols and praxis. These dimensions facilitate a construction of theological identity sustained over time. However, traditions are also part of religious cultures that do change, since cultures have porous boundaries that are open to and allow the assimilation of different ideas, languages, artefacts and practices. So, there is a stable and consistent set of values that remains operational and around which identity is constructed. Simultaneously there is some degree of evolution and change, as well as occasional rupture. From an academic perspective, this consistency provides an 'epistemological posture' from which to engage in the process of research and the exploration of various beliefs, values and practices. This consistency does not mean that the centre of the theological identity is never open to question, quite the opposite, but it does mean that there is a touchstone, an identity, that provides a theological location from which research proceeds. Research findings can precipitate change in posture or even on occasion quite dramatic rupture to one's position.

Given this brief description of religious tradition and identity in general terms, how does it influence how I conduct my own research in practical theology? I am someone who has combined participation in charismatic evangelical Anglicanism (I was ordained as a priest in the Church of England in 1989) with the discipline of practical theology and especially empirical approaches to the discipline. In addition, I have studied global Pentecostalism and supervised numerous doctoral dissertations in the field. I also interact with and I am embedded in the scholarship arising from the contemporary Pentecostal and Charismatic movements and which provides one of my main communities of enquiry. So, for me, there are different 'traditions', some religious and some academic, that together provide a nexus from which I engage in research and by means of which I have developed over the course of my professional academic life.

Traditions, and identities in relation to them, are living and growing. Much of our life within communities is an attempt to wrestle in an appreciative but critical way with what might be 'faithful' development – that is to say a 'handing on' which is not a 'handing over/betrayal'. Andrew Gilbert offers an analysis of the somewhat surprising support of the UK Conservative government for same-sex marriage in the *Marriage (Same Sex Couples) Act* of 2013 in terms of evolutionary development versus revolutionary change:

> . . . in the same-sex marriage debates it was clear that marriage was being redefined; an existing institution was being changed. How a Conservative perceived the change affected the likelihood that they would support and promote it. Does same-sex marriage *change* the concept of opposite-sex marriage, or do they just exist alongside each other, with each one catering for the needs of a different constituency? I would argue that where a Conservative MP perceived the legalisation of same-sex marriage to sit on a revolutionary/evolutionary scale of change affected how willing they were to support the

Bill (or perhaps causation was flowing the other way?). For example, Leigh, 'The Minister claims that marriage has always evolved. The Bill is not evolution, but revolution'; Howarth, 'This is a massive change'; Burrowes, 'This is indeed an historic change'. Compare with Peter Bottomley, 'It does not redefine marriage; it just takes away barriers'. Those who constructed it as a radical change – a redefinition of marriage – tended to oppose it (for example, Leigh, Howarth, Burrowes), whereas others who saw it as merely extending the marriage franchise to same-sex couples, approached it as an evolutionary change which could be accommodated within their conservative mindset (for example, Bottomley).

(Gilbert, 2014, p. 487; references to Hansard omitted from original)

In the case of the Conservative party discussion, revolution as opposed to evolution was not on the table; the question was whether the same-sex marriage act could be construed and accommodated within an evolutionary paradigm which did not betray fundamental values and beliefs. Within other contexts, including some contexts of religious faith and practice, something more like revolution is on the table, as will be discussed below.

Edward Shils' 1974 T.S. Eliot Memorial Lectures (Shils, 1981), were a groundbreaking study of 'tradition' as a concept in itself (rather than studies of specific 'traditions'). We cannot avoid being shaped by the past, but must face what Peter Berger describes on the book-cover as 'the sheer indispensability of tradition to human society'. Shils sets an appreciation of the role of tradition over against post-Enlightenment enthrallment to 'rationality and scientific procedure' (1981, p. 4). However, 'the metaphysical dread of being encumbered by something alien to oneself' (1981, pp. 10–11) contributes to the suspicion and neglect of tradition as something which curtails the freedom of the individual: 'Tradition hems an individual in; it sets the conditions of his actions; it determines his resources; it even determines what he himself is'. Notwithstanding this, he wishes 'to stress that traditions should be considered as part of the worthwhile life' (Shils, 1981, p. 330). These 'contraries' – human dependence on the continuities of past and present within community, and human need for autonomy, integrity and self-realisation – set the backdrop for an understanding of tradition.

Tradition is always an argument, and it is an argument within and between communities over time. Alasdair MacIntyre, defining traditions in terms of identity, narrative and community speaks of 'an argument extended through time in which certain fundamental agreements are defined and redefined' in relation to conflicts with critics external to the tradition and 'internal interpretive debates' within the tradition (MacIntyre, 1988, p. 12). This argument interprets and reinterprets the tradition which we inhabit, though it may also involve a deliberate stance against the interpretations of others outside our 'tradition within a tradition': 'tradition . . . is constantly at work, re-fashioning and re-creating our understanding of the world in which we find ourselves' (Prickett, 2009, p. 225).

THE NEGOTIATION OF TRADITIONS

Mandy Carr is a Jewish dramatherapist working on a professional doctorate. Interested in how religious faith may be expressed within dramatherapy, she explores the significance of ritual traditions in her Jewish heritage, looking at ways in which forms of Judaism have adapted traditional rituals in order to render them more meaningful in a contemporary context.

Progressive and Reform Jewish movements in the UK have adapted many aspects of more Orthodox services. In the Orthodox Synagogue in Liverpool, which I attended in the sixties and seventies, services were conducted almost entirely in Hebrew, although the prayer book (read from left to right) contained English translations, which seemed to my childish eye, to refer almost entirely to men. Men sat downstairs, whilst women looked down from the gallery and did not seem to participate actively in the service. Indeed for a service to take place at all, there had to be a 'minyan', a quorum of ten men needed before certain prayers could be recited. The clergy were all male. The Shabbat service included a weekly reading of a portion from the Torah scroll, always by an adult male. Whilst the above traditions are still largely observed by Orthodox congregations, it is interesting to note that Princes Road is clearly embracing the tensions between tradition and adaptation to change. Their website describes them as 'a friendly, Orthodox Jewish community in the heart of Liverpool, steeped in tradition and Victorian elegance. This community embraces its illustrious past whilst looking to the future' (Princes Road Synagogue, 2017). Indeed, this description illustrates the fact that one cannot categorise the orthodox tendency as 'traditional' and the more progressive as 'innovative' as there are overlaps, and the relationship between tradition and its application in modern life, remain concerns across the spectrum.

I am currently a member of a progressive synagogue, whose website explains, 'We recognise the reality of modern life and welcome not only Jews but also their partners and families, and all those who seek a Jewish connection and positive Jewish experiences' (Finchley Progressive Synagogue, 2017). 'We' could be said to include all of us, who may want to be included. The prayer book in liberal synagogues, often includes more English in the service, as well as transliteration of the Hebrew. The translation aims to be more contemporary, including the matriarchs Sarah, Rachel, Leah and Rebecca, along with the patriarchs, Abraham, Isaac and Jacob. There are women rabbis and mixed congregations and a minyan can include women. The synagogue aims to balance traditional values with contemporary meaningfulness.

Customs may be questioned and traditions (including 'invented' traditions) resisted; what is commonly simply known as 'tradition' is therefore often a site of alternative appeal to the past and contesting interpretations. The Protestant Reformation offers a rich and complex example of such an alternative appeal, through a re-appropriation of, involving inevitably some re-reading of, the past. It is not simply understanding of the present which is sought through engagement with traditions. The appropriation of past tradition is also politically dynamic; it is used to order, shape and influence future development.

In the service of such political ends traditions may be constructed: '"Traditions" which appear or claim to be old are often quite recent in origin and sometimes invented' (Hobsbawm and Ranger, 1983, p. 1). Such traditions are often used to transform present and future by legitimation of practices and beliefs through supposed continuity with historical antecedents. Hobsbawm and Ranger identify practices, rules and symbolic rituals as key elements in such 'invented' traditions and critically explore 'invented' national traditions (famously the 'highland tradition of Scotland') and the crucial role invented traditions play in processes of colonisation. Such examples throw light on analogous practices in religions and theology, where, arguably, the creative processes of inventing a usable past are particularly evident – see, for example, the project to reconceptualise theology with reference to premodern understandings that is fundamental to Radical Orthodoxy.

The weight of tradition may be felt negatively in a variety of ways. The 'anxiety of influence' (Bloom, 1973) refers to the pressure on writers to prove their originality and independence from the work of past 'masters'. Feminists have alerted us to widespread occluding of voices and experiences within hegemonic discourse. The current rightward turn in politics actively conceals the damage and destruction of inequality through reference to traditional values. Unease and felt dissonance drive resistance to tradition, just as they awake the urge to research – 'it doesn't have to be like this' (hooks, 1994, p. 61).

THE NEGATIVE WEIGHT OF MUTUALLY-REINFORCING TRADITIONS

Elaine Yip is a professional doctorate candidate conducting her research in Hong Kong on 'The Journey of Women's Empowerment in a Chinese Congregation with Missionary Influence'. She identifies within her work the stronghold of tradition and practice in which the missionaries' theology and Chinese culture mutually reinforce each other, but where she finds an opening within the community theology and practice and exploits it for change.

Through the research, I want to find out in what ways women have been empowered in the changes carried out ten years ago. Before the changes were introduced, the woman pastor was not allowed to give sermons in Sunday worship and the sisters were not allowed to lead the liturgical part of the worship. They were only allowed to lead the singing part. After the changes were introduced, the woman pastor could speak in the worship and sisters could lead the liturgical part of the worship.

> Before the changes were made, I had had the experience of being suppressed and had the awareness that my church had been very patriarchal in practice. I thus raised question about the roles of the woman pastor and the sisters in the worship to my pastor-in-charge at that time. A Task Group was formed to study the practice of other sister churches and also do exegesis on the related chapters in the Bible. Finally, changes were introduced afterwards.
>
> Why was there the patriarchal practice? It was because we had all along had the male dominance tradition. Men were elected to be the leaders. Even though there were also women leaders in cell groups or some ministry departments, the ultimate leaders, the Chairman of the Deacon Board and the Pastor-in-Charge, were men. This tradition has been implemented till now.
>
> The tradition was formed by the US missionary association which established our church more than thirty years ago. The way they interpreted the Bible bore a great impact on us. They treated the Bible as errorless and took every word of the Bible seriously. Therefore they adopted the teachings in 1 Timothy chapter 2 verses 11–14 that women should not teach men as man was made first, woman the second. They developed their theology of women's roles through this verse.
>
> My church, born and bred with the Chinese culture of being obedient and showing respect to the authority, had never questioned this interpretation, but followed faithfully. Leaders have been following this tradition, and the congregation has also been following the leaders in upholding and preserving this tradition.

The appropriation of tradition is a potential ideological tool in the shaping of both present and future. Its function is not only explanatory but also performative. As such it is politically tendentious: 'most discussions of tradition have always been concerned with defending or re-stating entrenched ideological positions' (Prickett, 2009, p. 13). The claiming of tradition is therefore normally both ambiguous and contested. To claim something is the case is to open, even to admit, the possibility that it might not be so or not be so always. Both precedent and propaganda are at work in the development of 'traditions'. 'There has always been a sense in which the "deposit of faith" [the gospel] has been a creation of the time or faction appealing to it' (Prickett, 2009, p. 221).

That written text which is part of, and even enshrines, the tradition is the scripture of the community. One universally important aspect of Christian traditions is the Bible, the 'scripture' of the Christian people. 'Scripture' is a meaningless term outside of a relationship with a community: '"scripture" is a bilateral term. By that we mean that it inherently implies, in fact names, a relationship' (Cantwell Smith, 1993, p. 17). The relationship to community is crucial to an understanding of any text which is treated as 'scripture'; there is 'an interactive relation between that text and a community of persons' (Cantwell Smith, 1993, p. ix). Cantwell Smith's examination of what is meant by 'scripture' centres on a living and organic process. There is not only a dialectical relationship between the text and the community of interpretation; there is also a dialectical relationship between the past, enshrined in and witnessed to by that scripture, and the present time of that community, who engage with the past for the sake of the present and the future. In understanding what is meant by 'scripture' there is a need for 'critical self-consciousness' (1993, p. 216) of what role that which various communities name as 'scripture, plays in contemporary life. In the emphasis on *self*-consciousness Cantwell Smith puts centre-stage the importance of reflexivity, communal and individual: 'The basic question is not about scripture, but is about us' (1993, p. 242). This is not only true of Christian scripture; Jewish, Muslim and other communities wrestle with their sacred texts in contemporary life, seeking to find what will contribute to human flourishing in their contemporary world. The Muslim writer Ziauddin Sardar puts the issue thus:

> I write as every Muslim; as an individual trying to understand what the Qu'ran means to me in the twenty-first century. I believe that every Muslim is duty-bound to accept responsibility for making this effort. I contend that one can only have an interpretative relationship with a text, particularly when that text is regarded as eternal.
>
> *(Sardar, 2011, p. xv)*

A SEARCH FOR TRUTH WHICH IS TRUE TO SCRIPTURE

Nick Ladd is Director of Practical Theology at St John's School of Mission, Nottingham, researching for a professional doctorate. With a strong evangelical commitment to the Bible, he has found that his research has involved the 'constant negotiation of shared knowledge' in relation to scripture.

I did the professional doctorate because I sensed it would help me to face the challenge of doing theology from practice as an evangelical. Evangelicalism places a high value on pietistic experience, but intellectually it is more suspicious. Safeguarding the truth intellectually creates an environment in which experience can be securely rooted; my tradition holds caution about the 'authority of experience' like a shibboleth. The preferred way for evangelicals to do theology is the 'one-way street' of applied theology; matters of theology are settled prior to practice and ministry becomes the application of academically-defined theology. This tends to generate idealised pictures of ministry practice, creating unnatural pressure upon practitioners to reproduce whilst at the same time failing to give them the tools to see and interpret the concrete realities of lived experience with which their theology must engage.

On the doctoral journey, I realised that as a minister, I had been doing theology from practice – a two-way street – for 30 years. There is no other way; 'experience' is how we engage with life. This experience had made me comfortable with complexity in personal, spiritual and ministerial matters. But in academic and intellectual terms, I was brittle and defensive, as if behind castle walls with a brief to defend evangelical doctrine from the siege engines of liberalism and modernity. The doctoral community of practice has helped me to allow 'otherness' and complexity into my academic identity. This creates the possibility of a search for truth which is true to scripture but nevertheless provisional as it is embodied and contextualised through a practice of dialogue and co-creation.

Whilst engaging critically with my evangelical heritage around the subject of experience, I became conscious that with the reification of experience and the privileging of non-theological disciplines, scripture was conspicuously absent in much practical theology; something that is reflected in pastoral practice and theological education. I wanted to offer an approach for attending to scripture in practical theology and pastoral practice that would take this concern seriously but would nevertheless help to fashion a practice in which scripture could be a distinct interpretative voice.

My research focuses on communal and personal maturity in which I have become convinced that attentiveness to the 'other' is a key marker. As I construed maturity as the ability to listen and co-create knowledge in dialogue and relationship, it seemed to me to be reasonable to consider scripture also as an 'other' (different and surprising) voice that we pay attention to in our constructing of knowledge in such a way that it takes a guiding role in helping us to form those provisional constructions of knowledge. Theologically this is grounded in Spirit-filled discernment as a community engages with scripture. Practically it is grounded in a growing maturity that is open to the insight of the other whilst maintaining one's own integrity and contribution.

In my research, an ethnographical study of a local church, I find that this constant negotiation of shared knowledge in the context of communal listening to scripture is an accurate description of the journey to maturity. This is both a contested and a constructive space in community and one in which at best people learn to listen, to negotiate and to create, at worst to distance, reject and isolate. For me, this journey represents a re-shaping of my evangelical identity, freer from the captivity to Enlightenment certainties and idealism than once was the case. It also, I believe, opens a door for an evangelical contribution to practical theology through a theory and practice of attentiveness to scripture in embodied communal learning.

Traditions and customs are invented, enacted, interpreted and inherited within communities. Benedict Anderson in *Imagined Communities* (1983) explores how communities are formed through the imaginative appropriation of traditions, highlighting the importance of language, political economy, geographical territory and conceptions of time. Like Hobsbawm and Ranger (1983), Anderson has 'nationalisms' primarily in view. His work, however, offers fruitful stimulus to the understanding of how religious traditions are formed, breaking open the 'taken for

granted' of our attachment to particular manifestations of Christian faith and practice, and inviting scrutiny of how these manifestations are communally 'imagined',
and how they elicit a deep shared emotional commitment, with 'roots in fear and
hatred of the Other', but with the power to 'inspir[e] love, and often profoundly
self-sacrificing love' (Anderson, 1983, p. 141).

The researcher and the researched in relation to (T/t) radition(s)

Practical theological research takes place within such communities, and can be in
itself a practice which contributes to such imaginative community formation. For
example, Action Research, particularly in its co-operative forms, is a specific site of
community engagement and transformation in practical theological research: '[i]n
adopting action research methods, practical theologians are not simply concerned
with change management or the techniques of activism, but with schooling people
in the well-springs of tradition from which practical wisdom flows' (Graham, 2013,
p. 178).

In practical theological research both researcher and the people and contexts
which are researched are embedded in traditions. These may be shared, not shared,
or most likely partially shared. The researcher needs to find a critical space in relation to both. Robert Orsi writes powerfully of his experience as a scholar of religion
studying Roman Catholic Christians in Chicago. He is both of their world and not
of their world. This ambivalence structures his understanding:

> the analogy is not of going behind the curtain like Toto in Oz to uncloak the
> imposter (although this is right for the modernist impulse in the discipline –
> see, Dorothy, it is social class pulling the levers, or the unconscious, the social
> or the psychological). Rather, the parallel experience is of a child glancing
> over his folded hands at his mother at prayer beside him, or watching her cry
> on a riverbank above a muddy baptism.
>
> *(Orsi, 2005, p. 160)*

The crucial thing is to be able to reflect on both worlds and on their connections.
Orsi stands in the traditions of his twentieth-century geographical and social-
class-related Catholicism, just as he also stands in the traditions of his academic
discipline – traditions of ethnography, cultural anthropology and the study of religion. What makes his work so powerful and indeed courageous is his ability to
be both analytical and appreciative of both, and of the ways in which they are
connected. He sees the hermeneutical power of self-involvement for good understanding. 'I had to involve my life in the process of reflection; I could not withhold
myself' (2005, p. 173). 'It is not sufficient to append an autobiographical prologue
or epilogue to the old studies' (2005, p. 175), but the critical process of clarify-
ing and understanding what is other is enhanced throughout research by reflective
attention to our own positioning, and by reflexivity.

While religious Tradition and traditions are central to the work of practical theologians, it is important to note that not all traditions share the features of religious traditions, and that cultural traditions, and concomitant representations and descriptions of reality, may intersect with religious traditions in a way which needs to be deconstructed. Such 'deconstruction', which is a part of self-reflexivity or self-in-community-reflexivity, while being necessarily critical is not necessarily iconoclastic but may take an appreciative form.

CULTURAL AND RELIGIOUS PERSPECTIVES – APPRECIATIVE CRITICALITY

Joe Luk is a researcher in Hong Kong, submitting for a professional doctorate in the UK, who found that Orsi's description of the insider/outsider perspectives enabled a critical perspective which is also appreciative.

I am researching my own practice of spiritual healing in terms of deliverance from the bondages of evil spirits under Christian belief and tradition. People who are 'demonised' are recognised as unfortunate and tragic, and they need deliverance as a spiritual healing. However, in another tradition of belief, for example, people of the Republic of Haiti identify being 'demonised' as an enviable spiritual blessing bestowed from the heaven. Moreover, my research participants are all Chinese Christians in Hong Kong, who may have grown up in a Chinese culture with worshipping ancestors and Chinese gods. As Christians, these forms of worship are related to partaking in the realm of evil spirits and viewed as idol worship, and they all need spiritual healing as deliverance. However, the purposes of them for worshipping ancestors and gods are to acquire wealth, peace, protection, victory and even to curse others, which they see as spiritual protection. Therefore, I see that different traditions will have different meaning of 'demonised' and worshipping gods, and I need to recognise the perspectives of other traditions.

Tone Stangeland Kaufman (2016) adds a further dimension to this discussion in highlighting the 'conundrum' of where to locate 'normativity' in practical theological work. The normativity embedded in both the field researched and the practice of practical theological work itself is organically related to the normative traditions which structure and govern the practices of research subjects and of researcher.

Furthermore, the theological tradition is not one, single Tradition with a capital T. It is a conglomerate of various traditions . . . Additionally, there are various understandings of how the Christian tradition should play a normative role in empirical practical theological studies. For example, is the tradition considered a once-and-for-all given entity available to us through Scripture and the various Confessions of different faith traditions, or is the Tradition (often with a capital T) considered a dynamic, ongoing revelation? Hence, there are several layers of normativity at work, and practical theologians doing empirical research face a conundrum in terms of how to handle these normative dimensions, and what role to give the theological tradition(s), whether that be a normative ecclesial tradition or the extant theoretical (and often normative) works of academic theologians.

(Kaufman, 2016, p. 138)

Arguing for a radical form of normativity which emerges from within the very act of research itself, in the dialectic between the field of what is researched and the activity of research on the part of the researcher, she criticises much contemporary conceptualisation of the task of practical theology and practical theological research as being forced to choose between what Zoë has called elsewhere 'the tyranny of the text (normative tradition) and the tyranny of experience' (Bennett, 2013). A 'normativity-from-within might prove helpful as an attempt to be more explicit about one's normative deliberations' (Kaufman, 2016, p. 159), thus encouraging the reflexivity which is a prerequisite of finding some form of critical space while recognising that this will be substantially an immanent rather than a transcendent space.

In 'That Don't Make It Junk' Leonard Cohen sings of fighting the bottle but having to do it drunk. He offers a powerful image of this kind of 'immanent' space, of the way in which critical spaces are won within, and not apart from, who we are, the way we have been shaped, the things we do and the painful and complex struggles in which our lives are immersed. There is no 'God's eye view' available to us, and there is no 'clean slate'.

Modes of finding a critical space

From our discussions thus far we suggest it is possible to identify four possible modes of inhabiting and interpreting traditions. These are each a kind of 'ideal type' – separated out as a heuristic device for better understanding but rarely in practice totally distinguishable from each other.

The *first* seems at first to offer little critical space – that is a mode of radical obedience in relation to one's tradition – but even here interpretation inevitably happens and contextualisation is often welcomed as part of inhabiting. Perhaps the most common mode of inhabiting and interpreting religious traditions is the *second* – the embrace of organic and evolutionary development. Here a critical space may be found, as the project of 'faithful development' invites interrogation of underlying values and of the practices whereby communities enact these. The prophet is welcome within bounds. But at times the weight of tradition overpowers and silences the experiences and practices of some, perhaps of many. So, in a *third* mode, voices struggle to speak out and communities to act out in defiance of traditions, in protest and in resistance to interpretations which smother and to ways of inhabiting which oppress and imprison. *Finally* we look at the seemingly contradictory possibility that traditions may call us from the future as much as determining or resourcing us from the past. This invites us to a rather different form of finding a critical space.

Individuals and communities work with the traditions in which they find themselves in different ways and often in criss-crossing or even contradictory ways. The four ways of inhabiting and interpreting traditions invite exploration of these processes. Few people or communities belong exclusively to one of these types, in that sense they are not realistic, but they allow us to interrogate the processes whereby traditions are formed, negotiated, 'handed on' and 'betrayed' – processes in which we are rooted, changed, lost and claimed and in which we negotiate our identity and search for that which we may call home.

Type one: radical obedience

What are people doing when they appeal to tradition (Tradition)? Many things. An appeal to tradition is an appeal to the past. It is an appeal to authoritative forebears which is believed to determine how individuals and communities should believe, think and conduct themselves today. It is an appeal to the accumulated wisdom of the past, and to precedent. It may, as in many religions, be an appeal to a site of once for all revelation in the past (the Bible), and/or a site of ongoing revelation legitimated by historical continuity (the Magisterium). It is a deliberate setting of human belief and action in ongoing communities whose relationship to their past involves the receiving of handed-on beliefs and practices. These may be expressed in narratives as well as in rules: 'you shall make this response before the Lord your God: "A wandering Aramean was my ancestor; he went down into Egypt and lived there as an alien, few in number, and there he became a great nation, mighty and populous . . . "' (Deuteronomy 26:5).

What such an appeal does is to legitimate certain understandings and actions; theology is amongst other things a language of power. The legitimation may be 'from above', justifications entrenched by the economic, intellectual or spiritual 'elite' and conformity enforced by institutional power. Or it may be 'from below', as boundaries which may not be crossed are policed by communities, and transgressors brought back into the fold or cast beyond the pale.

While such a mode of relationship to tradition may be seen from outside as imposing belief and practice through power not to be questioned, and operates with fixed boundaries which may not be crossed, it is not always the case that the approach to tradition of radical obedience precludes finding a critical space. Two examples may illustrate this. The first is from an evangelical, charismatic and mission-oriented women's movement; the second from research into the Orthodox Church and its involvement in the Ecumenical Movement.

Zoë was invited to speak at a meeting of women in Peterborough in the early 2000s, a group which was part of the *Women Aglow* movement.[1] The meeting took place in a ramshackle building on a trading estate on the very edge of the town, at night. The women were from working class backgrounds, poor, ground down by caring for children and by quarrels with difficult husbands. They had been converted, 'claimed' by a conservative Christian faith, which amongst other things enjoined obedience to husbands, including non-Christian husbands ('For the unbelieving husband is made holy through his wife . . . Wife, for all you know you might save your husband', I Cor. 7:14, 16). At this meeting the atmosphere buzzed – trials shared, feelings offloaded, problems desperately laid out for scrutiny, the meaning of faith in practice earnestly sought. Among equals. Seeking to live obediently to a fixed tradition, but seeking understandings and practices within it which were not yet given.

This nondescript room on the edge of town at the edge of the day offered literally and metaphorically a living critical space, within what the Pentecostal theologian Cheryl Bridges-Johns (1993, pp. 36, 44) calls 'the epistemology of obedience'. There are creative and empowering ways of inhabiting a tradition that may appear to outsiders as quite constraining. Such experiences in relation to women in particular are researched and explored in the work of Mary McLintock Fulkerson and Ellen Clark-King (Fulkerson, 1994; Clark-King, 2004).

The ancient traditions of the Orthodox Church are historically and culturally utterly different from the context and tradition inhabited by these women. The following example, however, taken from the research of a contemporary Orthodox scholar, illustrates those same possibilities of critical perspective, creativity and dynamic life, within an ecclesial tradition whose 'epistemology of obedience' to the early Church is an essential characteristic. The element of reflexivity (see Chapter 2), inherent in good practical theological research, allows this criticality, creativity and dynamism to be displayed *from within*. This exemplifies Kaufman's 'normativity-from-within', described above.

OBEDIENCE TO THE PAST AND MOVEMENT WITHIN GOD'S CALLING: A DIALECTIC

Razvan Porumb is Koga Postdoctoral Fellow and Vice-Principal of the Institute for Orthodox Christian Studies in the Cambridge Theological Federation. His doctorate, 'Orthodoxy and Ecumenism: towards active metanoia' is available at: http://arro.anglia.ac.uk/582334/

My research focused on the rapport between the Orthodox tradition and identity and the ecumenical practice of engagement with other Christian traditions. This rapport has for a long time been compromised by an underlying tension, as the Orthodox have chosen to participate in ecumenical encounters while – often at the same time – denouncing the ecumenical movement as deficient and illegitimate. This relationship proved to be all the more inconsistent since the core of Orthodoxy as professed by the Orthodox is precisely that of re-establishing the unity and catholicity of the Church of Christ. The Orthodox Church views itself as 'the right Church' in opposition with non-Orthodox traditions, viewed as imperfect or flawed. Consequently, Orthodox ecclesiology often places these traditions outside the boundaries of the Church – until such time as they have returned to the correct Orthodox faith. The Orthodox virtual 'excommunication' of other non-Orthodox traditions can thus be viewed as having a temporary, corrective aim. If this however is the fundamental calling of the Orthodox, it informs their identity as essentially a Church of exploration, of engagement and dialogue, a Church committed to drive all other traditions – but also itself – back to the 'right' primordial faith. The Orthodox are then often caught in the dialectic of guarding the truth of faith as it has been inherited from the early Church and fiercely rejecting any other perception or perceived innovation – while at the same time feeling it belongs naturally at the core of any ecumenical process, as intrinsically urged by their own identity. This 'existential' tension between Orthodox tradition/identity and ecumenical hands-on engagement impairs not only the quality of ecumenical interactions but also the Orthodox' self-understanding of their own identity, of their inner vector and vocation.

The Orthodox understand they have been keeping alive a spirit of energy and action – a vision of Tradition as a dynamic process of continuity and renewal in the Holy Spirit. This dual understanding of Tradition prevents an understanding of Orthodoxy as an institution confined to the past.

Type two: evolutionary and organic development

There is a rich 'tradition', with both literary and theological dimensions, of discussing and theorising how evolutionary development comes about in human practices through 'tradition'. Drawing on T.S. Eliot, Prickett offers a warm, living and organic view of tradition, 'in which the new, the truly new, changes all that has gone before it to establish, if not a 'new' tradition, then a new version of an existing tradition' (Prickett, 2009, p. 224) – or in Eliot's words, 'the past should be altered by the present as much as the present is directed by the past' (Eliot, 1951, p. 15). Eliot's essay establishes the view that a poet stands in relation to the tradition in which he finds him/herself in an active role which contributes to that very tradition itself, not as a mere inheritor of the past – '[tradition] cannot be inherited, and if you want it you must first obtain it by great labour'(1951, p. 14).

As the poet, so the theologian. Offering a sophisticated contemporary account of tradition seen as ambiguous and contested, but as essential to human life, and capable of living, breathing, growing and developing within human community, Rowan Williams laid out the inner workings of what faithful innovation might mean in *Arius: heresy and tradition* (1986): 'By the 360's . . . it had become necessary to choose what *kind* of innovation would best serve the integrity of the faith handed down: to reject all innovation was simply not an option' (Williams, 1986, p. 235). Religious tradition is not fixed; it should be exposed to critical view, and it should be understood as changing and organic. A key question is how religious tradition comes alive; fundamental to Williams' grasp of this is his rootedness in poetry and the conundrums of tradition in poetic influence.

In Eliot's essay, the poet makes the tradition something new even as s/he holds it within themselves and adds to it, however little, and the past is altered by the present, making 'tradition' a dynamic and growing thing. Williams presents a further dynamic of engagement with tradition – the way in which the past may offer a critical space challenging us to view the present not as fixed and normative but as relativised from the perspective of a time and place 'over against us' which is 'other' (Williams, 1986, p. 23). Such an understanding of the historical processes whereby our traditions of 'orthodoxy' are formed 'is to experience orthodoxy as something still future' (1986, p. 24); an insight interestingly echoed in the work of Razvan Porumb as an Orthodox theologian (above). Tradition is living, changing, growing – in short, organic.

Furthermore, this wrestling to understand the wrestlings of the past, allowing us to construct an 'other', be it scripture, tradition, or so-called heresy, is inevitably hard labour, but hard labour through which we win an organic connection to the past in faithful innovation.

> The loyal and uncritical repetition of formulae is seen to be inadequate as a means of securing continuity at an anything more than a formal level; Scripture and tradition need to be read in a way that brings out their strangeness . . . They need to be made more *difficult* . . . Otherwise, we read with eyes not our own and think them through with minds not our own; the 'deposit of faith' does not really come into contact with *ourselves.*
>
> *(Williams, 1986, p. 236)*

The inhabiting and interpreting of traditions within a paradigm of faithful development involves an element of volition/action which is important; inhabiting and interpreting are active verbs here. Such inhabiting and interpreting may primarily be seen in the *practices* of the communities and of individuals as in Tom Wright's powerful image of Christians improvising the unwritten fifth act of a drama in which they have seen and internalised the first four acts (Wright, 1991).

One of the key acts of practical theological research and reflection is the unearthing of what lies within and beneath this rich-textured drama. This may include exploring the extent to which the fifth act is faithful to the first four (see Chapter 3 and Graham, 1996). Such research and reflection is done by those both within and without the practices themselves, that is to say it is both emic and etic. This 'double vision' is essential so that both the operant and the espoused theologies are exposed and discussed, as in the method of *Theological Action Research* which works with these categories and deliberately engages both insider and outside researchers in a single process (Cameron et al., 2010). Research itself thus becomes part of the act of 'finding a critical space' in the interpreting and inhabiting of traditions.

Evolutionary and organic development of tradition occurs naturally as time and context changes. However, such development is subject to active human involvement. This involvement may take the form of hard wrestling with the past in order to discern the heart of the matter, and finding the critical space which that offers to present understanding and practice. However, what constitutes faithful development will be contested. And claims to faithful development may be used to legitimate current positions and or to shape future ends.

Type three: resistance, refusal and revision

Establishing in the midst of human life and human practices a radical break with existing tradition is complex. It requires ingenuity, persistence, courage and its own 'community of practice' to sustain it. Traditions are sustained, handed on and developed – and they are also confronted and challenged – within communities of practice, notwithstanding the role of the individual nonconformist and the lone prophet. It is never possible to be as if the past did not exist, as if we were not shaped by it. There are two fundamental tools for finding a critical space in relation to that handed from on past: one is the act of criticism itself, the unmasking of ideology, that is to say a questioning of the present and what lies beneath and behind it; the second is the exploration of alternative imaginative spaces, visions and possibilities lying beyond and in contrast to present reality, a horizon of hope.

The level of confrontation and challenge to traditions rises in so far as those traditions are experienced and analysed as oppressive and suppressive. So, for example, the work of feminist revisioning offers significant contemporary examples of resistance and suspicion towards dominant voices and traditions. Adrienne Rich's generative essay 'When we dead awaken: writing as revision' (1978) is frequently taken as the manifesto of a movement that seeks to expose the ways in which women have been silenced by dominant traditions throughout history and must now engage with imaginative and reconstructive work in order to create a sense of the cultural inheritance that they have been denied.

The term 'revisioning' emerged in the contexts of literary engagement with cultural traditions but such work takes place in the everyday life of believing communities, in preaching and pedagogy as we attempt to tell our stories differently conscious of the damaging power some of our traditional narratives have exercised in the past. It is also a fundamental aspect of pastoral care. People who have been abused or had their identity negated in ways sanctioned by dominant ways of telling sacred stories often experience deep renewal as they discover ways to revision their narrative inheritance and move out of silence into powerful speech. Revisioning is also integral to theological research as we attempt to uncover and articulate forms of spiritual wisdom that emerge out of experiences that have been ill understood or neglected in the past. Heather's work on infertility, for example, attempts to revision a theological narrative that places divine generativity at its core and asks what happens to our understanding of God when we place absence and loss at the centre of theological reflection (Walton, 2015). Her work draws on feminist literary revisioning, as the following extended extract explores.

Re-vision – the act of looking back, of seeing with fresh eyes, of entering an old text from a new critical direction – is for women more than a chapter in cultural history: it is an act of survival.

(Rich, 1978, p. 35)

In her famous essay 'When we dead awaken: writing as re-vision' (1978), the poet Adrienne Rich passionately articulates her conviction that women seeking a transformed future must not turn their backs upon the past. She argues that the weight of history cannot be 'shrugged off' but the burden it imposes upon women might be transformed into a strange blessing. In particular sacred traditions expressed through mythology, literature and art can be revisioned. Although the narratives that sustain culture are dangerous for women they also carry within them evidence of an unclaimed inheritance. Through attentive re-readings women may begin to claim their own erased genealogy. This will entail a painstaking effort of creative interpretation:

> To do this work takes a capacity for constant active presence, a naturalists attention to minute phenomena, for reading between the lines, watching closely for symbolic arrangements, decoding difficult and complex messages left for us by women of the past.
>
> *(1978, p. 13)*

Rich's essay represents a significant moment in the development of contemporary feminism. Women working in many cultural spheres sought to critique the male centred traditions through which they had been formed and also to engage with them in order that they might be reclaimed and transformed. The work of the pioneering feminist biblical scholar Elizabeth Schussler Fiorenza (1983) can be seen as paradigmatic of this painstaking revisioning labour. She interrogated biblical texts used to subjugate women but also lovingly examined these same scriptures for traces of the female past. Because the evidence of women's participation in the formation of culture must be assembled from fragments, gaps and silences Fiorenza soon came to realise that her work was creative as well as exegetical. The past is not only remembered it is recreated. This task requires imaginative as well as interpretative resources.

> Within the literary sphere feminist revisionists followed similar routes. They critiqued the way male authors employed myths and also sought to rediscover the spiritual wisdom of women which could then be used as a symbolic resource by women writers. This 'women's tradition' had to be both remembered and imagined and the development of revisionist mythology within women's creative writing came to be seen as a political move to address the history of women's cultural exclusion and transform the spiritual archives of Western culture.
>
> *(Walton, 2007, pp. 79–80)*

Type four: the call from the future

In a debate with Daphne Hampson in 1986, Rosemary Radford Ruether articulated a fundamental possibility for an approach to Christian tradition which neither discarded the past, or pretended to escape its influence, nor allowed itself to be entrapped into a historically determined ideological straightjacket which enabled oppression and stunted human flourishing. She identified a 'call from the future'. Christianity, she argued, is 'an eschatological faith. It lives by the norm of the reign of God in the still unrealised future of creation, not by a fixed, completed past' (Hampson and Ruether, 1987, p. 15).

Whilst some of Ruther's contemporaries within feminist theology, such as Mary Daly in the USA and Daphne Hampson in the UK, made the 'irradicating' move of uprooting themselves and leaving, believing that this particular family of traditions could never serve the flourishing of human beings, Ruether searched for the roots of Christianity in its prophetic critique of the *status quo* of religious traditions and practices, the 'shiny bits in the rubbish heap' (Ruether, 1995, p. 53). But this quest to root oneself in the past is crucially complemented by a looking forward into the future.

So we have here a complex mix of past, present and future: the present stirs up dissonance and dissatisfaction, the past offers resources from which to critique the present, and the future holds offers a horizon of hope which opens up an imaginative space for seeing that things might be otherwise: 'Peace with God means conflict with the world, for the goad of the promised future stabs inexorably into the flesh of every unfulfilled present' (Moltmann, 2002, p. 21). This horizon of hope is fundamental to the New Testament and to the Christian gospel; Jesus is the bearer of hope, Paul the strategist of hope and that strange and neglected book, the Apocalypse of John, the Book of Revelation, is the revelation of hope. 'The most significant discovery in modern New Testament scholarship has been the realization that without grasping the centrality of hope for a new age, we shall not understand the New Testament' (Bennett and Rowland, 2016, p. 33).

This approach to traditions, and to finding a critical space within them, is future-focussed and strategically transformative. Just as traditions may be invented to legitimate the present, the creative possibilities within traditions may be called on to shape the future. Memory and imagination are the two prongs of both evolutionary and revisionist developments of tradition. They are tools of discernment in the process of knowing handing over from handing on, betrayal from faithful development, and they are means of finding spaces critical enough to challenge traditions to and from their very depths. Memory and imagination are inextricably linked to a promise and a call from the future, for sometimes 'call is not memory but premonition' (Clarke, 2001, p. 201).

Implications for the researcher in practical theology

From this examination of the meaning and workings of tradition a number of key points stand out for the researcher in practical theology: that research will inevitably require attention to our own context and 'home'; that research raises the question of responsibility towards and within religious and cultural traditions; that communities of belief and practice are a fundamental element of how research is done; and that research has the potential to be transformative. The quest for a critical space involves an inward turn, an outward turn and a future turn.

The autobiographical act is an essential component in practical theological research. The recognition and the reconstruction of our stories are in dialectical relationship to the researching and the understanding of the stories of others. Our identities are thus formed not only in relationship to our complex and plural inherited traditions, and to our development of and resistance to these, but to the actual processes and products of our research itself. So research *itself* is part of the argument with and within traditions in which our identities live and grow.

While the four modes of developing a stance in relation to tradition do indeed point to substantial differences in approach and practice, there is in fact only one key question for the researcher in practical theology: how to engage old understanding with new understanding. Research on and within traditions may be interpretative and appreciative as well as suspicious and deconstructive. Indeed at its best it is both. All four modes of engaging with tradition present positions for research, and within each of them research has the potential to expose both hidden distortions and hidden treasures. Obedience does not need to be blind, faithful development requires understanding of the past and present, resistance and revision involve acts of unearthing and of imagining creative alternatives, the 'goad of the promised future' lays on us a calling and a claim that our research transforms some part of the world, however small.

As a conclusion to this chapter Zoë and Heather offer a comparison between Zoë's work on scripture and Heather's work in life writing as contrasting attempts both to inhabit and to deconstruct tradition. Zoë goes back to classic texts and Heather appears to go far away from them at times. But at the heart of all our work we are both still trying to work out our relations to tradition. The format of this section includes substantial quotation from work we have already published, in order to illustrate how our research exemplifies the positions we are seeking to lay out concerning our engagement with tradition(s).

Zoë

Critical self-consciousness, including an 'archaeology' of our commitments and loves, is the central theme of my *Using the Bible in practical theology* (2013). This book examines, specifically in the context of Christian traditions and scripture, how practical theologians might manage the 'dialectic of tradition and experience' in their work, their public theology and their research. The issue driving this discussion is the human tendency to succumb either to 'the tyranny of the text' (uncritical absorption of biblical and other traditional teaching) or the 'tyranny of experience' (uncritical acceptance of the experiences of our communities or our individual lives). Finding a critical space from which to interrogate tradition and experience, and from which to understand better our own constructions of these, is vital. Such a critical space, however, is not some Archimedean point above and beyond the world, but contextually located in the messy history and experience (and tradition) of human beings, in which we ourselves as researchers are inextricably integrated. It is about situated knowledge which knows itself to be such.

Research which is autobiographically self-conscious allows us to inhabit our traditions in a more critical and informed way. So while we are embedded in traditions we may explore our 'home' – and so inhabit critically rather than simply being embedded. The Bible has been central to my research journey because it is central to my home, but also because on it has been focussed my struggle and dissonance with the Christian tradition. These two factors are integrally related. If it wasn't 'home' it wouldn't matter. I have found a companion on the road for this research journey; the Victorian art and social critic John Ruskin. He has been a companion because in a different time and context he struggled with similar issues but never lost the sense that the Bible was part of home to him:

> I found a man with an extraordinary capacity to live with doubt, yet whose engagement with the Bible was robust, imaginative, centrally important to him and richly fruitful in the public domain. After my first visit to the British Library to look at Ruskin's annotations on the mediaeval Greek Lectionary he owned I recorded, 'The way Ruskin treated the text in this manuscript shows a man so utterly at home in the text of the Bible that he could afford to question, even be contemptuous, without losing his relationship with it.' Something he wrote in an open letter illustrates the point perfectly:
>
>> My good wiseacre readers, I know as many flaws in the book of Genesis as the best of you, but I knew the book before I knew its flaws, while you know the flaws, and never have known the book, nor can know it.
>> *(in Cook and Wedderburn, 1903–1912, Works 28.85)*
>
> Here was a man who lived constantly with questions about the Bible, agonising public and personal questions, but for whom it was a companion and a source of prophetic public passion all his life.
> *(Bennett, 2013, p. 2)*

So research on these detailed manuscript annotations gave me a way of engaging in the journey of change and loss without totally losing roots or home. And it gave me a hermeneutical strategy for relating practice and text, life and Bible, experience and tradition.

> Taking a historical approach of this kind makes two things possible. First it allows us to see how someone in another time and another place brought into dialogue his contemporary context and experience and the text of the Bible. This is a task which is central to our work as theologians with the Bible. Seeing this diachronically as well as synchronically, from a place and a point of view very different from our own, enables us to have a fresh perspective, bringing new insight and jolting us out of well-trammelled

grooves. The historical analogy awakes the imagination and the critical faculties and increases our range of possibilities for understanding the dialectic between the text of life and the text of the Bible . . . . While Ruskin is used as a historical hermeneutical dialogue partner to enable a critical perspective, he is also an inspiration, but not a model to follow slavishly. The archaeology of how Ruskin interpreted the Bible is not explored in order to suggest we have the same interpretative strategies as he did, but in order to encourage a similar archaeology of our own strategies in order to gain some critical purchase on them.

(Bennett, 2013, p. 53)

It was not, however, through my research on Ruskin, that I was 'claimed' by the Bible. It was through my work on feminist theology, liberation theology, and in engagement with the work of Christopher Rowland on William Blake on the Bible (Rowland, 2010). Here work on the Bible itself may mirror the work done through feminist literary revisioning. The crucial components for me are that the Bible engages the imagination rather than being a rule-book, and that within the Bible itself, through the medium of apocalyptic and eschatology, hope as a call from what is 'not yet' stands at the heart. So the Bible itself may become the means of finding a critical space within the reflective project of life:

What may cause surprise is the inclusion of such a substantial role for the Bible in the process of self-reflexivity, indeed in the process of critique more generally, when it has itself been the object of much criticism over the last 200 years. We have not denied the problems we have with the Bible but have seen its apocalyptic and eschatological perspective as a key part in the critical process which we deem to be the very stuff of existence. That strand in the Bible, along with others which complement it, has been crucial to the cultivation of a critical perspective, and we find it difficult to imagine ourselves developing a critical spirit, which is also affirming and informative without it . . . . [T]he Bible has helped us decongest our critical airways . . .

(Bennett and Rowland, 2016, p. 207)

Heather

I think it is interesting that my fascination with theology was first ignited through preaching. This giving-a-face-and-voice to theology is a provisional and performative act that seeks to make vital links between tradition and the needs of our times. My first experiences of preaching were as embodied, intimate and intense and, thus perhaps, rather unusual. In *Writing Methods in Theological Reflection* (2014) I describe how I first encountered preaching 'in my mother tongue':

I am nine years old and seated half way up the stairs in our new semi, and my mother is standing at the bottom of the steps. She is looking up at me and – preaching. Her first sermons were practised on me, and the hall was the quietest and best place in our house to do this work.

My mother had a definite call. It was delivered directly from God via the Chair of District, my 'uncle' Bill. 'We need you,' he told her. 'The Church has enough old men like me going back to 1900-and-frozen-to-death. We need young women who can speak directly from their own experience about their faith today.'

And hearing this she responded and began to speak exactly in this way about her life in the new semi with her husband and two small children and the garden that was emerging out of the mud, and how she had encountered God not only in the . . . new church with a flat roof but also *right there* in the midst. And elsewhere, of course, as well. She read, and she could read the signs of the times. Her text books were collected sermons by Martin Luther King and Paul Tillich. She preached that we shall overcome, and we shall live in peace some day. And half way up the stairs the foundations were shaken, and I heard the voice of God speaking in the depth of my being.

That is how I was formed as a preacher. I don't think it conforms to the norm.

(Walton, 2014, pp. 18–19)

These early experiences gave me a profound conviction that theology was integrally related to my everyday life and when I began to work as a preacher myself it was natural to me to root everything I said in lived personal and political contexts. This did not mean I despised the Bible. On the contrary I loved it. Not because of its status, infallibility or whatever. But because of its power; the work it could do. The Bible could sow fire on the ground. Reading from it I could hear singing as the Spirit sings in sighs (almost) too deep for words. However, there was a problem. The Bible did not engage with much of what was important to me. And so in the famous image, employed by many revisionists, I had to wrestle with it to obtain a blessing (Gen 32:22–31). In my early years, predictably, this was often a matter of searching for neglected female images of God and women's voices in the text. However, in my thirties I faced a harder challenge.

Struggling with the experience of infertility I had to ask what place is there in a tradition of hope, generativity and new birth to name the pains of the empty womb? Of course there were barren women in the Bible but their presence served only to make the blessings (on their husbands) more apparent. Their status did not stand as a challenge to the fecundity of the text or its divine author. Furthermore, I soon began to experience infertility less as a medical problem and more as a theological challenge. It obliged me to assume an alternative epistemological location (window on the world) from which to engage with theological reflection. It was infertility that drove me to creative and life writing as a means to pursue the theological challenges that life in this world poses and which cannot be adequately addressed by other means. This extract from my recent book *Not Eden* demonstrates how this creative process works both with and outwith the tradition to deliver 'new knowledge' the text cannot bring forth alone.

> I was Eve working in the garden tying in the raspberry canes and my hands and my lips were stained by mulberries too soft and sweet to gather. I wanted to bear good fruit but something happened in the night and there was blood on the grass in the morning and nothing would grow any more.
>
> So now I am that other Eve. A small, dark person who lives by her wits in the savage garden. You have been told that the universe is a place of constant growth and regeneration. I am compelled to contradict you and say that it is a barren, wasted place. For all the things that grow there are partners in things that never came into being. I am their mother and even if they are forgotten I shall remember them. I am their witness.
>
> Once the Spirit said to me 'See how much is given'.
>
> Now she whispers of what has been denied. So much has been denied. How many cold stars, how many frozen deep or burning hot stars for just this one green earth? And yet without them what motion, what fire or ice, except that which has been borrowed?
>
> Perhaps one day she will lead me out of here, show me a place to clamber out beneath the barbed wire fence and inherit a green and golden portion. In dreams sometimes I do seem to taste her milk and honey. But when awake I am captured by the strange beauty of this wilderness. See how sweetly blow my poppies. How brightly they flower even in the churned up earth, growing amongst the twisted metal, from the patch of earth that is stained dark. There are wild roses too. Wreaths and wreaths of briars.
>
> How beautifully grows the bindweed. It grows between the links of the wire mesh fence. It grows right to the top of the wire mesh fence. The only flowers they can see when they press their cheeks to the fence which is too high to be climbed and there is no escape from the beams of the arching lights. Mine are the only flowers that can grow in such a place. They are necessary.
>
> And there in the corner blooms a fragment of the true cross. Blossoms coming straight out from the bare wood. I confess that it does not grow very strongly but it is a miracle that it grows at all. You will have been told not to believe that this is the cross upon which the saviour hung. To you it seems a false and pagan relic. I am not so sure. To me it is a mysterious thing and it certainly is alive – though in a way I cannot understand. Standing close I can see that it is stained with blood. Perhaps this is holy blood? And perhaps also it is the blood of all those who treasured it, kissed it, fought over it, haggled for it, traded it, stole it, passed it from hand to hand and touched it in the hope of a healing that never came.
>
> I suppose that some of them were children.
>
> The blossoms have a lovely scent.
>
> *(Walton, 2015. pp. 136–137)*

Conclusion

Practical theology's work of transformation starts with the finding of a critical space, complexly both within and outwith the traditions researchers inhabit and study. Such a critical space will enable a vision that 'it doesn't have to be like this'. Or perhaps the researcher will have started with that perspective, and a critical space will begin to open up *why* it doesn't have to be like this, or how else it might be, or indeed how *this* might not be quite what it looked like at the beginning.

Practical theological research may unearth evidence in support of the need for change; it may enable the researcher to grasp conceptually, and report persuasively, on new understandings of how things are and how they might be better. In relation to the traditions we inhabit, which may be the objects we study and/or the pervasive context and world-view of our research practices, such research is part of the process of inhabiting, developing or challenging what we have been 'handed'; at its best it is the '*paradosis*' which challenges wisdom with fresh wisdom, and challenges foolishness with evidence of folly.

In our Introduction we wrote of four themes that underlie and characterise the kind of practical theological research commended and analysed in this book: *rooted, changed, lost* and *claimed*. All four themes may illuminate the relationship between the researcher and tradition. The researcher, like the poet, is inevitably rooted, and is working to 'obtain by great labour' the tradition in which she stands, and in so doing 'altering' the past by her present work as well as 'being directed' in it by the past she holds in herself and the past she discovers in her research. In this, and in the openness to inhabiting a critical space in relation to tradition, the researcher is changed, both in terms of self-deconstruction and in terms of understanding (getting under the skin of) what is being researched. She may feel lost. She may *be* lost. Traditions provide maps, maps we have internalised and maps we may consult. On the other hand new evidence and critical perspectives destabilise maps; that is their function. And in all this the researcher may experience being claimed, or perhaps reclaimed – claimed by a fresh understanding of the traditions they inhabit; claimed by the unexpected in the experiences and practices they research, and claimed by previously unimagined ways of mapping.

Home is a place where you have never *quite* been before. Home is a calling, a premonition, more than it is memory, though it is memory too. Practical theological research works in the space between the start of the journey and its end.

Note

1 Aglow International, Belief statement, www.aglow.org.uk/aboutbelief

References

Anderson, B., 1983 (revised and extended 1991). *Imagined communities*. London and New York: Verso.
Bennett, Z., 2013. *Using the Bible in practical theology: Historical and contemporary perspectives*. Farnham: Ashgate.

Bennett, Z. and Rowland, C., 2016. *In a glass darkly: The Bible, reflection, and everyday life.* London: SCM Press.

Bloom, H., 1973. *The Anxiety of influence: A theory of poetry.* Oxford: Oxford University Press.

Bridges-Johns, C., 1993. *Pentecostal formation: A pedagogy among the oppressed*, Journal of Pentecostal Theology Supplement Series 2. Sheffield: Sheffield Academic Press.

Cameron, H., Bhatti, D., Duce, C. and Sweeney, J., 2010. *Talking about God in practice: Theological action research and practical theology.* London: SCM Press.

Cantwell Smith, W., 1993. *What is scripture? A comparative approach.* Minneapolis: Fortress Press.

Cartledge, M., 2015. *The mediation of the spirit: Interventions in practical theology.* Grand Rapids, MI: Eerdmans.

Clarke, A.C., 2001. *Childhood's end.* London: Pan Books.

Clark-King, E., 2004. *Theology by heart: Women, the church and God.* Peterborough: Epworth.

Cook, E.T. and Wedderburn, A., eds., 1903–1912. *The works of John Ruskin.* 39 vols. London: George Allen (referred to as *Works*, volume and page number).

Eliot, T.S., 1951. Tradition and the individual talent. In: T.S. Eliot, ed., *Selected essays.* London: Faber and Faber (first published in 1932 by Faber as *Selected essays–1917–1932*). pp. 13–22.

Finchley Progressive Synagogue, 2017. *About us.* Available at: www.fps.org/our-team [Accessed 25 August 2017].

Fiorenza, E.S., 1983. *In memory of her: A feminist theological reconstruction of Christian origins.* London: SCM Press.

Fulkerson, M.M., 1994. *Changing the subject: Women's discourses and feminist theology.* Minneapolis: Fortress Press.

Gadamer, H.-G., ed., 1985. *The hermeneutics reader: Texts of the German tradition from the Enlightenment to the present.* New York: Continuum. pp. 256–274.

Gilbert, A., 2014. From 'pretended family relationship' to 'ultimate affirmation in British conservatism and the legal recognition of same-sex relationships'. *Child and Family Law Quarterly*, 26(4), pp. 463–488.

Graham, E., 1996. *Transforming practice: Pastoral theology in an age of uncertainty.* London: Mowbray.

Graham, E., 2013. Is practical theology a form of 'action research'? *International Journal of Practical Theology*, 17(1), pp. 148–178.

Hampson, D. and Ruether, R.R., 1987. Is there a place for feminists in the Christian Church? *New Blackfriars*, 68, pp. 7–24.

Hobsbawm, E. and Ranger, T., 1983. *The invention of tradition.* Cambridge: Cambridge University Press.

The Holy Bible, containing the old and new testaments: New revised standard version, anglicized edition, 1995. Oxford: Oxford University Press.

hooks, bell, 1994. *Teaching to transgress: Education as the practice of freedom*, London: Routledge.

Kaufman, T.S., 2016. From the outside, within, or in between? Normativity at work in empirical practical theological research. In: B.J. Miller-McLemore and J.A. Mercer, eds., *Conundrums in practical theology.* Leiden and Boston: Brill. pp. 134–162.

LeGuin, U.K., 1975. *The dispossessed.* London: Panther.

MacIntyre, A., 1988. *Whose justice? Which rationality?* Notre Dame: University of Notre Dame Press.

Moltmann, J., 2002. *Theology of hope: On the ground and the implications for a Christian eschatology.* London: SCM Press.

Orsi, R., 2005. *Between heaven and earth: The religious worlds people make and the scholars who study them.* Princeton, NJ: Princeton University Press.

Prickett, S., 2009. *Modernity and the reinvention of tradition: Backing into the future*. Cambridge: Cambridge University Press.

Princes Road Synagogue, 2017. Available at: www.princesroad.org/ [Accessed 25 August 2017].

Rich, A., 1978. When we dead awaken: Writing as revision. In: A. Rich, ed., *On lies, secrets and silences: Selected prose 1966–1978*. New York: W. W. Norton.

Rowland, C., 2010. *Blake and the Bible*. Newhaven and London: Yale University Press.

Ruether, R.R., 1995. Ecofeminism and healing ourselves, healing the earth. *Feminist Theology*, 9, pp. 51-62.

Sardar, Z., 2011. *Reading the Qur'an*. London: Hurst.

Shils, E., 1981. *Tradition*. Chicago: University of Chicago Press.

Walton, H., 2007. *Imagining theology: Women, writing and God*. Edinburgh: T&T Clark.

Walton, H., 2014. *Writing methods in theological reflection*. London: SCM Press.

Walton, H., 2015. *Not Eden: Spiritual life writing for this world*. London: SCM Press.

Williams, R., 1986. *Arius: Heresy and tradition*. London: DLT.

Wright, T., 1991. How can the Bible be authoritative? *Vox Evangelica*, 21, pp. 7–32.

Zuckmayer, C., 1966. *Als wär's ein Stück von mir. Horen der Freundschaft*. Frankfurt am Main: S. Fischer.

6

FRAMING THE VIEW

Method matters

Much literature concerning research methods in practical theology tacitly assumes that researchers choose their particular approaches and methods principally for pragmatic reasons. These might include:

- Seeking the best tool for the job;
- Thinking the research task itself suggests certain ways of approaching the topic;
- Aiming to generate academically credible knowledge;
- Being mindful of the methods currently deemed most reliable;
- Wanting research to be useful to others, so undertaking it with the methods that will best produce usable data;
- Hoping to promote social or ecclesial change so requiring a method that will complement this action-oriented process and be acceptable to stakeholders.

These are important considerations. However, the passion with which research methods are debated within the practical theological community suggests something more is at stake than these 'common sense' concerns indicate.

Debates over method, we suggest, often stand as proxy for fundamental differing understandings of the practical theological project. They are influenced by deeper forces than pragmatism and common sense. In this chapter, we go behind apparently prosaic, instrumental discussion about methods to expose their significance for practical theology research as a whole. Methods represent, and are freighted with, world-views and assumptions. It is for this, as well as for practical reasons, that method matters.

There are many approaches, methods and tools that can be used in undertaking research enquiry. Different methods and tools presuppose different understandings of evidence, data and interpretation based on different ways of understanding the 'object' of research and how it can be known and explored.

Historically, in many religions the divine is the phenomenon of which knowledge and understanding is sought. Obtaining this knowledge has often been primarily through devotion, worship, prayer, service and study of the scriptures. This is more of an absorption into the religious world and its lived, embodied understanding of the divine rather than a critical appraisal of it. The kind of religious knowledge sought and fostered is inhabited wisdom that deepens commitment. Reality is seen and engaged through the lens of religious understanding deemed to be pre-eminent in comprehending and living in the world. This is not the kind of knowledge that can easily be expressed in a critical academic essay. Hence the belief held by some that if you want to be a theologian, you must pray and be devout as a pre-condition (Farley, 1983; Ward, 2008). Monks and nuns undertaking *lectio divina*, feeding upon rather than analysing scripture, might represent an icon of this approach.

This contrasts with post-Enlightenment Western academic theological approaches to research. Here traditions, texts and practices may be inhabited, but they are also critiqued using rational analytic techniques such as textual scholarship and sociological insight. In this approach what is taken to be relevant theological knowledge is more diverse, complex and multi-perspectival; a variety of epistemological strategies (ways of knowing) are used to apprehend aspects of the reality being sought. Non-believers and the non-devout, as well as religious insiders can participate in gaining and making this kind of theological knowledge, since it can be assessed against supposedly universal and value-neutral criteria of articulation, reason, coherence, consistency and explanatory power within a shared and consensual epistemological framework.

In theology generally, and in practical theology in particular, there are many ways of pursuing research enquiry, depending on what kind of knowledge is valued and sought. Historical and textual research presupposes that some kinds of authoritative knowledge and insight can be gained from the experience and writings of people in the past. Enquiry into concepts and metaphors using literary or philosophical methods may be taken to reveal insight into contemporary beliefs and practices. Deep personal reflection on experiences of prayer in the light of scripture can be a valid method of theological enquiry in some cases.

'[A]ttentive listening to the internally held *habitus* or framework of faith', is how Quentin Chandler describes the element of prayer and listening in theological reflection, which his research among ministry students unearthed (Chandler, 2015, p. 111). This is a 'contemplative suspension of the conversation':

> The negotiation of the spiritual threshold concept has made me see that at the heart of theological reflection there needs to be a contemplative moment. Attentiveness to the canonical voice includes the discernment of Christ's presence in the world through contemplative practices . . . a suspension of the desire for cognitive mastery of the reflective conversation; a making-of-space so that the Holy Spirit can be heard; a 'letting go and letting God'.
>
> *(Chandler, 2015, p. 123)*

There may be diversity of ontologies (assumed deep understandings of what the world is fundamentally like) and epistemologies (ways of exploring and gaining knowledge of the assumed world). These lead to the selection of different methods and tools regarded as relevant and useful within these world-views. Thus specific research methods and tools reinforce and create ways of looking at the world at the same time as they provide means of exploring that world.

Every way of seeing is also a way of not seeing. The adoption of particular approaches, methods and tools is also a way of conveying significance, so that some things are seen and valued while others are ignored. The selection of research methods, like the whole practical theological enterprise, is not simply obvious, pragmatic, innocent or unimportant.

The chapter explores the ways in which research approaches, methods and tools reflect and help to construct worlds and world-views in practical theology. It does this by exploring some of the innovations in practical theological research methods over the last forty years. First, we use a case study of two different paradigms of research, empirical theology and feminist theology, to elicit the significance of different world-views or ontologies in research. This reveals how many different factors and commitments, intellectual and practical, can influence the selection of research paradigms and methods. This leads to further, deeper theoretical discussion of the importance of world-views and ontologies and how these then influence research enquiry and questions. With this theoretical discussion in mind, we then provide a critique of some important developments and debates in contemporary practical theology that often hinge on important world-view differences. Finally, some new, promising approaches to research that specifically attend to spirituality and creativity are outlined. These, like all ways of generating knowledge and insight, have their own understandings of ontology and epistemology, but use approaches and methods that are less distancing and more self-consciously constructive. They therefore offer an exciting model for engaging with the production of worlds, understandings and insights in research.

By the end of this chapter, readers will have a much clearer understanding of the importance, complexity and opportunities that can arise in the selection of research methods in relation to fundamental understandings of practical theology – and of reality itself.

Methods in tension: a case study

We turn first to a case study tracing two important research trajectories within practical theology that stood in painful tension at the turn of the century. This exposes some of the complex factors that can come into play in considering and selecting research methods.

Empirical theology emerged in the Netherlands during the 1970's under the inspirational academic leadership of Johannes van der Ven (van der Ven, 1988, 1993; Kay, 2003). The Department of Pastoral Theology at University of Nijmegen became the Department of Empirical Theology in 1990. Empirical theology soon became influential throughout Northern Europe, parts of North America, South Africa and beyond. Its basic principle is that the essence of practical theology lies in reflection upon the observable practices of people of faith. Thus, empirical theologians sought to gain credible and realistic understandings of significant religious phenomena (such as, the manner in which people come to faith, how religious believers make sense of suffering or how participation in religious communities influences attitudes to conflict).

These practices were examined using social research methods in much the same way as biblical scholars use the tools of textual criticism or systematic theologians draw upon techniques of philosophical enquiry. Empirical theologians believed that secular social scientists had neither the interest nor expertise necessary to interrogate faith-based practice. They therefore took a radical step, advocating that practical theologians should become proficient in social research methods in order to under-take work they believed to be of profound theological significance (van der Ven, 1993, p. 101).

Empirical theologians sought to bring the lived practice of believers into dia-logue with theology. In this conversation, the theological tradition was to have a normative, pre-eminent role in interpreting contemporary faith practice and cri-tiquing its expression. However, they recognised that if contemporary Christian practice was revealed to be at odds with the tradition, then serious theological reflection was imperative. This might eventually transform the tradition in small, or even significant ways.

From this brief outline of the nature of empirical theology it is possible to begin to imagine the research methods that it favoured. Having a strong belief in a social reality observable and interpretable through rational investigation, empirical theolo-gians first engaged in quantitative research, creating data through apparently neutral and value-free means like questionnaires. Qualitative methods were not excluded, and later played an important role in the movement. But a commitment to 'solid' empirical data that would speak authoritatively to academic and ecclesial institu-tions remained.

The final decade of the twentieth century saw the rise of another lively movement in practical theology. *Feminist practical theology* emerged as a radical voice through the publication of some very significant texts (see Bons-Storm and Ackermann, 1997; Graham, 1995; Miller-McLemore and Gill-Austen, 1999; Moessner, 1996). Femi-nist practical theologians drew upon the deep commitment to human flourishing enshrined within pastoral practice. They also valued the insights of liberation theol-ogy, including the conviction that Christian practice was not simply about living a Christian life within the Church, but also engaging in forms of transformative practice through which God was active in the world (Graham, 1996). Lacking the homogeneity and defined agenda of empirical theology, feminist practical theolo-gians nevertheless saw themselves as bound together in solidarity. They exposed how the practical theological community had neglected the social concerns and pastoral/ theological insights of women while also failing to acknowledge the emancipatory requirements of Christian practice. This approach placed less emphasis upon the normative status of tradition. There was also a very positive, open approach to the secular sociological research community where other feminist scholars were providing necessary conceptual and theoretical resources for feminist theological reconstruction.

Consistent with their critical ethos, there was a significant difference in the social research methods favoured by women scholars. They made use of quantitative, 'census type' data to affirm the significance of issues such as sexual abuse, domestic violence and women's economic marginalisation. However, they were suspicious of the way in which women's voices were lost in the abstraction and generalisation processes that characterise quantitative research. They tended to privilege case studies revealing aspects of women's experience previously ignored, and life story research where women reflected upon the constraints they had experienced and particular insights they had formed.

> [Q]uite a few women were willing to tell me about their experiences . . . The stories I heard form the basis of my knowledge about the topic at hand . . . They had come to a point where they could put their experiences into words. Hence, in actuality they are not silenced any more. They look back upon a stage of their lives when they felt silenced, but they found somebody who heard them into speech. They found their own voices.
>
> *(Bons-Storm, 1996, p. 37)*

They also adopted collaborative research methods with researchers fully engaged with respondents rather than standing apart from them to maintain a supposed neutrality. Personal history and autobiographical reflection were seen as positive assets in research practice and feminist practical theologians tentatively began to 'write themselves in' to their research projects (see Miller-McLemore, 1994).

Both groups of practical theologians were doing important work that impacted the way the discipline developed as the new century progressed. However, the relationship between the groups was often tense, sometimes acrimonious. The empirical theologians worried that their feminist counterparts' research was imprecise, emotionally charged and biased. It was unlikely to produce results credible within either Academy or Church, and was thus unhelpful in the development of the discipline. The feminist theologians thought that the production of statistical material on issues such as religious formation of young people in different countries was doing little to capture the particularities of experience, was not significantly conscious of issues of cultural difference, and was too narrowly focused on questions of faith rather than justice. They feared that women's concerns might be lost in a big picture that excluded the vivid colours and fascinating ambiguities of the world in which they laboured. The authors recall several conferences of the International Academy of Practical Theology in which methodological differences were keenly debated and very sharply felt.

With hindsight, it is possible to recognise how the world-views of both groups of researchers led them to prefer certain research strategies while discounting others.

Developments in empirical theology were overwhelmingly driven by a group of senior male scholars seeking to advance their discipline's reputation and place within the Academy by asserting its scientific credentials. However, as committed practical theologians, they also sought to make progressive changes to theological thinking that were radical and supportive to the flourishing of Christian communities in a rapidly changing cultural context. Empirical theology was most at home in Roman Catholic and Barthian environments where tradition/revelation was highly regarded as 'sure knowledge', and where established scholars were confident of receiving a hearing within academic and ecclesial structures. Only through generating equally robust, factual, reasonable and authoritative data could practical theology engage in serious conversation with the traditions of faith. Empirical theologians had a strong stake in defending the objective reality of the social world and its intelligibility, since it was on this basis that their research could be brought into conversation with religious thinking that understood revelation itself as pointing to an existing and communicable reality.

Feminist scholars, on the other hand, were more ambivalent about accommodating the discipline within established academic conventions. Many were pioneering academics, often amongst the first women to be employed in their academic institutions. Their sense of belonging within the Academy was 'complicated'. Academic work tended to be regarded as a form of political intervention, fueled by desire for social change and disruption of established understandings. Feminist scholars were similarly ambivalent regarding the theological tradition, frequently less concerned to acknowledge its normative claims than to expose places in which theology was used to support unjust, oppressive conventions, particularly those impacting women (Walton, 2016). Passionately concerned about both spirituality and social justice, they were often less interested in Church and easily forged communion with women from other religious traditions or none.

This case study shows how two movements within practical theology began to use different research methods to achieve their ends. Their choice of methods reflected David Tracy's consideration that Christian theology must locate itself in relation to the three 'publics' of church, academy and society and address their respective 'claims to meaning and truth' (Tracy, 1981, p. 29).

However, fundamental beliefs and commitments and beliefs about religious and academic world-views are not the only relevant factors in selecting methods. At a more mundane level, selection of methods is also influenced by factors like access to power, insider/outsider status, and access to money. A combination of factors creates and establishes the world-views that influence research design – and a sense of personal and/or institutional power must be counted amongst them (Pattison, 2007a, pp. 261–289). It is impossible to undertake large-scale survey research without the time and finance necessary to support it, whereas research on personal life histories or case studies, for example, is much easier to pursue independently and without gaining the *imprimatur* of church councils and funding bodies. People who are in secure employment are able to take paths that those without tenure cannot (and *vice versa*). Doctoral students may be led to use certain research methods because they hope their thesis will gain them a job. They may be rightly cautious about straying too far from established paths by using a new or radical approach.

From ontology to method in social research

EXPLORING INCOMPATIBLE WORLD-VIEWS IN LIFE AND RESEARCH

Alison Le Cornu, an independent consultant and coach/mentor specialising in adult education and adult theological education, undertook a research project exploring how people's Christian faith influences the way they learn for her doctoral research. Her PhD thesis at the University of Surrey was entitled 'People's Ways of Believing: learning processes and faith outcomes' (Le Cornu, 2004) and was subsequently adapted for publication as Le Cornu (2005).

In this short reflection, she explores how her personal world-views impinged upon, and were changed in, and by, her research.

My formative Christian years (as a teenager) in a strongly conservative evangelical church emphasised individual experience of God. I was encouraged to discern the peace of the Lord in my life, witness his many blessings and expect his active, positive, intervention. This worldview jarred powerfully against my real-life experience. I gradually began to develop an alternative 'from below' perspective where interpretation of my experience involved neither God nor the Christian tradition, and took far greater precedence in how I understood the world in which I lived and on which I acted. There seemed to be an irreconcilable gap between the two. I was uncomfortably aware that the/a 'Christian' understanding of the world to which I paid articulate lip service, was little more than that.

My PhD research methodology (in Adult Education Studies) deliberately aimed to bridge that gap, bringing together two worldviews, which until that point seemed incompatible. Semi-structured interviews offered not only a tried and tested method of investigation but an additional bonus of allowing me to see how others struggled to, or succeeded in resolving the challenges I wrestled with. The research therefore had one formal aim (to investigate and offer a response to my research question) and one informal, personal, beneficial spin off, permitting me to 'spy' on and learn from my interviewees' very varied ways of approaching the conundrum. My 'from below' worldview still dominated since I was investigating the processes of learning and reflecting. I was also keen not to fall into the trap of adopting a methodology and method that were so heavenly-minded that they were no earthly good! Interpretation of the data was strongly rooted in education and social science theory and in the scientific precepts that governed these. It was complex, but breakthroughs were not only part of my path to responding to my research question, but also personal, sometimes functioning on both planes simultaneously, sometimes entirely independently as I worked and re-worked the transcripts.

Nearly fifteen years on, I remain committed to a 'from below' worldview. I cannot imagine I will ever abandon my conviction that the Christian tradition must readily relate to my experience and I am still willing to allow experience to take precedence over that tradition if necessary, but rarely the reverse. However, my research has changed me. Unexpectedly, I have found a place for my conclusions in the theory and practice of practical theology since I realise I have conducted a study of the processes of theological reflection. Hence my worldview has taken some steps up the ladder from below to above. I have seen a middle ground in operation in concepts such as wisdom and mystery: places where both God and humans reside compatibly. And by introducing these into my own worldview and allowing them to play a role in my epistemology, my reflection and my faith, I have changed.

The question of how world-view and research strategy are related has not yet been sufficiently explored within the practical theological community. However, amongst social researchers this topic has been the subject of lively debate over many years. In a reflection upon these debates, and how these relate to her own research journey, Nicole Mockler (2011) uses the helpful image of concentric circles to display how researchers' convictions shape their methodological decisions.

Here ontology, what we term 'world-view', has central place. The convictions we have concerning the fundamentals of human existence form the heart of our research enquiries. From this, flow understandings of what constitutes knowledge (epistemology/ies) and what paradigms of social reality researchers adhere to. It is in congruity to these fundamental stances that preferred methodologies and methods take shape.

Mockler's attempt to illustrate stages in a research process is just a useful heuristic device allowing the examination of what is, in reality, a messy, ambiguous process. Nevertheless, its application is salutary. Within practical theology debate about social research often begins, and ends, with pragmatic discussion of the utility of particular methods. This prescinds from critical recognition of other possible world-views and ontologies that might suggest different, even more appropriate approaches and methods. 'Social research methods' are often blandly discussed in generic terms rather than recognising the heterogeneity characterising this field and the existential, ontological and epistemological questions that might exert lively, critical and creative influence upon research design. Inhabiting each layer of the circle, particular questions and challenges emerge for the practical theological researcher. These are considered below.

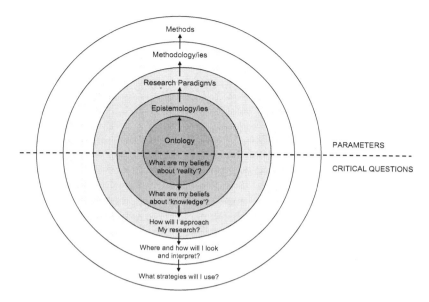

FIGURE 6.1 Elements of research design

Source: Adapted from Mockler (2011, p. 160).

Ontology

In the initial circle of Mockler's diagram, the practical theological researcher might ponder how their fundamental understandings of existence are related to the way in which they are planning their research project. Ontology is an intimidating word; we have preferred to use the term world-view. This is more accessible; it also helpfully unites two key aspects that shape ontology. First, it emphasises that the way we understand the world is a matter of deep enacted and embodied conviction (belief) and the related commitments that spring from a sense of belonging to traditions, communities of practice, and peoples of faith. Secondly, it reminds us of the importance of reflexivity; ontologies are generated from particular vantage points. For example, political developments in 2016 in Europe and North America revealed a deep polarisation between world-views within populations that are related to social class and access to cultural capital so that different groups actually appear to live in separate worlds with different ideas expressed in 'deep stories' that reflect what is real and salient (Hochschild, 2016). This shows that ontologies are always generated not only to explore and explain the nature of existence, but to also to predicate certain ways of being and seeing as more significant and valid than others.

Epistemology

In this circle the researcher will ask, what is the nature of the knowledge they are attempting to gain and represent through their research? Some approach research with confidence that it is possible to offer accurate, generalisable and convincing accounts of social reality. This will often be linked to a 'high' understanding of the nature of revelation and the normative status of tradition, as we saw with the empirical practical theologians. Others may be convinced that knowledge is fundamentally situated and incline towards forms of standpoint epistemology. Here, the goal of research might be to articulate understandings that are generated from within a particular or marginalised social location (e.g., that of a kidney dialysis patient, a female deacon).

This approach to epistemology is often coupled with a view of faith as something that takes form and life – in other words, incarnated – in particular situations and contexts. It is an embodied practice rather than a universal set of normative tenets to be adhered to. A third perspective that might shape the epistemological stance of the practical theologian is that our current knowledge of the world is itself produced through the operations of power within our society. Only when we attempt to address the distortions to our understandings of reality caused by oppressive forces will we gain a better understanding of our situation. From this perspective the pursuit of knowledge is inseparable from change directed practice, 'praxis' (Boff and Boff, 1987, p. 39; Pattison, 1994, pp. 32–33). This approach to epistemology is often linked to liberative and kingdom-based understandings of the theological tradition.

IDENTIFYING CLEAR EPISTEMOLOGICAL THEORETICAL UNDERPINNINGS

Susy Brouard, an adult educator working for a Catholic development organisation describes and illustrates the clear theoretical and value underpinnings for research, demonstrating the need to find practical strategies and approaches that are in line with these. Her 2015 professional doctorate thesis, 'Using theological action research to embed Catholic social teaching in a Catholic development organisation' is available at: http://arro.anglia.ac.uk/580464/.

My pedagogical instinct is that adults learn best when content relates to their experience, when that experience is acknowledged and drawn on, and when what is taught is seen as relevant to their lives. I was looking for a way of 'teaching' Catholic social teaching (CST) to people from diverse faith backgrounds and none that would put this instinct into practice. The teaching/learning method would need to be rooted in staff's practice and encourage not just intellectual appropriation, but a capacity to inhabit the principles of CST in their work. My involvement in two cycles of an emerging method of theological reflection known as Theological Action Research (TAR) made me think I had found a way to embed CST in a manner consistent with my pedagogical practice.

Reading Freire, Groom and other contemporary Christian adult educators and practical theologians, I identified five aspects of educational theory which I believed to be key to the practice of Christian theological education. These were:

1   *The telos of educational practice: education as political and transformative*
2   *Teaching as rooted in the lives of the learners*

> Given the philosophical underpinnings of my pedagogical practice, I concluded that, within my own practice, TAR was potentially an ideal method of teaching CST to staff from a diversity of faith backgrounds.
>
> Indeed, TAR revealed itself to be a strong tool for adult theological education since it contains within it many key educational and theoretical concepts. TAR also steers participants towards encountering others and entering into dialogue with them. It allows people to tell their story in conjunction with the Christian story, to sit round a table and come to see practice and the Christian story in a different light, and to share insights with others. With its emphasis on conversation and shared learning, participants can own their learning, increasing the chances of it being integrated into practice. TAR also offers a way of involving those of a diversity of faiths and none in the conversation with the Christian story itself, its tradition and theology. TAR as a form of theological education reminds us that, in the words of one of the participants at the end of the project: 'theology is a living thing, that it is alive'.

Research paradigms

Research paradigms and approaches spring directly from the ontological and epistemological considerations discussed above, even if researchers are unaware of them (a world-view is most powerful when it is unnoticed and inhabited as common sense 'reality'). So, for example, a practical theological researcher may adopt a positivist paradigm (sometimes described as a realist or empirical approach). This assumes that reality can be apprehended by investigation, experimentation, observation and various types of measurement. Alternatively, they might take a constructivist approach. This assumes that what is called reality is socially constructed so that people make the meanings that create the world. The researcher's task then becomes to enquire into these meaning-making processes themselves. Finally, a researcher might be less concerned with either structure or meaning and be looking for a transformative paradigm which emphasises processes of change.

Positivist researchers will tend to favour quantitative methods (particularly survey research). Constructivist researchers will tend to rely upon the wide range of qualitative approaches that seek to determine how people assign meanings to situations and events. The third group of researchers might be quite pragmatic in their use of research tools but would prefer research strategies allowing them to observe and evaluate processes of change, e.g., those currently employed with action research.

It is important to remember that the categories we are discussing do not have clear boundaries between them; in practice, they can easily 'bleed' into each other.

Methodologies

Methodologies are closely related to research paradigms. Methodology, however, refers more particularly to the 'research home' which sustains the concrete practices of the researcher.

Gaining a firm understanding of methodology often causes problems for researchers in practical theology as the social research literature employs the term in a variety of ways. It can be used to describe a research tradition in which the investigator stands (for example, as a phenomenologist or action researcher). Alternatively, it may be employed in more overtly political ways to describe a critical position which the researcher adopts and which structures their research activities (e.g., as a queer researcher, a Marxist, or a postcolonial researcher). Yet however the term is employed,

> methodology is . . . the organizing system through which researchers make use and sense of data and ideas, engage critically with theories and literature, reflect on material practices and actions, ask questions and seek answers to weave research in a cohesive and systematic way.
>
> *(Grierson and Brearley, 2009, p. 5)*

A methodological awareness reminds us that we do not come to the creation of knowledge as innocent enquirers. Our practice is creatively enabled and critically constrained by methodologies employed. These are the research 'dwellings' we inhabit and construct. Researchers will often not be fixedly constrained within one methodology. Very commonly practical theological researchers, like those in other fields, will draw upon more than one methodological tradition (Lincoln and Guba, 2005, p. 167).

It is crucial that research methodologies are 'fit for purpose', not only in a pragmatic or technical sense, but insofar as they can demonstrate coherence and consistency in terms of addressing the initial research question and fulfilling the objectives of any given project. Our research design must demonstrably achieve our criteria of verifiability, reliability, responsibility (in ethics – see Chapter 7) and rigour. This is about whether or not we as researchers, and our data/evidence as generated by the research process, can be *trusted*.

Methods

Methods are the varieties of tools and techniques used to generate data. Within practical theology a number of methods are frequently used. These include survey-based research, focus groups, interviews and close ethnographic observation. Even when these common methods are employed, there will be differences in practice springing from the researchers' world-views.

For example, quantitative researchers might use focus groups to undertake small-scale surveys with carefully chosen, predetermined questions. They would calibrate the membership of the groups in relation to the population they intended to study to claim the statistical reliability and validity of the data generated.

By contrast, a qualitative researcher might employ focus groups to discover how understanding of a particular issue is communally formed through informal processes of social interaction. The agenda here would be more open. Members of the group might not be representative of a larger population, but be drawn from those having most interest in the topic being investigated. Data analysis would be a hermeneutical process undertaken without statistical outcomes in mind.

As well as these common techniques there are many other research methods available to practical theologians. These include established tools such as discourse analysis, and life story research which are now finding an acknowledged place (see Kappler, 2009; Moschella, 2016). Emerging methods such as arts-based research and autoethnography offer challenging alternatives to dominant practices, and will be discussed later.

Whatever research method is chosen, it will carry implicit ontological and epistemological 'baggage' into the research process. There is always more at stake in selecting methods than finding the best tool for the job.

Going round in circles?

The image of concentric circles represented in Figure 6.1 helps us to recognise that research design always contains implicit ontologies and epistemologies. However, there is a danger in employing this heuristic device that a straightforward movement from ontology to method is assumed and that this progresses unidirectionally, always towards predetermined outcomes.

This is not the case in research practice. Movements take place backwards and forwards between categories. Research methods generate world-views as much as the other way round. So, for example, a person may find that the process of using a particular research method generates unexpected questions of an epistemological or ontological nature for them. Or, in the process of working with more than one methodological framework, they might find that they have to abandon former convictions by being challenged by critical insights from another tradition. The researcher may be challenged to change, experiencing confusion and loss alongside new callings (Dreyer, 2016; Wigg-Stevenson, 2013).

MOVING IN AND AROUND FRAMEWORKS AND METHODS

Susan van Scoyoc is a psychologist and a Buddhist who has undertaken professional doctoral research bringing these two areas together in a thesis entitled: 'Meditations of a solitary Buddhist Psychologist using action research to consider dilemmas experienced whilst practicing in Criminal Court settings'. Here, she describes the way epistemologies, methods and approaches may need radically to change in the course of a research project.

> The focus of my original research plan was on something outside of myself: psychological science blended with the Buddhist methods of practice. I was avoidant of the real issues at hand: the need for meditative inquiry into myself, my thoughts, feelings and behaviours. As I immersed myself into Buddhist interpretations of my experiences, the awareness of my central place in the research increased. I moved from outsider research, into insider research, and finally another stage: inside-my-head research.
>
> I moved from living inside my head to encompass the Buddhist concept of heart-mind. In Buddhist philosophy, mind is not understood as in the head or brain. Instead there is simply experience. This experience is represented by the concept of heart-mind where the experiences (thoughts, feelings and more) are one and the same, responding together, influenced by the practice of loving kindness, compassion, joy and equanimity. Owen Flanagan in a 2006 address introduced the phrase 'cramps in the heart-mind' when we encounter 'intuitive discomfort, cognitive and affective dissonance'. This is a wonderful description of my personal experience of such dissonance, providing the energy to embark on this research project. 'Cramps in the heart-mind' descriptively moves beyond the sense of only turning one's mind to intellectual logic. The more I practise meditation the more I feel myself moving from the constant conceptualisation that arises from living in my head to purer experiences, accepting the pleasant and unpleasant of living a full life.
>
> This research journey challenged me to let go of the influence of early positivist approaches and to value my experiences as valuable and researchable in their own right. I have learned to take notice of the discomfort within myself. I see I became complacent; I thought I understood my professional role only to discover I do not understand or even approve. I learned to practise Buddhism rather than conceptualise about Buddhism.

The contemporary research context

The case study presented at the beginning of this chapter revealed sharp polarities concerning research practice within the practical theological community at the turn of the century. Interestingly, two of the most vibrant movements within practical theology today are explicitly identified through their methodological stances.

The *Ecclesiology and Ethnography* network has generated inspiring new scholarship and has renewed the discipline of congregational studies (Ward, 2011). Alongside this network, and with overlapping participation, is the *Theological Action Research* (TAR) network (Cameron et al., 2010). This uses theologically informed processes of action research to enable Christian communities to reflect upon their identity, mission and communal life.

These movements are more diverse, in every sense, than those which preceded them. Many women scholars are active within them, and an inclusive approach is

taken to a variety of research techniques – most of which are focused upon understanding, being and practising Church. The ecclesial focus is significant. Because
the Church is viewed simultaneously as a human and a divine institution, both
theological sophistication and research acumen are required to engage with the
place where revelation meets practice in a unique encounter (Watkins, 2015).

Although some scholars continue to view themselves as empirical or feminist
practical theologians, these older groupings are now less antagonistically positioned.
Superficially at least, a more healthy, constructive atmosphere prevails. There is a
growing consensus about research paradigms; most of those involved in both networks proceed in their research as 'critical realists' (Swinton and Mowat, 2016, p. 36).
They acknowledge that humans are meaning-making creatures who construct their
social realities – whilst also affirming that these realities are tangible, intelligible
and exist in some sense beyond their members' imaginative construction. Qualitative approaches to research are now favoured, with particular attention afforded to
detailed ethnographic observation and the reflective processes of action research.
With many scholars now speaking the same research language, inter-institutional
and international research collaboration has been enlivened. There is a welcome
sense of confidence in the importance and efficacy of research in practical theology
compared with the situation a decade ago.

However, this positive assessment should not prevent critical evaluation of our
current context. What issues are at stake in the contemporary consensus? What
new academic developments in social research might need to be noted? And what
visions do we have for the future of practical theological research?

Concerns about consensus

Practical theology researchers appear more relaxed about processes of self-
identification and methodological allegiance than formerly. However, this smooth
surface reflects a rather disturbing homogeneity in outlook. Despite the healthy ecumenism evident in the networks discussed above, considerable theological consensus
is shared by those within them who would identify as radical Catholics, progressive
Barthians or inclusive evangelicals. All tend to hold the theological tradition as normative; believe that theological issues should set the research agenda; assume that the
location of research should be ecclesial; and display concerns that the methods of
social science should not lead the ecclesial researcher astray. Thus Swinton insists that
practical theological researchers must resist the temptations that come from 'those
who have fallen in love with the social sciences and want to offer them too much
creative power over theology' (2011, p. 92). Indeed, some commend a 'Chalcedonian'
model for research in practical theology (Swinton and Mowat, 2016, pp. 79–86).

From this perspective, there is a clear distinction between theology and the social
sciences, with the former enjoying precedence (see Swinton and Mowat, 2016).
Others hold less firmly to such boundaries, affirming that the simultaneously human
and divine nature of the Church should challenge both the research agenda and the
theological tradition (Ward, 2011, pp. 2–3). In practice, however, an ecclesial focus

and context in the bulk of research undertaken militates against forms of theological critique and development long regarded as important by feminist and liberation-orientated scholars. As our case study has already highlighted, these scholars tended to be less interested in exploring the practices of faith and more interested in how social analysis, in various forms, becomes revelatory of divine imperatives requiring transformative responses. An ecclesial turn may downplay this important under-standing of practice – one that has inspired much of our own work in the field (Graham, 1996; Pattison, 1994, 1997, 2013).

Catholic, evangelical and reformed researchers do not share a single vision of the Church. There are significant differences between those who see the Church as *lumen gentium*, a light to the world, in the spirit of the Second Vatican Council and those who see the Church as a radically alternative community necessarily in contradiction to its cultural context, seeking to be obedient to its prophetic vocation – although there is now more commonality between these perspectives than formerly (see Graham, Walton and Ward, 2005, pp. 100–102). Nor do practical theological colleagues working on ecclesial research have a narrow, exclusive view of mission. We share with them an understanding that the Church is required to be prophetic and active in the world. For them, however, the ecclesial location is assumed to be the base from which to address these issues. But our reading of Christian traditions leads us to the view that the divine calling frequently addresses us from unexpected and 'unholy' places beyond Church as we currently understand it. Thus, our fundamental world-views and assumptions about where theology is to be done, and how and where research might be undertaken, differs.

FUNDAMENTAL THEOLOGICAL ASSUMPTIONS DETERMINE METHODS AND APPROACHES

John Swinton, a prominent academic practical theological researcher, has written extensively about theology and methods (Swinton and Mowat, 2016). He explains how his theological assumptions articulate with the selection and use of methodologies and methods.

My starting position is that practical theology has a certain telos, or perhaps better an eschatology, that locates it in the world in a quite particular way. It begins with the assumption that all research occurs within creation. So, certainly we can and should examine human culture, neurology, biology or psychology, but all of these things have an underlying theological context. We don't do our fieldwork research and then reflect on it theologically. Rather all of it is always done within a theological context. Methods from varying worldviews are grafted in and sanctified, that is, put to the purposes of the coming Kingdom. That being so, practical theological research is always participatory; participation relates to the continuing redemptive work of God in, to and for the world.

That is the basic methodology that I assume underpins all of my work and I gauge the appropriateness and effectiveness of my methods accordingly. As a practical theologian, I perceive myself as working in the Kingdom and for the Kingdom.

Methods are modes of participation in such a task. They are basically tools that we use to gather the information that we want to look at. At this level they are purely pragmatic. However, at another level, they are deeply formative. Methods provide a lens through which we examine the world. A lens allows us to see some things very clearly, but in seeing them clearly, we see other things less clearly. Methods are therefore guides which have a tendency to determine what we see. For example, a psychological method will allow us to examine certain aspects of religious behaviour in great detail. So we might conclude via a psychological method (questionnaires and statistical analysis) that prayer and meditation are 'good for our health'. However, if we allow a psychological method/lens to determine what we mean by 'health', then we have problems. Psychological health/ worldview, often means the absence of anxiety and restlessness; theological health is always about the presence of God irrespective of our current psychological state. Using the methods and methodologies of psychology we may produce good psychological research, but if we accept that without critical theological reflection based on a quite different worldview, then the faithfulness of our research comes under scrutiny. Psychological methods can be useful of course, but only when they are carried out and interpreted within a theological context.

New academic developments in social research

In this book we cannot provide detailed accounts of all new trends arising in social research. However, in concluding this chapter, we want to draw attention to two significant developments deserving attention in practical theology. The first is an increased openness to, and positive appreciation of, spirituality and religion in the world of social research. This challenges the common assumption that there is a lack of interest in this area amongst social scientists, a conviction that was axiomatic in empirical theology. The second is a new interest and engagement with research methods traditionally associated with the creative arts rather than the social sciences.

The spiritual turn

A new eagerness to engage with religion and spirituality has arisen in the world of social theory. This springs from belated acknowledgement that religion continues to play a significant role in contemporary culture that will not disappear. Many 'secular' scholars, including feminists, are now reassessing their approach to religion, recognising that spiritual commitments and religious understandings cannot be unthinkingly dismissed as socially reactionary (Badiou, 2003; Žižec and Milbank, 2009; Braidotti, 2013; Calhoun, Mendieta and Van Antwerpen, 2013). They may actually contribute positively to challenging and changing alienating and oppressive practices.

The recognition that we are entering what is widely viewed as a 'postsecular' age (Gorski et al., 2012) is also changing approaches to social research – once viewed as an 'enchantment-free' zone (Knowles and Cole, 2008a, p. 60). Leading social researchers are reconsidering their previous reticence towards naming spiritual concerns:

> If we had to do it all over again we would make values, or more correctly axiology (the branch of philosophy dealing with ethics, aesthetics, and religion) a part of the basic foundational philosophical dimensions of paradigm proposal. Doing so would enable us to see the embeddedness of ethics within, not external to, paradigms . . . and would contribute to the consideration of and dialogue about the role of spirituality in human inquiry. Arguably, axiology has been "defined out of" scientific inquiry for no larger reason than it also concerns "religion". But defining "religion" broadly to encompass spirituality would move constructivists closer to participative inquirers and would move critical theorists closer to both (owing to their concern with liberation from oppression and freeing of the human spirit, both profoundly spiritual concerns).
>
> *(Lincoln and Guba, 2005, p. 169)*

Some scholars explicitly affirm that ethical social research must be transformative, even utopian (such as Denzin, 2010, pp. 261–262). This indicates an important shift in thinking. It is connected to the macro trends in social theory and to local developments within the social research world itself. Amongst these are:

- An acknowledgement that if qualitative research is fundamentally concerned with meaning making processes it is academically unjustifiable to maintain silence about the spiritual meanings people place upon experiences;
- The development of postcolonial research methodologies affirming spiritual worldviews and employing spiritual practices (such as deep attentiveness and community consciousness) to engage with social phenomena;
- The turn towards creative and arts-based research methods as a means of social research.

This last development in particular has the potential fundamentally to shift understandings of what constitutes fruitful research practice in practical theology.

Creative research practice

USING CREATIVE WRITING TO DEEPEN UNDERSTANDING AND ANALYSIS

A professional doctoral researcher, Steve Dixon, formerly an adviser on children's ministry, used creative writing in attempting to deepen his understanding and analysis of adults working with children. His 2012 thesis, 'In the light of a child: adults discerning the gift of being' is available at https://chesterrep.openrepository.com/cdr/bitstream/10034/253596/8/stephen+william+dixon-dprof.pdf Dixon. See also Dixon (2014). He explains and gives an example of his approach here.

Linked to George Fox's view of theological 'knowing', and my long-standing acceptance of the position that we can never fully share or know the experience of another, my epistemology has always been heavily based on my personal experience. This probably led me to frame a research question examining the personal effects experienced by those working with children in the Church, and it certainly caused me to make significant use of autoethnography in conducting the research.

The prominence this approach gives to creative writing particularly recommended itself, as I have been a writer since childhood. My first degree was in literature and my worldview, as a child of the 60s, has always given a high value to all areas of creative expression and exploration.

In my research, I used creative writing to portray analysis and produce reflective dialogue between theological perspectives, and I employed a literary criticism approach to reflect on personal narrative. A lasting effect of this experience has been to bring more of the researcher's rigor to my own creative writing.

As an example, my research revealed that I had 'issues' with being under and exercising 'authority'. To reflect on this, I 'free associated' personal experiences linked to the topic. I jotted down one of them as:

Dad – ulcerated & worried by his responsibility

I created a composite narrative from my experiences, including the following passage in which 'Wilf' represents my father:

Wilf was scratching his head over a set of ledgers. He was trying to make an impossible situation work out right. He knew before he started that it was impossible. But he had to try to do something. The firm was sliding slowly beneath the waves. Like the Titanic, it would take some considerable time to go down. There was still dancing going on in the ballroom – or the boardroom. But the hull was ripped and they were shipping water. And only Wilf seemed to be able to see it, or to care . . .

Wilf felt a sharp twinge in his stomach. This always came on when he wrestled with the impossible. It was about as near to panic as he ever got in his life. There was no point crying and moaning about things. Just get on with it. That's how he'd been brought up. 'KBO' as Churchill used to say – 'Keep buggering on'. But there was just this stab in the stomach – his body protesting. He closed the ledger. No amount of staring at it would make money appear where it wasn't. He was in his office – more like a kiosk really, in the middle of the factory floor. The women's sewing machines

> *were hammering away all around him like something about to reach a crescendo, but never quite getting there.*
>
> *The narrative was 'automatic' – written without pause for thought or revision. I analysed its uses of emotive language to reveal major themes. One of these was 'Fighting, drudgery, suffering and torture', exemplified in the Wilf passage by [terms such as]:*
>
> > *"wrestled with the impossible"*
> > *"hammering away"*
> > *"something about to reach a crescendo"*
>
> *I sent my narrative, the themes, and some 'difficult questions' they raised to others who could comment from social (SOC) and theological perspectives; and informed by their responses I created a 'conversation' between myself (SD) and these other voices in the same 'automatic' way as the narrative. The following is a snatch:*
>
> SD   *Why shouldn't we avoid pain? If God's made a world in which pain is inevitable, where's the love – or sense in that? When we find ourselves in an impossible situation, is that God's doing – should we just accept our lot and 'keep buggering on' as my dad did, and Churchill said.*
> SOC   *I suppose we have to say from a purely factual point of view – everything seemed impossible to Churchill, but thanks to him buggering on rather than buggering off, things took a turn for the better.*
> SD   *Not for my dad though.*
> SOC   *I wonder. Did nothing good come out of his efforts?*

The UK Arts and Humanities Research Council evaluates research projects according to how they advance 'creativity, insights, knowledge and understanding' in a particular area (www.ahrc.ac.uk/funding/research/researchfundingguide/introduction/definitionofresearch/ [Accessed 15th February 2017]). Conventional social methods of social research achieve much of this. However, it is increasingly recognised that the creative arts also generate insights about humans and their worlds in ways that enhance understanding. These can stand alongside ways of knowing that have looked to the sciences for their epistemological reference point.

> Arts-informed research brings together the systematic and rigorous qualities of scientific inquiry with the artistic and imaginative qualities of the arts. In doing so the process of researching becomes creative and responsive.
>
> *(Cole and Knowles, 2001, pp. 10–11)*

Greater openness to creative approaches has been evolving in social research. This has been part of an epistemological shift, particularly related to feminism and other emancipatory movements, which has highlighted the significance of reflexivity, standpoint epistemology and the active identification of the research practitioner in the research process (see chapter 2 above). Alongside this, the increasing importance of hermeneutical (focused upon interpretation rather than explanation) and phenomenological (stressing the importance of the lifeworld and embodied location) methodologies has paved the way for acceptance of hybrid modes of inquiry such as autoethnography. These cannot be confined within traditional social scientific forms (Brearley and Hamm, 2009; Denzin and Lincoln, 2005).

Autoethnography is now becoming a very significant methodological resource in practical theology (see Pattison, 2000, pp. 5–6; Walton, 2014). It gestures towards ethnography as this has developed in anthropology and beyond, seeking to understand a cultural issue from the vantage point of personal experience. However, it also looks towards the arts, employing the tools and techniques of creative non-fiction and creating invocations of situations often occluded or marginalised in social discourse. These might include, for example, experiences of mental distress, enjoyment of material and bodily pleasures, the search for sexual identity or role-disempowerment. In a refusal to 'leave themselves off the page' (Graham, 2013, p. 150), practical theologians have turned to autoethnography, often in fruitful combination with other methodologies, in order consciously to 'write themselves in' to their own research texts. These works often display challenging intimacy and accounts of particularity that would be difficult to comprehend in more conventional forms.

Creative writing is only one arts-based method now employed by social researchers. From photography to performance-based interventions, from bricolage to body art, a diverse range of media are adopted to explore social phenomena (Higgs et al., 2011; Knowles and Cole, 2008b). Creative freedom enriches research by adding new tools to those conventionally employed. More importantly, it enriches it by adding another layer to the concentric circles discussed above. In arts-based research generating knowledge is a making process.

Adopting this perspective, we need to place 'making' after 'method' as a vital stage in the research journey. No methods, however mechanical or quantitative, produce meanings automatically, channeling data into predetermined outcomes. Researchers *always* shape and craft the materials their research has produced into new forms. These do not present a mirror to some pre-existing reality. Rather, they are new makings that change the way we see the world and so our basic epistemology and ontology. They generate insight.

An understanding of 'research as making' is deeply consonant with the approaches to practical theology discussed in this book (Walton, 2012). Realising that as researchers we may also become creative practitioners is energising and liberating. Furthermore, thinking about research as creative practice (as has been common now within the arts for many decades) allows the rediscovery of ways of linking back to older ways of understanding practical theology in terms of the arts of ministry. This approach was subjected to considerable critique during the latter years of the twentieth century for being overly clerical and skills-based (for a discussion of this debate see Miller-McLemore, 2007). This critique was salutary.

But something important was lost when reflections in depth on homiletics, liturgy, sacred music and spiritual discipline were displaced in practical theology classrooms, and curricula. A renewed engagement is now possible with these areas of creative practice, understood to be places where insight and knowledge are generated in ways that may be just as important (theologically, ecclesially and politically) as what takes place in congregational studies and public theology.

USING CREATIVE AND COLLABORATIVE METHODS IN RESEARCH PRACTICE

Clare Louise Radford is a doctoral researcher with experience of a range of faith-based community and anti-poverty work undertaking a study of practices of sharing experiences of marginalisation to create social change. Here, she reflects on the value of using participative, creative and collaborative methods throughout the research process.

Practical theological research is a reflexive process in which worldview and research methodology are reshaped alongside one another. The feminist, creative, collaborative methodology I work with encourages the recognition that, as a researcher, I am being shaped by the research process. Simultaneously, I am also shaping the research.

A belief in the agency and creativity of participants means being open to what emerges in the research process, both from being with participants and communities, and from being with texts, theories, images and the material world.

Currently, I partner with socio-economically marginalised groups to research the ways in which speaking out about their experiences can create change. Taking seriously participants' creative agency is therefore also an important political act, recognising the margins as spaces of critical resistance and people as interpreting the meaning of their own lives.

I use methods such as interviews and participant observation alongside creative workshops and research journals. In workshops and interviews participants emphasised the importance of creating situations in which those listening can reciprocate and respond sensitively to the speaker, recognising the reality of their experiences.

As a result, as well as using creative methods for gathering participant insights, I have been making creative pieces such as artists' books that reflect the key insights, themes and questions arising from this research, sharing these pieces with participants. This has enabled the research to continue developing collaboratively, in this instance into a community curation project.

As well as enabling accountability, using creative pieces continues the shared process of making meaning between the participants and me. Rather than checking that 'my interpretation' is correct, responding creatively has become crucial for keeping the research open to the nuanced and multiple meanings emerging in collaboration with others. This reminds me to look not for what is academically viable, but for what is life-giving, liberating and of the divine.

What if?

It may be easy to talk about the enriching possibilities of arts-based research. However, art disturbs and discomforts as much as it refreshes and renews. Embracing creative methods may enrich research, but it may also disrupt it, making it more difficult. Creative methods do not take us neatly from A to B (Behar, 2003). They are ways of setting out towards the unknown or navigating in the dark. They are faith based, certainly – but this is a faith characterised by the surrealist principle that the experimental 'joining together of incongruous things can bring about an unexpected awareness, a slant of sharp, sublime light, an edgy form of knowing that dares to surprise the knower too' (Behar, 2003, p. 24).

Herein lies the chief difference between artistic and conventional research methods. We may embark on research processes assuming that they will help make the world more comprehensible, intelligible and habitable for us, that the research journey will lead us safely home. However, research through creative practice is a wandering, wayward kind of exercise. The researcher often begins their making process with little idea of what will eventually be revealed as the making takes shape. They cherish the expectation that what they make will probably render the world stranger, not more familiar to them. In other words they are looking for something they do not expect to find. The only way to encounter it is through the leap of faith that is the creative act. As in any artistic or craft practice,

> New knowledge is made possible through the materiality of practice itself. Such practices can be of the most challenging order . . . the most revealing and moving emotionally, the most embodied physically or the most disquieting politically. Often they expose the cutting edge of imaginative ideas and new forms of thought as they reveal uncertainties in the human condition or subvert known forms of language, text and social practices.
>
> *(Grierson and Brearley, 2009, p. 5)*

Can a discipline so earnestly titled 'practical' affirm and benefit from expanding its own horizons to engage with creative research methods that, whilst interesting and engaging, do not appear to be as self-evidently 'useful' as the established analytic tools with which it is familiar? For many of us, a main guiding principle of practical theology to date has been to undertake work that makes a practical difference to the life of Church and world. The 'so what?' question is one which we apply as a litmus test to judge the validity and appropriateness of all our scholarship (Pattison, 2007b, p. 8). However, perhaps it is now time to recognise an alternative plane upon which our research might function.

The challenging work of Terry Veling has consistently called upon the practical theological community to realise that making a difference is not simply a matter of asking 'so what?' but also 'what if?' (Veling, 2016). What if we employ our mystical, prophetic and spiritual inheritance in order to envision new possibilities in theological thinking, social engagement and ecclesial practice? For Veling (2016, p. 127), this imaginative process requires a poetic turn in practical theology. This welcome development could generate renewed understandings of practice as *creative making* which would provide a counterbalance to the notions of *useful doing* which currently form the ideological subtext to our work.

References

Badiou, A., 2003. *Saint Paul: The foundation of universalism.* Translated from French by R. Brassier. Stanford: Stanford University Press.

Behar, R., 2003. Ethnography and the book that was lost. *Ethnography*, 4(1), pp. 15–39.

Boff, L. and Boff, C., 1987. *Introducing liberation theology.* Tunbridge Wells: Burns and Oates.

Bons-Storm, R., 1996. *The incredible woman: Listening to women's silences in pastoral care and counseling.* Nashville, TN: Abingdon Press.

Bons-Storm, R. and Ackermann, D., 1997. *Practical theology in feminist perspective.* Campen: Kok Pharos.

Braidotti, R., 2013. *The posthuman.* Cambridge: Polity Press.

Brearley, L. and Hamm, T., 2009. Stories from the spaces between indigenous and non-indigenous knowledge systems. In: E. Grierson and L. Brearley, eds., *Creative arts research: Narratives of methodologies and practices.* Rotterdam, Boston and Taipei: Sense Publishers. pp. 33–54.

Calhoun, C., Mendieta, E. and Van Antwerpen, J., eds., 2013. *Habermas and religion.* Cambridge: Polity Press.

Cameron, H., Bhatti, D., Duce, C., Sweeney, J., and Watkins, C., 2010. *Talking about God in practice: Theological action research and practical theology.* London: SCM Press.

Chandler, Q., 2015. *Conversations beyond the threshold: An exploration of theological reflection among lay ministry students.* Unpublished PrD thesis. Anglia Ruskin University. Available at: http://arro.anglia.ac.uk/700185/

Cole, A.L. and Knowles, J.G., eds., 2001. *Lives in context: The art of life history research.* Walnut Creek, CA: Alta Mira Press.

Denzin, N.K., 2010. *The qualitative manifesto: A call to arms.* Walnut Creek, CA: Left Coast Press.

Denzin, N.K. and Lincoln, Y.S., 2005. 8th and 9th moment in qualitative research. In: N.K. Denzin and Y.S. Lincoln, eds., *The Sage handbook of qualitative research.* 3rd ed. Thousand Oaks, CA: Sage. pp. 1115–1126.

Dixon, S.W., 2014. What's so special about children? A reconsideration of the use made of scriptures such as Matthew 18: 1–5 in advocating the importance of children in the church. *Journal of Childhood and Religion*, 5(1), pp. 1–33.

Dreyer, J., 2016. Knowledge, subjectivity, (de)coloniality, and the conundrum of reflexivity. In: B.J. Miller-McLemore and J. Mercer, eds., *Conundrums in practical theology.* Leiden: Brill. pp. 90–109.

Farley, E., 1983. *Theologia: Fragmentation and unity in theological education.* Philadelphia: Fortress Press.

Gorski, P.S., Kim, D.K., Torpey, J. and VanAntwerpen, J., eds., 2012. *The post-secular in question: Religion in contemporary society.* New York: New York University Press.

Graham, E., 1995. *Making the difference: Gender, personhood and theology.* London: Mowbray.

Graham, E., 1996. *Transforming practice: Pastoral theology in an age of uncertainty.* London: Mowbray.

Graham, E., 2013. Is practical theology a form of 'action research'? *International Journal of Practical Theology*, 17(1), pp. 1–31.

Graham, E., Walton, H. and Ward, F., 2005. *Theological reflection: Methods.* London: SCM Press.

Grierson, E. and Brearley, L., 2009. Ways of framing. In: E. Grierson and L. Brearley, eds., *Creative arts research: Narratives of methodologies and practices.* Rotterdam, Boston and Taipei: Sense Publishers. pp. 1–16.

Higgs, J., Titchen, A., Horfall, D. and Bridges, D., 2011. *Creative spaces for qualitative researching.* Rotterdam, Boston and Taipei: Sense Publishers.

Hochschild, A.R., 2016. *Strangers in their own land: Anger and mourning on the American right.* New York: The New Press.

Kappler, W.A., 2009. *Communication habits for the pilgrim church.* New York: Peter Lang Publishing.

Kay, W.K., 2003. Empirical theology: A natural development? *Heythrop Journal,* 44(2), pp. 167–181.

Knowles, J.G. and Cole, A.L., 2008a. Arts-informed research. In: J.G. Knowles and A.L. Cole, eds., *Handbook of the arts in qualitative research.* Thousand Oaks, CA: Sage. pp. 55–70.

Knowles, J.G. and Cole, A.L., eds., 2008b. *Handbook of the arts in qualitative research.* Thousand Oaks, CA: Sage.

Le Cornu, A., 2005. People's ways of believing: Learning processes and faith outcomes. *Religious Education,* 100(4), pp. 425–446.

Le Cornu, A. and University of Surrey, School of Arts, Department of Educational Studies, 2004. *People's ways of believing: Learning processes and faith outcomes.* Guildford: University of Surrey, School of Arts, Department of Educational Studies.

Lincoln, Y.S. and Guba, E.G., 2005. Paradigmatic controversies, contradictions and emerging confluences. In: N.K. Denzin and Y.S. Lincoln, eds., *The Sage handbook of qualitative research.* 3rd ed. Thousand Oaks, CA: Sage. pp. 163–188.

Miller-McLemore, B.J., 1994. *Also a mother: Work and family as theological dilemma.* Abingdon: Nashville.

Miller-McLemore, B.J., 2007. The clerical paradigm: A fallacy of misplaced concreteness. *International Journal of Practical Theology,* 11(3), pp. 19–38.

Miller-McLemore, B.J. and Gill-Austen, B.L., 1999. *Feminist and womanist pastoral theology.* Nashville: Abingdon Press.

Mockler, N., 2011. Being me: In search of authenticity. In: J. Higgs, A. Titchen, D. Horsfall and D. Bridges, eds., *Creative spaces for qualitative researching.* Rotterdam and Boston: Sense Publishers. pp. 159–168.

Moessner, J., ed., 1996. *Through the eyes of women: Insights for pastoral care.* Minneapolis: Augsburg Fortress.

Moschella, M.C., 2016. *Caring for joy: Narrative, theology and practice.* Leiden: Brill.

Pattison, S., 1994. *Pastoral care and liberation theology.* Cambridge: Cambridge University Press.

Pattison, S., 1997. *The faith of the managers: When management becomes religion.* London: Cassell.

Pattison, S., 2000. *Shame: Theory, therapy, theology.* Cambridge: Cambridge University Press.

Pattison, S., 2007a. *The challenge of practical theology.* London: Jessica Kingsley.

Pattison, S., 2007b. *Seeing things: Deepening relations with visual artefacts.* London: SCM Press.

Pattison, S., 2013. *Saving face: Enfacement, shame, theology.* Farnham: Ashgate.

Swinton, J., 2011. 'Where is your church?' Moving toward a hospitable and sanctified ethnography. In: P. Ward, ed., *Perspectives on ecclesiology and ethnography.* Grand Rapids: Eerdmans. pp. 71–94.

Swinton, J. and Mowat, H., 2016. *Practical theology and qualitative research.* 2nd ed. London: SCM Press.

Tracy, D., 1981. *The analogical imagination: Christian theology and the culture of pluralism.* London: SCM Press.

van der Ven, J., 1988. Practical theology: From applied to empirical theology. *Empirical Theology*, 1, pp. 7–27.

van der Ven, J., 1993. *Practical theology: An empirical approach*. Kampen: Kok.

Veling, T., 2016. A reserve of vitality: Poetics and practical theology. In: C. Wolfteich and A. Dillen, eds., *Catholic approaches in practical theology*. Leuven: Peeters. pp. 117–131.

Walton, H., 2012. Poetics. In: B. J. Miller-McLemore, ed., *The Wiley-Blackwell companion to practical theology*. Oxford: Wiley-Blackwell, pp. 173–182.

Walton, H., 2014. *Writing methods in theological reflection*. London: SCM Press.

Walton, H., 2016. The history of feminist theology in the academy: An autoethnographic research journey. In: L. Gemzöe, M.L. Keinänen and A. Maddrell, eds., *Contemporary encounters in gender and religion: European perspectives*. Cham, Switzerland: Palgrave Macmillan. pp. 285–306.

Ward, P., 2008. *Participation and mediation: A practical theology for the liquid church*. London: SCM Press.

Ward, P., ed., 2011. *Perspectives on ecclesiology and ethnography*. Grand Rapids: Eerdmans.

Watkins, C., 2015. Practising ecclesiology: From product to process. *Ecclesial Practices*, 2(1), pp. 23–39.

Wigg-Stevenson, N., 2013. Reflexive theology: A preliminary proposal. *Practical Matters*. Available at: http://wp.me/p6QAmj-sP [Accessed 10 February 2017].

Žižec, S. and Milbank, J., 2009. *The monstrosity of Christ: Paradox or dialectic?* Cambridge, MA: MIT Press.

7

ETHOS, PROCESS AND OUTCOMES

If we all lived on our own, outside any kind of human group, we would not need to think about ethics. Ethics in its broadest sense is closely related to ethos, the nature, character and purpose of the communities to which we belong and whose ends we wish to help realise. It concerns what is broadly conceived of as 'the good': whether that is defined in terms of orienting oneself towards particular virtues, maximising the good of the greatest number, a categorical imperative, or even how various goods and benefits may be distributed (Junker-Kenny, 2013). It is another way of understanding perspectives and limitations as well as possibilities – issues with which we have been concerned throughout this book as part of our discussion of the relationship between experience, practice, theology and tradition.

Within this overall vision and set of purposes, characterised very broadly as ethics, it is possible then to work down to specific commandments, guidance and practices that help to realise that ethos at a procedural and practical level. But in this chapter we will try to place practical theological research within the 'higher' or 'meta-level' of thinking about the broad context, values, significance and accountabilities that come from engaging in investigation that both involves humans (including researchers themselves) and is undertaken to promote desirable change and transformation at a number of different levels. The chapter broadly follows the process of research from motivation through research design and fieldwork to analysis and presentation of data. At each stage, we present questions and issues that researchers will find it useful to reflect upon in their pursuit of 'the good' in research.

At the outset, we make two important assumptions, picking up on themes in this book. First, we suggest that the approaches and methods used in research, even the idea of research, is part of constructing a value-laden moral world-view (Browning, 1991; Cresswell, 2013). All approaches to research, together with particular research methods, bear witness to particular ways of understanding and inhabiting the world. They are transmitters of particular 'action-guiding worldviews' (Pattison,

2007, p. 11), vehicles of a moral and ethical approach to the world in which certain things are taken to be significant whilst others may be ignored or devalued. Indeed, they help to construct and maintain the worlds that they claim to investigate. See-ing and attending to some kinds of data is to privilege and make them visible, while making other things less significant. So the very matter of setting out to do research is not just about exploring a world that is essentially independent and observable, but bringing that world and the subjects/objects of research into being (Cresswell, 2013).

Secondly, and in line with this perception, the process of doing research is as sig-nificant as any outcomes in creating a moral universe. Ethics and morality, broadly understood, are not just about the effects of the results of research. The process of doing research is itself inexorably involved in affirming or questioning world-views and practices.

We do not wish to consign the business of meeting the specific ethical require-ments to the various codes that exist in Universities and professional bodies, along with primers in ethical theory and practice (Russell, Hogan and Junker-Kenny, 2013; Danchev and Ross, 2014). These are, of course, important. But our purpose here is to continue to situate practical theological inquiry within a broad quest for complex transformational knowledge that is responsive and responsible to a variety of different communities. Practical theological research should be ethically aware, as well as theological, all the way through, in its ends, approaches, methods and outcomes, not just in its procedural ethical phase of empirical investigation – where that occurs.

A key word throughout the discussion of ethics in this chapter is *trust*. Can we be trusted, can we trust ourselves, to be acting appropriately? How do we know what methods and evidence to trust? What sort of trust can we repose in the endeavour as a whole and in the outcomes of it?

Another of the ongoing themes we are exploring in practical theology in general which also pertains here is that of *complexity*. The fullness of contemporary experi-ence, including experience of the divine, is diverse and complex. So the business of finding one's way through and around it is not a simple, linear matter. Thinking about all this through the lens of ethics then helps to usefully enrich the complexity of undertaking inquiry in practical theology, providing another 'take' on it.

A third theme is that of *relationality*. Practical theology is not undertaken in a vacuum or for its own sake or theoretical beauty. So having a clear understanding of responsibilities and expectations in relationships and in our accountability to wider groups of stakeholders is an important underpinning part of understanding and developing practical theological inquiry.

Finally, but perhaps most importantly, the theme of *vulnerability* enters in here. If theological activity endeavours generally to be 'healing work' (Bondi, 1995), then researchers in this area must seek to be aware of their capacity for wounding and being wounded, for healing and being healed. This could be called risk manage-ment of, and for, self and others. Research is not risk or cost free. It promises gains and potential losses. These must be consciously assayed at all points in the research process, from initial conceptualisation to final publication.

Honouring ethics in research is not simply a matter of compliance but essentially a matter of desiring and seeking 'the good' – which encompasses excellence, justice and integrity.

SEEKING 'THE GOOD' IN PRACTICAL THEOLOGICAL RESEARCH

In his professional doctoral research ('Supporting and interpreting virtue: a chaplaincy narrative', submitted 2017, http://arro.anglia.ac.uk/701524/) Peter Hayler decided to work directly on identifying how he might use his professional efforts to good purpose in trying to pursue the good of an institution using the classic Aristotelian and Christian virtues as a guide not only to the ends, but also to the process and methods of the research.

During my first year as Chaplain to Cambridge University Staff, there was a great deal to get to grips with. Universities are complex, yet rather atomised institutions. My work among administrative staff in many different secular disciplines was to make a pastoral contribution to their wellbeing. I had attend to the growing multi-faith realities of the university community liaising with Equality & Diversity officers, in the face of new equalities legislation, whilst also facilitating access to a multi-faith space.

Quickly, I had to face fundamental ethical questions: What shall I do with my time, effort and other resources . . . why . . . and to what end?

Alasdair MacIntyre attempts to rehabilitate the Classical and Scholastic tradition of virtue ethics for late modernity. Locating my work within this philosophical approach, I came to understand the place of chaplaincy within the polity of the university better. In my work, I was constantly deliberating with others over means and ends (prudence), seeking a fair deal within the constraints of the law for those on the margins (justice), learning to rein in my passions (moderation) or to let the reins out appropriately (courage). As a Christian, I sought to be guided by the virtues of faith, hope and love. Here was virtuous chaplaincy in a nutshell.

I developed this approach into an intentional form of reflective practice, meeting with six non-chaplaincy colleagues for five terms, to narrate our work for the common good of staff wellbeing under the titles of the virtues. With my interpretative support, they found this exercise accessible and meaningful. More importantly, I witnessed them experiencing a sort of micro-political solidarity with one another, an antidote to their experience of silo-ed working and isolation.

Working as a researching professional on a doctoral programme opened up a critical space in which I was able to conceive, enact and inhabit a new, viable and fruitful model of chaplaincy, in my own context and to open up a new, practical, ethical dimension within chaplaincy studies.

Reflexivity and motivation

[G]ood practice in research ethics begins with a commitment to self-critical reflection and with a determination to pursue each research programme with integrity and honesty.
(Hogan, 2013, pp. 4–5)

Hogan's comment about reflexivity reinforces our invitation in this book to become more consciously aware of who you are as a researcher, what you bring to the research in terms of hopes, values and aspirations and what you hope to gain from it. So far, we have constantly drawn attention to the importance of researchers taking themselves and their own contemporary experience seriously as a first, reflexive move. If honesty is the foundation for trust in ethics and in everyday life, the first place to be honest is in looking at yourself and what you bring to any putative research project: your own motives, values, strengths and weaknesses.

This may embrace a broad spectrum, from professional advancement, to social idealism, or even a passionate need to address a pressing social problem. It will include personal dispositions that draw you to particular issues and methods (or push you away from them), your ideological pre-commitments, for example to a feminist view of the world, and even your skills and temperament, such as your willingness to be in highly social situations or your ability to analyse statistical data.

THE POWER OF PERSONAL MOTIVATION IN RESEARCH

Ros Lane, a former Prison Chaplain, reflects on a deeply personal motivation for her research. An incident from her own past made her acutely sensitive to similar un-met needs in those with whom she worked and to the lack of research or understanding around a particular phenomenon: see 'Imprisoned grief: a theological, spiritual and practical response' (Doctor of Professional Studies in Practical Theology dissertation, submitted 2015, http://chesterrep. openrepository.com/cdr/handle/10034/620349).

My interest in one of the concepts at the heart of this research – that of 'disenfranchised grief' – had its origins not just in my professional life but also my personal life. I found myself a "disenfranchised griever" when my grandmother died whilst I was away from home during my curacy in Huddersfield, aged twenty five. I could easily identify that being away from family and friends was not an ideal position in which to grieve. In my role as a prison chaplain I was conscious that there was often little consideration given to the feelings and emotions that prisoners experienced on receiving sad news. This weighed heavily on top of the experience of loss through imprisonment, hence their experiences of grief and loss accumulated.

A random group of practical theology doctoral students offered a wide range of motives for undertaking their research:

'Research allows me to question things.'

'I need to get a job.'

'Being a doctoral researcher means people take me more seriously when I talk.'

'I want to understand the place of women from ethnic minorities in my religious denomination.'

'I need a language to describe the experience of ministry so I can communicate it to others.'

'I need a goal and a structure to make me study.'

'I want the opportunity to be able to speak into my organisation.'

'I am making up for educational opportunities not grasped in the past.'

'I want to reflect on my work.'

'I want to prove to myself that I can do this work.'

MOTIVATION IN PRACTICAL THEOLOGICAL RESEARCH

One of the authors, Stephen, here describes his very mixed motives in undertaking research at the beginning of his academic postgraduate career. The thesis he describes was submitted in 1983 and became, in a modified version Pattison, 1994.

I don't think I really understood or was totally honest with myself about my motives for doing a PhD project when I started. Looking back, I think I had two main conscious motives. First, I was very committed to making the world a more just place and saw the PhD as a way for doing this. I was a card-carrying socialist and wanted to see the world becoming more egalitarian and for there to be radical social change that would privilege the under-privileged. Second, if I am really honest, I wanted to increase my own sense of intellectual and personal importance in the world. I studied the situation of people with mental health problems in a psychiatric institution. This brought me face to face with social injustice and an analysis of why people experienced extreme inequality in society generally and in health care in particular. However, because of my humanities education I shied away from doing empirical work and did the thesis basically conceptually from secondary sources.

I think I had mistaken ideas about what a PhD research project could 'do' in the world. I thought rather grandiosely that one only had to write such a large work to 'make a difference', and that it would create a stir with its radical analysis. However, I did succeed in buttressing my own sense of ability and importance in the world and doing the degree ended up with my going into an academic job, which was not one of my conscious ambitions when I started. Whether anyone else benefitted in the long run, which was my original overt intention, I don't know, though I think they probably did marginally judging from written citations the work. My greatest regret is that I saw the project as a very personal explora-tion and did not involve others, particularly health care service users, in it more – a painful irony, because it was about community and justice. There is a sense in which I think I 'used' the people and situation I was concerned about for my own ends – ouch!

My advice to myself if I were starting again would be: 1) Try to be more con-scious of your real motives, altruistic, selfish or other; 2) Keep research degrees and projects in proportion and understand what they are and what they can/ cannot achieve – research might make a difference but it may not be much of a difference or even the difference that was initially hoped for; 3) Be aware that you may not achieve what you set out to achieve, but may do something else inadvertently; 4) Grandiosity and a desire to enhance one's personal significance can be good motivators, but you need to have a community of reference who care about the work as well or all the responsibility and pressure devolves onto one person – you!

Readers will have very different experiences and backgrounds from the people in the vignettes above. But it is worth thinking about issues that may affect your basic approach to research such as:

- What are my basic social, religious and other beliefs and values?
- What are my motives and aspirations in undertaking research?
- What benefits will accrue to me and to others from the project?
- What enthusiasms, passions, fears and aversions are aroused by the project?
- What are my hopes for myself and others in doing research?
- What are my own vulnerabilities and what am I putting at risk in myself by undertaking this research project?

This kind of reflexive self-knowledge may be very helpful in designing and executing a project in ethically responsible ways. Reflexivity and self-monitoring in research represent the practices that will safeguard ethical thinking and acting, alerting us particularly at times when we are suppressing or 'blocking' our own critical perspective (McNiff, 2017, pp. 170–172). Indeed, reflexivity may help to improve the quality of the project in making it more complex and self-aware. It is also an act of self-care. This is important as researchers must treat themselves as significant moral subjects as well as any others with whom they work. You are required to attend to yourself as well as others in undertaking research as yourself a member of the 'kingdom of ends' (Paton, 1948, pp. 95–96). It is, then, to the wider communal dimensions and aspects of research that we now turn.

CULTIVATING CRITICAL REFLEXIVITY IN SITUATIONS OF VULNERABILITY IN RESEARCH

David Beedon, an English prison chaplain undertaking professional doctoral research, here gives a critical account of some of the reflexive and other issues pertaining to his research with an extremely vulnerable group of long-term prisons in a very sensitive situation. Risk of harm was high, including to the researcher himself.

My research is amongst prisoners serving a sentence of Imprisonment for Public Protection (IPP). It is an indeterminate sentence; thousands of IPP prisoners remain in prison years after the minimum sentence length set by the courts. The sentence was abolished in 2012.

Prisoners have a higher suicide or self-harm rate than the general population. Indeterminately sentenced prisoners are even more likely to harm themselves. My research interest concerns pastorally caring for those who live with a deferred hope of liberty. Many have given up proving themselves to be a manageable risk in society. This is a lived experience contrary to the human flourishing practical theology seeks to foster.

Vulnerability is a key ethical issue when researching amongst such a group. This was particularly acute in the invitation and consent phase of my fieldwork. Through reflexive journaling and reflective supervision (both academic and pastoral) I identified three contextual factors that were a cause of concern: passion, persuasion and informed consent.

- *Passion. Having a 'heart' for your research interest is important for good fieldwork. Mine was emotionally and psychologically focused around the self-inflicted death in custody of an IPP prisoner I had been pastorally supporting. But I found myself asking: Was it fair to use this emotive story amongst the group to encourage participation?*
- *Persuasion. In the penal hierarchy I am a suit-wearing chaplain with a management grade. I am also a persuasive preacher. Engaging one-to-one with potential participants during invitation follow-up, I was conscious of a skewed power dynamic. As an embedded researching practitioner did I carry an authority that was ethically detrimental?*
- *Informed Consent. Group members have low literacy levels and their lived experience contains a sense of constrained human agency. My passion as a practitioner researcher, coupled to my imagined persuasive powers as a trained preacher initially raised reflexive concerns. How could I be sure consent was not unduly influenced by a benign form of brow-beating? Was I adequately allowing those who were initially reluctant (to participate) to exercise what little agency they had in the penal context?*

Close academic and pastoral supervision, combined with regular reflexive journaling, helped me to remain sensitive to these issues and mitigate their effects

> *where possible. Fifty percent of those originally invited to participate declined to be involved in the fieldwork suggesting my benign form of brow-beating may not have been such an undue influence!*

Ethos and community

Like ethics, research of any kind would be meaningless without a community of reference. Even if a particular piece of research is undertaken by solitary individuals, they will be bound by social conventions and seek to communicate their findings to a wider group. So it is important to explore the ways in which research can recognise and respond to its surrounding communities of reference, and the conventions that have arisen to protect that (Higginbottom and Liamputtong, 2015).

What constitutes the "good" in research?

This is the classic conventional ethics question that underlies all research, indeed all human moral activity (Beauchamp and Childress, 2013). It can be asked of the minutiae of research methods by research ethics committees, but it should certainly be asked in a complex, wide-ranging way by practical theologians seeking to enhance and increase human well-being. It is not an easy question to address. Research and knowledge-generation can be seen as goods in themselves that trump others, that a researcher's good intentions and curiosity will guarantee the value of a project. But there are many different kinds of goods, moral and other, and these may have to be balanced against each other. There are goods intrinsic to research itself, such as the value of understanding and learning for its own sake. But there are also extrinsic goods (and potential evils) such as the ways in which research findings may be used to inform policies and actions.

There will always be many potential goods that might emerge from a research project: knowledge, insight, greater and more critical professional competence and intentionality, acquisition of skills, increased awareness, mutual understanding, desired communal and organisational change and much more. But these must be weighed against each other and against potential 'evils' or harms, direct and indirect, foreseeable and unforeseen, that may be possible. It may also be the case that benefits accruing to one group of stakeholders (such as professional advancement, for example) may have to be weighed against harm or negative outcomes for others. The dedication of resources and time to research is in itself a decision to pursue particular objectives, and this may be at the expense of other, greater goods.

What constitutes valid research, and how can it be undertaken with integrity?

It would be possible to research many things that would be interesting in and of themselves but which might be fairly trivial or have limited validity in practical theology. While not exhaustive, here are some of the issues that you might want to think about in determining whether or not your proposed endeavour has validity and value.

1 Does it have the potential to contribute significantly to human flourishing and understanding, whether one's own or, preferably, that of others, also?

2 Does the research really come from clear background work that establishes its potential value so that it is properly connected to fields and communities of scholars and research users, thus ensuring the likelihood of its making a useful contribution?

3 Does the project have a clear question it seeks to answer? Is it addressing a problem that cannot be resolved by any other means – so only research and rigorous enquiry will do?

4 Are the methods proposed to attempt to answer the question robust and clearly thought through as the very best way (at least provisionally) to engage with the question?

5 Is the project realistic and modest in the methods that it uses, acknowledging their real limits and problems?

6 Is there a commitment really to attend to the evidence that may emerge from the enquiry and to engage with it openly and honestly, even if it may be inconvenient or inconsistent, and contradict the researcher's hopes and even fundamental assumptions about life and God? And by the same token, is there the flexibility to change directions and methods if the original ones prove unsuitable or unworkable?

7 Finally, is there a commitment to understanding and being honest about the limits of the methods, knowledge and insights used and gained?

Positive answers to all these questions do not guarantee the validity or integrity of research projects, but they may help in establishing the degrees of integrity and validity that pertain. Once again, acknowledging that research does involve some uncertainty, even risk, and that contingencies need to be anticipated and managed, is not an admission of failure but a commitment to act responsibly. It is this basic realism about the limits and hiatuses in research that is fundamental to its honesty and which provides the basis for trustworthy integrity.

What ends and outcomes should practical theological inquiry seek?

In life and in research there is always the possibility of unintended consequences and outcomes. Research which focuses on humans and professional practice must be rigorous in its considerations of what ends research should serve, and how interests of competing participants or stakeholders may need to be negotiated (Liamputtong, 2007; Reason and Bradbury, 2008).

Once again, this is not simply a matter of courtesy or compliance, but about the nature, character and ethos of research itself. Research which is self-consciously undertaken with others' interests and views at its centre will be different in tenor, methods and outcomes from research undertaken by autonomous individual researchers who define all aspects of the research questions, process and outcomes themselves without reference to others. For practical theology means, attitudes and actions should not inadvertently be allowed to subvert significant ends such as empowering the poor and oppressed.

Similarly, change is not always desired or for the better. Even understanding can be subversive of values that a community or individual holds dear. This means that researchers need to be sensitive and careful in thinking through the transformative or change oriented ends of their research, particularly when others may not really have assented to this or have helped to define the nature and boundaries of change and transformation, so feel alienated and ignored.

Arguably, all research is a step into the unknown – if we are able to control or predict the outcome, it may be we have not framed our question correctly! The recognition that the future is not entirely predictable and that serendipitous discovery and outcomes are possible is an important corrective to the rather restrictive kind of rational instrumentalism that surrounds much contemporary research (Pattison, 2007, pp. 261–289). It raises the question of how far research ethics can eradicate uncertainty and risk entirely, or whether it should simply aim to anticipate and seek to manage them.

Nonetheless, it is worth thinking carefully as far as it is feasible about the possible outcomes of research activity. What is it really going to achieve, and for whom? Is it all right to do research to satisfy individual personal educational and curiosity needs? Will a piece of research activity create differences in communal understanding and practice? Will it contribute to theology as well as to other kinds of academic theory? Will it create new professional understandings and choices or allow an organisation to change its habitual ways of doing things? It is part of the responsibility of researchers to try to ensure that, thorough thoughtful design, careful monitoring and comprehensive evaluation, negative consequences are minimised and positive ones are maximised.

To whom are researchers and practical theology research communities accountable, and in what ways?

There are often multiple interest groups and stake holders in practical theological research (Costley, Elliott and Gibbs, 2010). These include employers, religious communities, academic authorities and peers, family members and researchers themselves. Frequently, the investment and hopes of these different groups may be very different. An individual researcher may want to get a degree or a book out of a project, a community may want ideas about how to be more effective in its work, while an employing organisation might want to know how allowing and encouraging research will improve its profitability or credibility. Meanwhile, academic peers may be most interested in the methodologies developed or the contribution that a project might make to theory and theology and be far less interested in social usefulness for its own sake.

The issue for the researcher is then to clarify the possible accountabilities that pertain to a particular project, to balance these against each other, and then to work out in what ways accountability is to be discharged. This may be simple if demanding in the case of academic expectations – a large book will do nicely. However, it may be much more difficult to work out accountabilities to individuals and potentially diffuse groups who may have an interest in how they are researched and represented in research but may not easily be able to articulate how they would like to be engaged and consulted. An employing church may have a different notion of how research should be accomplished and used from the local people amongst whom the research is conducted. Accountability literally means to be able to give an account of actions and decisions made, not necessarily to do what others want. However, it needs to be taken seriously in the light of the need to empower and engage in practical theology, or again, we see the ethos of practical theology being violated in practice even if it is maintained in theory.

Cui bono? Who should benefit from research and learning in practical theology? Whose interests should it serve?

There may be many, and many different, kinds of stakeholders and interests involved in research. These may be direct and indirect; interests and investments may be very different, and even conflict. An employer or sponsoring body might vaguely want to support a person's research project in the interests of their continuing professional education and training, or to further evidence-based practice. However, if this results in, for example, that person neglecting other duties (or being perceived to do so), or asking uncomfortable questions in the course of their enquiries, then tensions or outright conflict may develop.

Bruce Moore, a student on a professional doctorate in business administration, found that the process of undertaking research changed many relationships in his life, ultimately forcing him to change his job and organisation. In Moore's case this was at some cost to himself, and, eventually, to his doctoral research.

> From a personal perspective, I had hoped that undertaking a doctoral degree would enhance and demonstrate my intellectual credentials. What I seriously underestimated though was the impact that acquiring new insights and understandings might have on my relationships both at work and with my family. I did not anticipate the extent to which I would upset the equilibrium that I would establish in my life by taking on research responsibilities or that in particular these would require me to question and reassess my appreciation of and contentment with my privileged position.
>
> *(Moore, 2007, p. 29)*

Moore had to come to terms with a factor very familiar to many postgraduate researchers and even established academics: the damage that may be incurred to one's family relationships, even one's health, in pursuing a demanding research project, whatever the outcome.

COSTS AND BENEFITS – A BIG QUESTION

John Barnett, a Church of England minister and professional doctoral student exploring multiple religious belonging, reflects thus as he comes near to the end of his research and his paid ministerial career in his research log:

Dwelling on Carlton Turner's challenge in a research seminar over the cost of study. Realise I have spent 13 years of ministry doing degrees (as well as 7 beforehand). How much has that cost to ministry and family? Only now perhaps can I begin to face that. Calling? Or self-indulgence? How I am made? Doctorate gives a more communal element and more vocational, so more defensible. But what is going on here? The question I haven't dared to ask. How is it that I am facing it now? Is it just because I am in a retrospective mood, or is it safe to ask these things now because I won't be stopping so close to the end anyway? Or is this a natural phase for any researcher?

As with the other issues raised here, there are no simple solutions to the complexity of demands and relations surrounding research. However, it is important for those involved in this activity to really think through who might benefit from what they are doing, in what ways, and also to think about how they can really be given the opportunity to benefit. Related to this is the need to ensure that there is a clear understanding of the interests involved so that research is not designed or undertaken in such a way as to serve, for instance, the interests of the powerful over the relatively powerless. Thus, churches may want to understand the behaviour and interests of parents and children in order to ensure increased involvement so that these organisations have a secure future and religious training can be administered; but it may have to be asked what the interests of children themselves are. It may not be appropriate to devise and test more effective methods of engagement before discerning whether it is in the interests of children to have a different experience of religion and spirituality which is not necessarily mediated through church engagement.

Here again, beneficent intentions and enthusiasm to 'make a difference' must be screened against a background of hard-headed evaluation and critique. Unsurprisingly, this kind of self-conscious evaluation may lead researchers involved in professional practice to have to question the ethics of some of their routine work activities with, for example, children or vulnerable adults (Danchev and Ross, 2014; Liamputtong, 2007). This is no bad thing and it is an integral part of practical theological research which aims to raise sharp questions about practice as well as to provide theoretical and theological insights.

What (and who) should determine the priorities for research?

If research is undertaken that is accountable to stakeholders, takes into account the interests and needs of communities, and attempts to discern positive and negative possible outcomes and effects, then setting priorities in research, such as what is researched and when, what opportunities are to be seized and which are to be neglected, becomes a fundamental consideration. As noted already, researcher reflexivity and communal engagement will help in discerning the rank of priorities that are to be sought. Material and contextual restraints such as time and resources will also help in gaining focus. It may be a highly appropriate and principled decision not to undertake a particular piece of research at all if academic curiosity or training in skills are the only real outcomes. But if a particular project is to be undertaken, there needs to be a clear, and publicly defensive reasoned account of why it should be given priority.

Research design: visions, values and voices

So far, we have reviewed some of the general issues and questions that pertain to undertaking research and which might be considered in the period before a project is actually commissioned or implemented. In this section, a similar line of questioning designed to help researchers be properly sceptical and critical in designing research is developed. The aim is not to debunk or demoralise researchers, but to ensure that there is a critical clarity about all aspects of research.

Who should be involved in designing the research process?

By this point, it will come as no surprise that thinking carefully about who should be involved in designing research and the use that is made of different voices and interests is really important. On the one hand, projects need direction and clarity if they are to succeed. In that context, too much and too diffuse consultation may scupper any prospect of research actually occurring, especially if it is not a priority for the people who are being worked with. On the other hand, engaging with the voices and interests of others can deepen and give added purpose, depth and significance to research (Cooperrider, Whitney, and Stavros, 2008, Higginbottom and Liamputtong, 2015).

So here again, a complex, self-aware approach needs to be taken to discern who are the groups and individuals who might usefully (which does not mean uncritically and positively) influence research design. It might be helpful to think of those who stand most obviously to gain from the process and outcomes of the research, and then to think of those who would be likely to be sceptical and/or indifferent. Then it might be appropriate to try and access the views of both groups.

A particularly difficult issue arises when people who might have an interest in research are not themselves in a position to easily or competently comment on it. People may be too busy, insufficiently articulate, or too damaged really to help shape projects that might affect them as subjects or beneficiaries. These people are of particular value in practical theological research insofar as it makes options for the disempowered and excluded. Thinking carefully about how people who may not easily be able to be actively involved can make a contribution that is respected and valued is important. Involving them may require subtle methods of dialogue and consultation that might involve others like advocates, carers and organisations. At all points, it is useful to ask, whose voices are being listened to, how and why? It is not always the most articulate and powerful voices that have most to offer and to gain in designing research.

What sort of values should inform and guide research design?

There are many values that might inform and guide research design. First, there is a commitment to human flourishing, to undertaking research that will enhance human life, individually (the researcher's own life) and corporately and to avoid approaches and methods that might diminish self and others. Secondly, practical theology reckons to promote research that is experience- and reality-near so that it can actually provide insight into the contemporary world. So relevance and realism are important values. In the actual conduct of research it is important to be committed to maintaining values such as dignity and respect. This enhances the possibility of trust between the various actors in the research project, as does honesty, which can be understood as a commitment to tell the truth about the project and its limits, not to deceive or intentionally participants in any way without their real and informed consent, and to share its findings openly in intelligible, empowering ways as the project develops and at its conclusion.

Similarly, there can be awkward moments in research projects where researchers become aware of findings that they suspect those who have helped them will not appreciate or understand. At points like this, candour is an important virtue, as is courage, which might be relevant at all points in a project from starting out and daring to propose it, through undertaking challenging field work, to feeding back findings and outcomes.

INTEGRITY, HONESTY, ACCOUNTABILITY AND DISCRETION IN A MULTIPLE STAKEHOLDER CONTEXT

Here, John Barnett describes some of the ethical issues arising in the design and conduct of research within a very complex environment of multiple stakeholders as he undertakes research into multiple religious participation with Christianity and Sikhism.

My research is an autoethnographic study of the experience of multi-religious participation (Christian and Sikh).

Informed consent for fieldwork was needed from my own Christian congregation and from the gurdwara at which I am regularly worshipping. Issues arising were my own position of authority in the congregation, and the vulnerability of an ethnic minority at the gurdwara.

At church I withdrew from the church council when it was discussed, and also invited them to share any concerns with the archdeacon. They approved the research and have been encouraging throughout.

The gurdwara committee has also been encouraging, though I was anxious when a member of the gurdwara who supported the application said it would be helpful for the gurdwara, making it known as a welcoming place. I did not question this at the time, but am rather burdened by that expectation. I gave both groups an interim report after twelve months which they discussed with approval.

In my fieldwork I sometimes note things of discredit to my hosts, snarking in the congregation, or caste issues, or dishonesty in the gurdwara. When I write up my research I will refer to these issues for completeness, but without details or emphasis for three reasons. First, this is research on the effect of multiple religious participation on me rather than an ethnographic study of the settings, and these issues have not affected me much. Second, I have the aim of not just investigating but also improving – or at least not harming – interfaith relations, so my approach shares the positivity of appreciative enquiry. Thirdly, I am considering divine friendship as a key theological motif. Aelred, a key Christian writer on the subject, emphasises the role of discretion in friendship, and my writing should match my theology.

Where does power lie in research processes and relationships?

Because a lot of research in practical theology is practice-based and aims to illuminate people's real work and experiences, inevitably it will often involve working with people with whom researchers have ongoing relationships and responsibilities. This is absolutely consonant with the underlying value of practical theology that it seeks to find theology in the 'here and now', not in the 'there and then', but it raises very important questions of how issues of power and inequality are to be handled in research projects.

UNANTICIPATED CONTINGENCIES IN RESEARCH ETHICS

Aloys Ojore recounts his experience in Kenya when researching the phenomenon of levirate union among Roman Catholic widows within his own Luo people, in research for his thesis entitled 'A new model of pastoral care: resources from Luo widows in Kisumu archdiocese' (Anglia Ruskin University, 2017). Acting responsibly requires flexibility and the willingness to respond to the unexpected in a spirit of trust.

In keeping with Anglia Ruskin University Policy and Code of Practice for the Conduct of Research with Human Participants, my research on Luo levirate custom received required approvals from all bodies involved. Since Levirate custom involved discussions on death and on widows' sex life, I knew it was likely to cause pain and embarrassment. Consequently, I engaged two women research assistants to interview widows.

I, therefore, began the sessions by introducing myself, the research assistants, explained about the participant consent form and participant information sheet and then left [the room]. I wanted to respect the sensitivities about lack of gender parity and to allow the women to discuss the issues without the constraints the presence of a man might have imposed. However, participants in the three focus groups in the three different deaneries, called me back after 10 to 15 minutes. They insisted that I sit through all the discussions and hear their stories, because it is we, Luo men, who are responsible for their miseries. Luo widows were telling me that eradication of forced levirate unions starts with men listening very carefully to what they have to say. The widows were already moving from victims into protagonists of their own change, by taking control of how they wanted the debate to be conducted. Research ethics demand that researchers treat respondents with dignity and respect.

During tea breaks, I was struck by the animated exchanges by widows among themselves and with me. The relief and the sense of peace on their faces hinted to me that some kind of healing process had started. It is possible that for many of them, their sad stories had finally been heard and their hope was that something would be done about it. I was convinced that by telling their stories to a listening man, some kind of cathartic healing had occurred.

My listening to the widows discussing painful experiences of abuse at the hands of Luo men, transformed me from a mere sympathiser into an active participant in their struggle to dismantle an oppressive cultural practice. My research experience compelled me to put the liberation of Luo widows first. I have made a leap from orthodoxy (correct doctrines) to orthopraxis (correct actions). The opinion shaper in the study has been shaped. All these have come from productive listening to the dreadful experiences of widows.

At all points in research, it is vital to be aware of how inequalities of race, gender, age, power, class might be present overtly and also in covert ways. Thinking through what this means for research also allows a greater awareness of these issues in every day professional practice. Asking people to take part in a research project with informed consent and all that is required can very helpfully raise the issue, how is it that I feel free to ask people to do things as a matter of course in everyday work without really getting their permission? Thus the process of research can helpfully sensitise people to everyday issues of power and inequality. As ever, it is not that there is an ideal of power and inequality neutrality that can be sought as an ideal of perfection amidst the research process. The point is that awareness of these issues can deepen and enrich both analysis and practice if subtly and conscientiously undertaken. Thus greater intentionality and awareness can be nurtured both in professional practice and in research.

INTENTIONALITY IN RESEARCH AND CONTINUING PROFESSIONAL RELATIONS OF RESPONSIBILITY

Mark Pryce, Anglican clergyperson, poet and adult educator who completed a professional doctorate at the University of Birmingham ('The poetry of priesthood: a study of the contribution of poetry to the Continuing Ministerial Education of clergy in the Church of England', submitted 2015 http://etheses. bham.ac.uk/5772/3/Pryce15DPT_Redacted.pdf, later published in a modified version (Pryce, forthcoming) here discusses some issues of power and responsibility emerging from researching his own practice with people for whom he had responsibility in an asymmetrical relationship of power.

Researching my own professional practice with people for whom I had some ongoing professional responsibility gave rise to unexpected ethically-related insights. As a Continuing Ministerial Education (CME) Adviser, I have organisational responsibilities towards clergy in a particular Church of England diocese. This involves some careful keeping of boundaries. For example, it is important that a priest can share with me in confidence her sense of needing to develop capacity in an area of ministry, knowing that this will be received as a constructive initiative rather than as a professional deficiency. This sense of confidentiality and trust is mostly implicit within the church structures.

Participating in research made these codes explicit. For example, an integral part of my CME practice with clergy was to facilitate poetry sessions as a means of reflecting on ministry. When I proposed to systematically evaluate the efficacy of these poetry groups as a means of reflective practice, the clergy involved became research participants, and research practice helped to clarify that I needed to think more explicitly and critically about participant well-being and issues of confidentiality and dual responsibility.

Research practice led me to articulate in a clear and specific way what had previously been assumed between clergy: that if a participant shared something in one of the groups I facilitated, this would not be judged, and would remain confidential to the group, so that participants could reflect in an uninhibited way, knowing that this would not adversely affect their careers and our relationships beyond the group. This usefully problematised the assumptions that I had made about my practice down the years, giving me new insights into CME practice. Research ethics gave an opportunity to think about the range of professional relationships that I had, dynamics of power and trust, and the efficacy of work that I was doing. Initially, this critical examination of assumed codes in my professional practice was uncomfortable, but ultimately my work has benefited from the intentionality and clarity that research introduced.

How should the pragmatic (what is possible and practical) be related to the ideal (what is desirable and best)?

Having dealt with ideals and virtues underlying research practice, it is really important to recognise that research is a very practical activity which is constrained by reality. Many researchers start out with clear plans and ideals about what they would like to do, who they would like to interview, how many groups they would like to observe, and so forth. Then they find out that this is not realistic for all manner of reasons, such as time, resources, or people's sheer lack of availability. This is a real part of the research journey so that a completed project is really often an idealised and tidied up version of what was possible after it proved that the idealised goals and plans turned out not to be feasible in all respects.

As with most of the questions raised here, there is no right answer as to how idealistic or pragmatic researchers have to be. The point is to encourage researchers to be open and honest about the nature of the research journey so that others can see and learn from the choices they make and the limits and mistakes they identify. To be able to change and respond is human and humane in research with people, especially in qualitative research where humans affect each other directly (many research subjects seem to find being interviewed in some way therapeutic – they feel attended to and so better – even though that may not be the primary intention of the interviewer). Cultivating virtues of realism and pragmatism in research may, indeed, lead to better research and results as it allows the possibility of turning aside from a main train of enquiry to pursue something more interesting and perhaps more relevant. Consequences and outcomes may be predicted or unpredicted, expected or unexpected, positive or negative, and the impact research has may be surprising and take place in places where it was not expected. All of this is quite normal – predictably unpredictable, if you like.

What are the risks of undertaking research and to whom?

We have already considered the ethical dimensions of research in terms of unintended outcomes or complex consequences, but it is also important to remember more conventional aspects of risk inherent in the research process: to physical, psychological, emotional, financial or even intellectual well-being.

Clearly, there are people who are involved in research who can easily be recognised as vulnerable and at risk. These include the elderly, children, sick people, people with various disabilities, and anyone who might find themselves in an inferior position in terms of power or dependence to the research initiator (Liamputtong, 2007; Dickson-Smith, James, and Liamputtong, 2008). Unwelcome though this thought might be, this includes people who are managed or cared for by researchers who may feel that they have to collaborate or respond in certain ways in order to preserve good relations or to please the researcher. And these are people who can be easily and directly injured, deliberately or perhaps most often, accidentally in the research process, for example, if things they say in private become public or are misrepresented so that they are cast in certain lights.

But, less obviously, there may be risks to researchers themselves. Not only might they jeopardise relations with people they have to work with and need to respect if they mismanage a project and don't adequately assess risks, they may find that they are in a risky situation. So, for example, working with at-risk groups like asylum seekers or criminals may expose a researcher to physical danger. But more likely are non-physical and intellectual dangers (Behar, 1997), such as, for example, if research subjects' experience makes a researcher realise that their fundamental beliefs and assumptions about themselves and the world are wrong, or no longer fit for purpose. This is the risk of enquiry and education and all of this could be labelled 'growth'. But it is demanding, and change may be disillusioning.

Collecting, analysing and interpreting evidence

There are clearly ethical issues inherent in the part of the research process that is concerned with collecting and analysing research data. It raises issues about the nature of evidence, the way it is interpreted, its status and the uses to which it is put (McNiff, 2017, pp. 195–226). Much practical theological research makes a pre-commitment to lived experience that is in the present moment and context, rooted in human activity and problem-centred, arguing that this is where theological and other kinds of insight and truth are to be found, at least in significant part. This means there is already an epistemological commitment to the empirical and the contextual, and to using critically insights and methods from disciplines and approaches that will allow that to be better and more fully understood. This would thus tend to favour qualitative approaches drawn from disciplines such as sociology and psychology. Of course, these approaches and methods have their own epistemologies and anthropologies which affect how reality is understood and analysed – all practices and approaches are theory and theology laden, implicitly or explicitly (Browning, 1991; Swinton and Mowat, 2016). So it is important for researchers in practical theology not only to think about methods and what they may or may not allow to become visible and significant, but also to think about the authority and value of the evidence that their use produces. In this regard, a number of useful questions can be asked.

What should be valued and recognised as evidence?

In practical theological research people undertake surveys, interviews, observations, focus groups, actions for change and many other activities to gain understanding of the world. Often they will use a range of approaches and methods in the service of a particular research question. So the issue is, what kinds of data are to be collected and how are the different kinds of data to be weighed against each other? Selecting and evaluating data sources in critical and reflective ways entails making value decisions about what the nature of the world is and what matters within it (Cresswell, 2013). What sort of data is to be valued and taken as significant while other data are discounted or side-lined? As ever, there is no right answer here, but critically evaluating the kinds of data and evidence available and the importance given to them in answering a research question is vital as this process is as much a construction of a moral world in itself as a description. It contributes to making the world a certain way and so has important moral and ethical implications.

How should evidence be interpreted, and by whom?

If the weight given to different kinds of data and evidence is important in terms of making decisions about the fundamental nature of reality and whose perspectives are taken seriously, the issue becomes even more important when it comes to the process of interpreting and theorising data. Many researchers at the stage of analysis reserve to themselves the right to interpret data and then to theorise and generalise on its basis, for example, about the state of Young Black Men, of Alzheimer's sufferers, of prison chaplains. It will by now be apparent that this move cannot be unquestioningly assumed. It might be very important to get other people involved in the process of analysis and interpretation, perhaps by wondering with others about the significance of what has been found out, or talking to them about data they have themselves produced in interviews or observational work. They may have very different ideas about the really important elements in the data, about their significance and generalisability.

Engaging in this wider interpretative community itself raises ethical issues about sharing and making data available, but it opens up the prospect again of deeper, more multi-variate analysis. In this connection, it is worth remembering that the theological tradition itself is multi-variant and invites many different kinds of interpretations, all of which are in some ways contestable and provisional. So there is no need to seek a single stable meaning from a theological perspective. Polyvalent symbolisation and hermeneutic complexity involve many different voices and perspectives in a contestable space. There is no reason why this should be forgotten or ignored as a potential resource in bringing into being communities of interpretation round research data.

How are issues, findings and persons to be represented in research?

Representation is a key issue in the presentation of data, findings and interpretation in all empirically based research. How people and communities are portrayed and presented can have substantial implications both for people's own self-perception and for the ways in which they are regarded by others (Eakin, 2004). This issue can start in the data collection process – do people themselves get an opportunity to comment on what they have or have not said or done and what it means? Or are they just passive objects within the researcher's own portrayal and narrative about them? Some people and groups will not have strong feelings about this. But minority and unheard groups may feel that research positions them in a way that is unhelpful and unacceptable to them. Hence the importance of allowing their voices to be heard at all points in the process and also of trying to create mechanisms for ongoing dialogue and discussion of findings and what they might mean.

Often, what is needed is mutual understanding and engagement. A researcher may genuinely hold one perspective which has its own integrity and validity, but this may be very different from that of others whose experience and data is used in the research. The various parties involved therefore need to be involved in a reasonably equal mutual discussion so that possibly different representations can be laid beside one another and be drawn into dialogue (Higginbottom and Liamputtong, 2015). This is not a bad way of understanding ethics in practice. Ethics is really a careful conversation which takes place over time so that respect and trust can emerge and be enhanced (Cooperrider, Whitney, and Stavros, 2008). If this kind of conversation is engaged in at all points in the research process, including when people and communities are represented, then research is likely to be ethically accountable and justifiable, even if its conclusions are controversial.

REPRESENTATION AND CREATIVE ENGAGEMENT OF RESEARCH 'SUBJECTS'

Michael Paterson, a psychotherapist and supervisor who completed a professional doctorate at Glasgow ('Kinship in the borderlands of practice: a theological performance autoethnography', submitted 2016), here demonstrates his learning about how researchers can both exploit and affirm participants in analysis and representation.

Several years ago I was interviewed by a researcher. I signed the consent form, reviewed the transcript and agreed that she could extrapolate whatever she found useful for her research. What I never anticipated however was finding myself three years later, in a bookshop, reading my entire interview as a book chapter with all identifying characteristics visible.

That boundary violation led me to make three ethical commitments in my own auto/interethnographical research: 1) to pay careful and explicit attention to gaining consent at every stage of the research process; 2) to counter the tendency for researchers to loot interviewees' lives in pursuit of their own speculative research ends; 3) and to ensure that my research would leave those who would participate in it not with more rather than less ownership of their stories through a process of co-performative witnessing in which at the end of each interview I used a playback theatre approach to offer back to the 'teller' the impact their story had had on me.

An additional, distinct ethical issue arose in explicitly choosing to work with intimates rather than strangers. That decision arose out of a desire to see what would happen if, rather than dispassionately standing back from the research field, I allowed myself to be in and of the data in a committed, intentionally subjective way. I began by engaging in creative life writing provoked by external stimuli which spoke to me of my own internal situation. I then interviewed friends and colleagues offering them the chance to perform their stories either in words, images, movement or music. Gathering the data was the easy part. Finding a way to bridge from private performance to public staging within the thesis presented enormous ethical challenges. Carol Gilligan's work with teenage girls in which she extracts every sentence that begins with 'I' to create what she terms 'I Poems' offered a way of preserving proximity to what emerged in the interviews. Having created the individual 'I Narratives' (some accompanied by the interviewee's chosen images), I then sent them back to the participants for their approval. Participants reported finding such self-renditions stark yet revealing, concise yet kerygmatic. To my relief, only minor changes were requested.

The final challenge came in synthesising what would traditionally be termed data analysis. Conscious that the whole research project had been characterised by intimacy rather than distance, I had to find a way not to step back and take an objective look at what I had found. What emerged was considerable dis-ease with the temptation to act either as a stenographer relating an unfolding drama or as a video artist creating a digital archive of events. In keeping with my commitment to being in and of the data I realised that I was a co-participant in the plot, a conspirator in determining outcomes and co-constructor in the search for meaning. I ruled out traditional 'analysis' and instead presented a four minute musical composition (with commentary) which reflected the impact on me of all that I had seen and heard.

What does it mean to be honest, truthful and trustworthy in using and presenting evidence?

As will now be apparent, these adjectives, honest, truthful and trustworthy are not static virtues or entities in practical theological (or any other kind of) research. They denote a commitment and approach to complex processes so that their meaning changes as events proceed. In many ways, they are relational and contextual words, not constant states of being. To be trustworthy, truthful and honest demands taking into account the complexity of situations and of the individuals and groups involved in them.

Honesty cannot simply mean being willing to tell all, however irrelevant or hurtful it might be. Truthfulness is not just about exposing situations in a simple and open manner, no matter what the consequences of this might be. Trustworthiness is not just about giving people answers which bolster and support people's self-understandings or wishful thinking – telling people what they want to hear or things that only affirm them does not necessarily inspire trust, while nuance and complexity of interpretation might. All of these features need to be integrated into some kind of integrity whereby researchers commit to living with a variety of complex data, factors and possible consequences and remain willing to enter into dialogue about this in responsible and responsive ways that prescind from over-simplification and obscurantism. Again, this is all a matter of discernment, *phronēsis*, wisdom – practical, critical, dialogical understanding that allows facts, data, interpretation and findings to be gained and shared in constructive ways.

It should not be forgotten, either, that there are criteria within the academy for what constitutes 'good research', which include such things as: originality, rigour, engagement with relevant scholarship and good communication. Most people would say that, in addition, principles of good conduct in research should also embrace broader ethical questions such as 'fairness' and 'transparency' – both in dealings with research subjects and with potential readerships. And of course, regulations regarding plagiarism are designed to ensure that any researcher gives due credit to those scholars whose work has informed their own (Neville, 2010).

RESPECTFUL AND CREATIVE REPRESENTATION OF SUBJECTS AND DATA IN RESEARCH

Jo Whitehead undertook an interview and focus-group study of students and tutors on a youth work course of which she was a staff member in connection with her professional doctorate. Here, she reflects on how to represent people she knows and large amounts of data in a way that is transparent and fair.

In the data analysis process, I found myself wrestling with the question of how to work with the huge amount of transcribed material. I was conscious that interview and focus group transcripts represented real people with backgrounds and situations I knew well. I was working with material that had emerged from people that I knew and worked with personally. They had given their time and input. In some cases, they had talked very personally about their journeys and experiences. Searching the data for emerging themes, I found myself highlighting huge sections of text and wondering how I might represent with integrity, the complexity of what I was reading. I was aware that I could easily pick out small sections of text randomly to make points that fitted with my argument, but was keen not to do this. I was equally concerned to avoid having huge chunks of direct quotation in the final thesis.

Using the phrase 'body of data' in my research journal was the catalyst for a reflection on 'embodiment'. For this, I spent some time creating a line-drawing of a female figure (life-drawing classes I was attending at the time were helpful here) and wrote reflections around the image to reflect on my feelings around the issue – basically a series of questions about how I could allow the 'body of data' to express itself. I wondered how I could allow each part to speak in its own way, 'to flex and stretch and dance and play.' I was drawn to 1 Corinthians 12 as I drew and wrote, particularly thinking about how I could value and honour those parts that seemed critical, awkward, insecure, inappropriate or particularly vulnerable.

One outcome of this reflection was the decision to use 'I poems' as a way of retaining the integrity of the original voice, whilst framing it in a more accessible way for the reader.

Sharing and disseminating research

If the initial premises outlined above – which are that research in practical theology should benefit a wide variety of people and communities as much as possible – are accepted, it follows that ownership of knowledge and insights of research activity should as far as feasible be shared and equally that this knowledge and insight should be disseminated and shared as widely as possible. Interestingly, this makes publication and other kinds of dissemination an ethical responsibility and not just a personal option for those who like the idea of publicising their work. If research is worth doing in the first place, it is certainly worth sharing and maximising its use at all points, particularly since it is likely to involve the efforts, resources and good will of others. In this context, it is important to consider questions like the ones that follow.

Who 'owns' and should have access to research outcomes?

There are different kinds of putative 'ownership' that can apply to the outcomes of research. If it has been commissioned by a funding or other body, or sponsored or facilitated by them, then there may be a moral right, even a formal contract governing access to and use of research findings. Similarly, a body that is being researched may insist that it should have the right to comment upon and have a say in what findings are published and how because it may have consequences for how they organise themselves or are publicly perceived.

Researchers themselves who have collected and interpreted data clearly have an ownership stake in research outcomes and what is done with them, but arguably so too do communities and individuals who have been involved in the research and anyone like them who might benefit from understanding them. For example, the findings of a study of Black Young Men and why they find themselves in trouble with the law and alienated from the churches in a particular location may be valuable for them, for local churches, but also for churches nationally and for all kinds of people who are concerned with the future of ethnic minorities and with social cohesion (Anderson, 2015). Ownership can be a tight or a loose term, but it should be taken as broadly as possible and then the issue is how to ensure that interested groups have the opportunity of access research outcomes (Higginbottom and Liamputtong, 2015).

Traditionally, researchers have regarded it as enough to publish their results in thesis, book or journal article form. But this means that the results may not really reach a wide and relevant audience. So in this connection, it may be important to think about how audiences might really be able to access and engage with findings. Perhaps media appearances, short reports, blogs, popular articles, even cartoons, plays, or playing cards might be helpful in engaging people, along with meetings where they can play with findings, critique them and suggest extensions or alternative interpretations that may create further dialogue and greater depth of analysis. One of our student colleagues, Peter Babington, designed a short course on ageing as part of his professional doctorate studies. This has been re-used with his own congregation and is available for use in other churches. This is the sort of activity that is now labelled 'impact' as well as dissemination within the research world, and it usefully draws attention to the desirability of intentional and planned sharing of research in different and appropriate ways rather than just assuming that research is a good thing in itself. However, there may be conflicts of interest in terms of deciding whether to publish in a formal, academic journal in order to gain professional *kudos* (and to justify funding), or to aim for more 'popular' dissemination – personal, professional, institutional and community pressures may diverge quite radically in this respect. Once more, the researcher's core values – their priorities, objectives and intentions – need to be clear in helping them make tough decisions.

How should research be presented?

For an academic audience, it is reasonable to assume that a fairly straightforward, linear presentation of methods and results will be most helpful so they can see how research was carried out and what has eventuated from it. However, even academic audiences do benefit from seeing familiar issues from new angles, and can be very appreciative of a non-traditional or creative presentation of the research journey (Grierson and Brearley, 2009; Kara, 2015). It is also important to give attention to how to engage non-academics as well as scholars in research. Would it be better to provide case studies or narratives that quickly allow people to see what has been arrived at? Could pictures, poems, or stories be used to engage people's attention and concern with research findings, and to open up conceptual and imaginative understanding in ways which go beyond that which discursive argument is able to achieve? Short audios or videos might be more accessible and more widely available than conventional written materials.

The point is that applying critical thought at this stage is as important as at any other stage in the research. If material is presented in over-simplistic ways, or if it mis-represents perspectives that are important, or if it cannot be understood, this can weaken the moral commitment of practical theology to promote flourishing in the widest possible ways. Indeed, it can reinforce hierarchies of power in representation and organisation in such a way as to be disempowering and distorting. This reinforces the importance of allowing the people involved in the research and similar groups to talk back to the researchers and not merely to have to listen quietly to what 'they' have to say about 'us'.

Conclusion

In this chapter we have laid out a vision of the critical ethos that might underlie practical theological research endeavours. We have alluded to fundamental pre-commitments and values that inform the conception, design, prosecution, analysis and presentation of research. Throughout, we have emphasised the need for creating trust and acting with integrity within the context of engaging with a complex range of interests and questions. The management of a complex conversation is what we have characterised as the heart of being ethical in practical theological research. Research is a personally demanding and challenging activity at all points. Thinking about the values that underpin it and how they are operationalised at various points in its prosecution is a very important part of articulating the nature and importance of the whole project for all concerned.

Good research ethics – researching well, for the well-being of all – demands space, time and a willingness to listen to and engage with hard questions from a variety of different quarters. Engaging in such a complex ethically informed and intentioned conversation will not guarantee that research is 'Ethical' with some kind of formal stamp on it. But it may go a long way to ensuring that research is properly accountable, responsive and responsible; and that it is consonant with humane and theological concerns to promote individual and communal flourishing on a variety of levels and for a variety of groups, particularly the disempowered and ignored.

References

Anderson, C., 2015. *Towards a practical theology of effective responses to Black Young Men associated with crime for Black Majority Churches.* Unpublished PhD thesis. University of Birmingham. Available at: http://etheses.bham.ac.uk/5977/

Beauchamp, T. and Childress, J., 2013. *Principles of biomedical ethics.* 7th ed. Oxford: Oxford University Press.

Behar, R., 1997. *The vulnerable observer.* Boston: Beacon Press.

Bondi, R., 1995. *Memories of God.* London: Darton, Longman and Todd.

Browning, D., 1991. *Fundamental practical theology.* Minneapolis: Fortress.

Cooperrider, D.L., Whitney, D.K. and Stavros, J.M., 2008. *Appreciative inquiry handbook: For leaders of change.* 2nd ed. San Francisco, CA and Brunswick, OH: Crown Custom Publishing, Inc.

Costley, C., Elliott, G. and Gibbs, P., 2010. *Doing work-based research: Approaches to enquiry for insider-researchers.* London: Sage.

Cresswell, J., 2013. *Qualitative inquiry and research design: Choosing among five approaches.* 3rd ed. London: Sage.

Danchev, D. and Ross, A., 2014. *Research ethics for counsellors, nurses and social workers.* London: Sage.

Dickson-Smith, V., James, E.L. and Liamputtong, P., eds., 2008. *Undertaking sensitive research in the health and social sciences.* Cambridge: Cambridge University Press.

Eakin, P.J., 2004. *The ethics of life writing.* Ithaca, NY: Cornell University Press.

Grierson, G. and Brearley, L., 2009. *Creative arts research: Narratives of methodologies and practices.* Rotterdam: Sense Publishers.

Higginbottom, G. and Liamputtong, P., eds., 2015. *Participative qualitative research methods in health.* London: Sage.

Hogan, L., 2013. Developing ethics as a core competency: Integrity in scientific research. In: C. Russell, L. Hogan and M. Junker-Kenny, eds., *Ethics for graduate researchers: A cross-disciplinary approach.* London: Elsevier. pp. 1–5.

Junker-Kenny, M., 2013. Recognising traditions of argumentation in philosophical ethics. In: C. Russell, L. Hogan and M. Junker-Kenny, eds., *Ethics for graduate researchers: A cross-disciplinary approach.* London: Elsevier. pp. 7–26.

Kara, H., 2015. *Creative research methods in the social sciences: A practical guide.* Bristol: Policy Press.

Liamputtong, P., 2007. *Researching the vulnerable.* London: Sage.

McNiff, J., 2017. *Action research: All you need to know.* London: Sage.

Moore, B., 2007. Original sin and insider research. *Action Research,* 5(1), pp. 27–39.

Neville, C., 2010. *The complete guide to referencing and avoiding plagiarism.* Maidenhead: Open University Press.

Paton, H., 1948. *The moral law: Kant's groundwork of the metaphysic of morals.* Translated by H. Paton. London: Hutchinson.

Pattison, S., 1994. *Pastoral care and liberation theology.* Cambridge: Cambridge University Press.

Pattison, S., 2007. *The challenge of practical theology: Selected essays.* London: Jessica Kingsley.

Pryce, M., forthcoming. *Practical theology, poetry and reflective practice.* Abingdon: Routledge.

Reason, P. and Bradbury, H., eds., 2008. *The Sage handbook of action research.* Revised ed. London: Sage.

Russell, C., Hogan, L. and Junker-Kenny, M., eds., 2013. *Ethics for graduate researchers: A cross-disciplinary approach.* London: Elsevier.

Swinton, J. and Mowat, H., 2016. *Practical theology and qualitative research.* 2nd ed. London: SCM Press.

8

CONCLUSION

Moving on

In this book, we have invited you to journey with us around the burgeoning field of research in practical theology. We have looked critically and selectively at some of the assumptions and methods that have become common in this activity to provide a kind of critical horizon for research. More than that, we hope you will have gained a real sense of what it feels like to engage in research in practical theology, not only from the experiences of the main authors, but also from the material we have included from our colleagues and co-researchers. Research in any field is not, or should not be, a solitary activity. In practical theology, it is undertaken by, for and with other people. As you will have noticed, those who undertake advanced research in practical theology have very varied experiences and the course of their work often does not work out in a simple, linear way.

This, of course, reflects the reality of human existence. Life is in many ways unpredictable. It would therefore be strange if practical theological research that claims to take both life and the transcendent seriously were to be smooth and unproblematic.

Teilhard de Chardin wrote many years ago,

> The great objection brought against Christianity in our time, and the real source of the distrust which insulates entire blocks of humanity from the influence of the Church has nothing to do with historical or theological difficulties. It is the suspicion that our religion makes its followers *inhuman*.
> *(Teilhard de Chardin, 1964, p. 68; italics original)*

As practical theologians, we believe that religious belief and practice, the discipline of theology and the pursuit of academic research should all aspire to enhancing and developing human potential and flourishing. But to be human is to be imperfect and in a perpetual state of incomplete transition. Research in practical theology is a profoundly and inescapably human activity in its intentions, processes and outcomes. In many ways, research project reports (books, theses, articles and so on) are maps of problems identified and often only partially addressed. They are interim statements about directions undertaken and destinations frequently unreached or changed as the research process has evolved. This is a partial, in some ways unsatisfactory, characterisation of activity which is time- and energy-intensive. But it would be unrealistic to present a picture of research that is not experience- and life-near. And we hope that you will have been able to see that there are joys and satisfactions in the voyages of discovery and understanding that constitute varied types of research activity as well as frustrations and limitations.

One of us, Elaine, has famously talked of practical theology enabling people to 'practise what they preach' (Graham, 2000, p. 106): to ensure that they enact their beliefs and thoughts authentically, and that their actions are consistent with their deepest convictions. Commenting on this, however, Stephen has observed that the inverse also applies, and that practical theology should help people of faith to 'give a public, critical account of the truth claims that they enact in practice' (Woodward and Pattison, 2000, p. 105). Actually, this only serves to reinforce our conviction that 'preaching' and 'practising' should be of a piece: a single moment of praxis, of critical engagement at all levels with ideas and material reality. 'In this sense, practical theology helps communities of faith both to articulate and practice what they preach or believe and also to better articulate or preach what they practice' (Woodward and Pattison, 2000, p. 105).

It is to this that we aspire, and this is what we encourage fellow researchers to do, reflecting upon their own practice and giving an account of their journey of enquiry, struggle and discovery. So it seems only fair that we should evaluate and reflect upon the extent to which we have practised what we preach and preached what we practise in writing this book together.

The process of writing this book, like all research — and especially collaborative research — has been challenging for us. We have different ways of thinking and acting, different availability, different concerns and pre-occupations and, in particular, different habits of writing and organisation. Anyone undertaking research involving people will know that this immensely complicates things as well as providing interest and added value — in the end! It has taken us much longer to write the book than we had hoped; that is because we have had to be patient and wait with, and for, each other. This is a parallel enactment of research process that takes people as subjects and collaborators in research seriously. It is undoubtedly costly.

We feel proud of the fact that we have embodied many of the processes and practices that we (perhaps glibly!) commend to our students and (less glibly) follow in our own individual research. We are members of a growing community of practice in practical theological research, focused in many ways around a common postgraduate research programme. We have used our authorial group as a base in which creatively and critically to develop ideas, to test them and to expound them. From time to time, we have gone out to the wider research community to share concepts and writing and to gather in the perceptions of others, some of which have caused us to stop in our tracks ('Is this your book or ours?' Our doctoral students ask. 'How are our voices going to have the place that they deserve? Are you just using us?')

Within our authorial group, we have real differences on the nature and importance of theology, on how critical we should be of ourselves and other researchers, on what style the book should be written in, on what voice should come out of it. As it happens, we have all worked on all of the book, so we have been neither homogenising or individualising in authorship. But this has been the result of considerable discussion over the years. Any author/researcher reading this will not be surprised to know that we have even had long discussions over whether practical theology should be spelt with, or without, capital letters through the text, whether we should be Zoe and Elaine, or Bennett and Graham, whether we are a 'we' as authors, or should appear to be more impersonal. Not all research decisions are monumental in their importance, but even these minor issues need discussion, and are time-consuming. Yet they are important, too, as they have a bearing on matters of voice and representation. After all, however pressing its initial questions, however ground-breaking its findings, research that is not disseminated to others can never hope to make a significant impact; so the manner of our communication is part and parcel of the contribution, ultimately, we seek to make to the field.

The impression is often given in research that the final, well-honed linear text appeared more or less as expected with few problems in either process or construction. This is a misleading fantasy. All research and writing is demanding and emotionally involving. This has been our experience in writing this book. Some of us have been ill, others despondent or impatient at times. We have often felt like giving up, like most research students. We have all had difficulties in meeting deadlines and sometimes we have sat in front of screens and felt unable to begin writing. In moments like this, we have used our co-authors as friends and encouragers. In other words, we have turned to the research community. We have also employed our own easily-given but not easily followed advice ('Don't get it right, get it written!' Or, 'Take an inch, life's a synch, take a yard, life is hard!') True, this is folksy 'craft wisdom' embodied in annoying aphorisms; it is corny and sounds very basic. But research is basic. The process of research and writing finds you out: at all levels, personal, organisational and communal. It reveals things to the researcher and those around like collaborators which is as much about persons, emotions and relationships as it is about the topic ostensibly being researched. Inside every thesis or book, alongside literature, methods, findings and analysis there are human beings and communities with feelings, needs, hopes and fears trying to get out.

A range of emotions can accompany the final conclusion or interim completion of writing up a research project. These can include relief, regret, anxiety about reception, pleasure in achievement, bereavement, frustration, excitement – possibly even joy. These reactions are not necessarily mutually exclusive. The authors of this work now have to leave it, imperfect as it is, and throw it open to the world and to our fellow researchers – which was the whole point of writing in the first place – to get it out to people who might find it useful as a source of information and stimulus.

We hope that you will have found in this text some ideas, approaches and material that will inspire your own research endeavours within the wider community of scholars aspiring to add critical value and understanding to life and work.

References

Graham, E., 2000. Practical theology as transforming practice. In: J.W. Woodward and S. Pattison, eds., *The Blackwell reader in pastoral and practical theology*. Oxford: Blackwell. pp. 104–117.

Teilhard de Chardin, P., 1964. *Le milieu divin*. Glasgow: Fontana.

Woodward, J.W. and Pattison, S., 2000. Introduction to practical theology as transforming practice. In: J.W. Woodward and S. Pattison, eds., *The Blackwell reader in pastoral and practical theology*. Oxford: Blackwell. pp. 104–105.

INDEX